Totalitarianism on Screen

TOTALITARIANISM ON SCREEN

The Art and Politics of *The Lives of Others*

Edited by

Carl Eric Scott and
F. Flagg Taylor IV

UNIVERSITY PRESS OF KENTUCKY

Scholarly publisher for the Commonwealth,
serving Bellarmine University, Berea College, Centre College of Kentucky,
Eastern Kentucky University, The Filson Historical Society, Georgetown College,
Kentucky Historical Society, Kentucky State University, Morehead State University,
Murray State University, Northern Kentucky University, Transylvania University,
University of Kentucky, University of Louisville, and Western Kentucky University.
All rights reserved.

Editorial and Sales Offices: The University Press of Kentucky
663 South Limestone Street, Lexington, Kentucky 40508-4008
www.kentuckypress.com

Photographs courtesy of Sony Pictures Classics/Photofest © Sony Pictures Classics.
Photographer: Hagen Keller.

Library of Congress Cataloging-in-Publication Data

Totalitarianism on screen : the art and politics of The lives of others / edited by Carl Eric
Scott and F. Flagg Taylor IV.
     pages cm
  Includes bibliographical references and index.
  ISBN 978-0-8131-4498-6 (hardcover : alk. paper) — ISBN 978-0-8131-4499-3 (pdf) —
  ISBN 978-0-8131-4500-6 (epub)
  1. Leben der Anderen (Motion picture) 2. Totalitarianism and motion pictures. I. Scott,
Carl Eric, editor of compilation. II. Taylor, F. Flagg, editor of compilation.
  PN1997.L383T68 2014
  791.43'72—dc23   2014010372

This book is printed on acid-free paper meeting
the requirements of the American National Standard
for Permanence in Paper for Printed Library Materials.
∞

Manufactured in the United States of America.

Member of the Association of
American University Presses

CONTENTS

INTRODUCTION

Carl Eric Scott and F. Flagg Taylor IV

"Don't I need this whole system? What about you? Then you don't need it either. Or need it even less. But you get into bed with them too. Why do you do it? Because they can destroy you too, despite your talent and your faith. Because they decide what we play, who is to act, who can direct."

These are the words of Christa-Maria Sieland, actress and girlfriend of writer Georg Dreyman, East Germany's most celebrated playwright. She is being blackmailed by the minister of cultural affairs: sexual favors in exchange for permission to continue her work on the East German stage. Christa-Maria is about to attend to her duties with Minister Hempf, when Dreyman, who has recently discovered the affair, implores her not to go. "You don't need him," he says. Her reply, seen above, brings home an ugly truth to Dreyman. Their work, their art, their success are not theirs. Dreyman and Christa-Maria live well. They have a nice apartment with nice things. They have many friends. Best of all, they have audiences who laud their artistic endeavors. But all of this merely conceals the putrid core of the system, the "really existing socialism" of the German Democratic Republic (GDR), which dominates their lives.[1]

The Lives of Others, written and directed by Florian Henckel von Donnersmarck,[2] has been widely praised for its overall excellence, especially its dramatic portrait of dissident activity and pervasive surveillance under the GDR. Released in 2006 in Germany as *Das Leben der Anderen,* the film would go on to win international acclaim and many awards. *Lives* was victorious in seven categories at the German Film Awards and in four at the German Film Critics Association Awards. In the United States, the film won Best Foreign-Language Film at the Academy Awards and was honored at the Independent Spirit Awards and the New York Film Critics Circle Awards. It was similarly honored in England, Ireland, France, Spain, Poland, Brazil, Argentina, and Canada.

The brilliance of Donnersmarck's film is that it brings the utter strange-ness—the peculiar horror—of life in the GDR to audiences who have no experience of such a phenomenon. His accomplishment is all the more impressive in its recreation of this world "precisely because," notes Timothy Garton Ash, "it was so banal, so unremittingly, mind-numbingly boring."[3] As the then thirty-three-year-old writer/director explained, "It's not a Stasi film. . . . That's just the setting."[4] Donnersmarck said to John Esther, "I don't want to present someone with two hours of communist drabness."[5] After all, who would pay to see such a film? So Donnersmarck set out to make what John Podhoretz has termed "a character study in the guise of a stunning suspense thriller."[6] In the view of Matthew Bernstein, *Lives* "explores canonical themes of surveillance and voyeurism, using hierarchies of knowledge and recalling Hitchcock's best thrillers and especially Coppola's *The Conversation* (1973)."[7]

Lives tells the story of two men whose lives intersect in dramatically illuminating ways. Gerd Wiesler, a captain in the Staatssicherheit, or the Stasi (the East German Ministry for State Security), is tasked with spying on Georg Dreyman, heretofore the regime's approved and award-winning playwright. Dreyman's life reveals to Wiesler that the ordinary goods of love, beauty, and friendship are utterly absent from his own life. And in turn, Wiesler's actions wind up bringing Dreyman to see the extent to which he has quietly compromised his own moral and artistic integrity for the sake of success. Wiesler and Dreyman each attempt to extricate themselves from a world of appearances and lies. So as the film brings to the fore the iniquity of communism, it also succeeds as a drama of the human soul.

In Germany, the film attracted 1.7 million viewers during its first year.[8] *Lives* would become the subject of much debate (sometimes quite heated) for its portrayal of the Stasi in particular and life in the GDR more broadly.[9] It has thus attracted a good deal of criticism—some even before the film-ing started.[10] Some critics charge Donnersmarck with distorting the truth about the Stasi by demonizing it. Others, by contrast, object to the heroic portrayal of Wiesler, a Stasi officer—there is no record of such an officer betraying his orders and protecting a subject of surveillance. Many of the essays in this volume touch on this criticism in particular. For reflections on the historical accuracy more broadly, see the contributions to this volume by Peter Grieder and Manfred Wilke.

For three basic reasons, the film merits continued attention and study. First, a strong case can be made—one we endorse—that it is a masterpiece of the cinematic art form. Second, it is one of the most insightful works in any literary medium about the nature of communism in general. Third, it is one of the best portrayals of the particular communist regime known as the German Democratic Republic.

Viewing *The Lives of Others* leaves most people deeply moved and still intrigued by the plot's complex development. It is a film that invites discussion and multiple viewings, and that invitation becomes even clearer upon listening to the director's DVD commentary. While much of Donnersmarck's commentary rightly focuses on the excellence of the actors, he also reveals the great care he took with all the details of the script and filming.[11] We learn, for example, that he insisted upon recording with analog sound, that he obtained authentic Stasi surveillance equipment for the relevant scenes, that he chose the names of the characters very deliberately, that he took pains to borrow a particular painting for the apartment set and, astoundingly, that he had the entire costume and decorative scheme coordinated to exclude certain colors, blue and red, that he felt were uncharacteristic of the look of the GDR.[12] Closer viewing and consideration show that these are not the only details that Donnersmarck attended to—as many of the essays in this volume demonstrate, plot structure, dialogue, music, composition, and even props are all deployed to create a fully realized poetic "world" and drama. Time will tell how this finely wrought artwork holds up when judged according to the highest standards of cinema, that is, when compared with the greatest films, and whether it achieves lasting popularity, but obviously, the initial judgments have been remarkably favorable. It is our hope that the essays in this volume, which in our estimation are far from exhaustive of the interpretational discoveries available to students of the film, will demonstrate the literary depth and landmark stature of Donnersmarck's achievement.

A truly great work of art typically requires a truly great subject. There can be no question that the triumph of totalitarian ideology, occurring more briefly but more catastrophically with Nazism in Germany and at far greater length with communism in the Soviet Union and a number of other nations, has a powerful claim to be the signature event of the twentieth century. It is our contention that *The Lives of Others* deserves a place as one of the truly great works of art touching on the phenomenon of communist totalitarianism. Though there are many great literary works on communism—George Orwell's *1984,* Arthur Koestler's *Darkness at Noon,* Czesław Miłosz's *The Captive Mind,* to name a few—the number of good films on the subject is surprisingly small.[13]

The Lives of Others is particularly successful in elucidating the nature and function of ideology in a totalitarian regime. A communist party in power rests its claim to authority upon its purported knowledge of history and its claim that the dream of communism has been at least partially realized. Thus, communist regimes must insist on mass participation in a multifaceted and constant endeavor to maintain the appearance of the triumph of the ideology. They likewise insist that everyone attribute deficiencies to the predicted resistance of class enemies. This is why such systems, according to Václav Havel, are "so thoroughly permeated with hypocrisy and lies: government by bureaucracy is called popular government; the working class is enslaved in the name of the working class; the complete degradation of the individual is presented as his ultimate liberation. . . . Because the regime is captive to its own lies, it must falsify everything. . . . Individuals need not believe all these mystifications, but they must behave as though they did. . . . For this reason, they must live within a lie."[14] Donnersmarck's film communicates the anguish of living under such circumstances and how and why people might have become captive to the illusions of such regimes.

The film's central character, Wiesler, is a Stasi captain. Security organizations like the Stasi were central to the maintenance of obedience in all of the countries of the Eastern bloc. Through their monitoring and surveillance of their captive populations (whether directly, through official employees, or indirectly, through an informant network), state security services enforced compliance and ferreted out dissent. Here the Stasi was exceptional in the extent of its power and reach. In 1989, before the fall of the Berlin Wall, there were 91,015 full-time Stasi employees and 173,000 informants. In its prewar phase, the Gestapo—the Nazi secret police—employed only 7,000 people for a population more than three times that of East Germany. And the Stasi stands out by comparison with its brethren in the communist bloc: while the Stasi had one full-time officer for every 180 East German citizens, the ratio in other countries was not as high: USSR (1:595), Czechoslovakia (1:867), and Poland (1:1,574).[15]

The Stasi, then, was a remarkable instrument of totalitarian control. Yet one must draw important distinctions between the Stasi and the Gestapo or the Soviet secret police during the 1930s. As Gary Bruce points out, outright murder was by no means a routine occurrence for the Stasi. "Instead, the Stasi employed more refined methods of control—extensive behind-the-scenes monitoring by a vast army of informants, psychological methods to disrupt individual lives, prisoner neglect, blackmail, coercion—methods, no matter how distasteful, that do not equate with a shaft to the eye or, in real terms, to the brutal torture methods of the Gestapo."[16] Bruce's point here is a salutary reminder not to associate totalitarianism with mere terror and violence. Over the course of the latter half of the twentieth century, critics of the concept of totalitarianism argued that though the term once seemed to capture the reality of communist oppression, with the decline in terror and violence after the 1950s the term lacked descriptive power.[17] Just as the term was being abandoned in the West in academic circles, it was being picked up by many anticommunist dissidents in the East throughout the 1970s and 1980s. Though the regimes of this period lacked, to a large extent, mass physical terror, labor camps, and deportations, everyday life was defined by bureaucratic inertia, an omnipresent secret police, mass fear, and apathy.[18] Thus, *Lives* is important for its effective portrayal of totalitarianism in this later phase and for the way it captures communism's coercive and seductive power.

Though we will not rehearse the long debate around the concept of totalitarianism here, we should point out that a version of this controversy has played out in East German historiography specifically.[19] While historians sympathetic to totalitarianism as a concept were in the ascendancy shortly after the fall of the Berlin Wall, by the turn of the century other scholars stepped in to argue that the totalitarian approach failed primarily due to sins of omission. By focusing too much on the state, its instruments, and repression, these scholars argued, the totalitarian approach failed to capture the full and textured reality of life in the GDR. Mary Fulbrook, for example, faulted the totalitarian approach for the "near total exclusion from [its] account of the people themselves, except when engaged in attempted escape, political resistance, or popular uprising."[20] She has been struck by how a political and social life that appears "bizarre" and "unintelligible" to some seems "perfectly normal to many who grew up within the parameters of the state."[21] Here we think Fulbrook's critique misses the mark and she fails to understand the nature of totalitarian rule. As Peter Grieder puts it in his contribution to this volume, "What [Fulbrook] does not acknowledge . . . is that totalitarian polities rule *through* rather than *over* society." Scholars continue to grapple with the question of how "East Germans [led] 'perfectly normal lives' in a country with the Berlin Wall and the largest secret police per capita in world history."[22] The debate has yielded strikingly different answers, but Bruce is certainly correct to offer this assessment: "Daily life in East Germany cannot be reduced to the Stasi, but daily life in East Germany cannot be understood without taking it into account."[23]

An accurate view of the GDR is of course significant not simply for humanity's fuller understanding of communist regimes, but also for the German people themselves. Nor is this only or primarily a debate for scholars. The divide between the Ossis and the Wessis remains quite economically, culturally, and politically visible, and there are yet other divides among Germans from both Eastern and Western backgrounds about how to approach the legacy of the GDR. As Joachim Gauck has remarked: "We have two political cultures in Germany: the culture of a society in transformation in the East, and a halfway stable structure of a civil society in the West. When the two meet, of course misunderstandings occur. In my opinion, these differences stem more from the way mentalities are shaped than from participation in the communist ideology. Only a few people really believed in communism. But many people still feel that a free society is something very alien."[24] With sensitivity to these divides and the legitimate differences of opinion they can reflect, there can be no question that German society has a duty to deal with the memory and aftermath of its second totalitarian regime.

Confronting this legacy is a varied and difficult task. One element would be the pursuit of justice for the victims of communist tyranny. But there has been no process akin to denazification with former communists or Stasi employees. As Bruce reports, "Of the more than 91,000 full time Stasi officers in 1989, thirty-three were sentenced by the year 2000. Twenty-eight of the sentences were suspended, four were settled financially."[25] John Rodden reports in *Dialectics, Dogmas, and Dissent* that many victims of the Stasi express "rage and anger that Germany—more than six decades after the close of World War II—widely publicizes and regularly funds new memorials and conferences devoted to exposing the crimes of the Third Reich yet pays little attention to their suffering in the quite recent past."[26] The comparison of Nazism and communism is a vexed question—many recoil at the suggestion that the two could be morally equivalent or even comparable phenomena. "The Soviet Union," Flagg Taylor has written, "was wildly successful in imposing its own ideological vision of the political landscape on the West."[27] Nazism became the incarnation of the Right and communism the incarnation of the Left, despite the fact that both movements had socialist roots. As Jean-François Revel argues, "The left's vigilant refusal to acknowledge the equivalence of Nazism and Communism or even to make comparisons between them, despite their evident affinity, has a practical rationale: the daily execration of the one serves as a barrier against careful examination of the other."[28]

Even more problematic from the point of view of these victims of communist oppression is the nostalgia (*Ostalgie*) expressed by some Eastern Germans for the GDR. Bruce reports that "the image of an East Germany where life was simply a connection of happy events was reinforced in the early 2000s with several major German TV stations running variety shows about the GDR."[29] The former Olympian ice skater Katarina Witt appeared on television wearing a Young Pioneers (the Communist Party youth group) shirt and reminded viewers that "there were also some very nice times" in the GDR. Anna Funder, author of *Stasiland,* the acclaimed collection of personal stories about life behind the Wall, notes the increasing aggressiveness of ex-Stasi who continue to defend themselves in print and via protests while "conducting lawsuits against people who speak out against them."[30] Polls taken to gauge attitudes on post-reunification Germany have shown that large numbers of East Germans report that they "want the Wall back" or that "socialism is the superior system" to the present government. For Rodden, such replies indicate both an "appalling ignorance" about the true nature of the GDR and an "insulting indifference" to the human costs of communism in Germany.[31]

Countering such ignorance and attitudes is a task for diverse instrumentalities and arenas such as policy, law, scholarship, education, psychology, ethics, and religion. But surely the fine and popular arts have an important role to play as well. Indeed, a strong case can be made that filmmakers have a special responsibility here, since a widely seen film can decisively shape a nation's imagistic impression or, we might say, "cinematic consciousness" of its own history. As Stephen Brockmann points out, "For Germans born after the early 1980s, films like *Good Bye Lenin!* and *Das Leben der Anderen* necessarily became key ways of understanding the German Democratic Republic."[32] Though the topic of East Germany first came to post-unification Germany with a number of films in the early 1990s,[33] the subject gained widespread attention with the success of Leander Haussmann's *Sonnenallee* (1999)—a comedic love story that was very attentive to East German material culture, making it a good example of Ostalgie.[34] As Haussmann candidly noted after its release, "We wanted to create a movie that would make people envious that they hadn't lived there [in the GDR]. Since politicians like to compare the GDR to a concentration camp in order to preen themselves with their historical mission. And that's what GDR citizens can't stand: they are always supposed to have been either camp commanders or camp inmates—but what was in between was people's daily life."[35] Following *Sonnenallee* in 2003 was Wolfgang Becker's enormously successful *Good Bye Lenin!* which gained more than 6 million viewers in its first eighteen months.[36] The film follows the travails of Alex Kerner, whose mother goes into a coma just before the fall of the Berlin Wall. When she wakes up after the fall, Alex is advised by doctors that any sudden changes could adversely affect her health. So with the assistance of his sister and friends, Alex, in effect, reconstructs the GDR for his mother. Though the film is often placed into this Ostalgie category and described as a comedy, not all critics agree on this characterization (see the essay by James Pontuso and the interview with Joachim Gauck in this volume). But *The Lives of Others* clearly was a departure in tone from its predecessors. It took a more serious, critical look at the GDR and its most infamous political institution, the Stasi. This fact, among others, explains the fairly intense and at times apparently nitpicking criticism of *The Lives of Others* for purported historical inaccuracies.

One of the more important of such critiques comes from Funder; she calls *Lives* "a beautiful fiction" that sits over an "uglier truth."[37] For Funder, no Stasi officer could have acted in the manner of Wiesler because the totalitarian system, with its multiple hierarchies and division of tasks, made such action impossible. But she makes a second charge that is perhaps more interesting. Not only did the system not offer the possibility for Wiesler-like rebellion but, even more frightening, Stasi employees had no desire to engage in such behavior. "The institutional coercion made these men into true believers; it shrank their consciences and heightened their tolerance for injustice and cruelty 'for the cause.'"[38]

It is useful to compare Funder's contention here with the portrait provided by the historian of East Germany and the Stasi Gary Bruce. His book *The Firm: The Inside Story of the Stasi* is the product of extensive archival research and, more important, of many interviews of ex-Stasi employees in two districts, Gransee and Perleberg. Bruce captures the distinctive characters of his interviewees and uses the device adopted by Czesław Miłosz in *The Captive Mind*. As Miłosz had given his exemplars of the mind and character of an ideologue taglines such as "the moralist" and the "disappointed lover," so we see in Bruce's chronicle "the ambivalent one," "the repentant one," "the earnest one," and "the intellectual" (to name a few). In support of Funder's first charge, Bruce points out that none of his interviewees was "remotely close to treason." Though some Stasi employees expressed dissatisfaction with the party and the state, they remained loyal soldiers and did what was asked of them. As Bruce puts it, "In spite of their inner concerns, in spite of their slight moral protest, in spite of their hostility toward their party bosses, they continued and indeed increased their exhaustive work of societal repression and, it should be emphasized, at no point did any of them indicate that they feared reprimand should they not fulfill their duties." Save for one interviewee who expressed "profound remorse" for her actions, all of these ex-Stasi seemed to have clean consciences. On the other hand, except for one "committed ideologue," none of these individuals were "chest-thumping patriots or bloody-minded," and they were "the furthest thing from fanatical."[39] We think Bruce's more nuanced portrait of the ex-Stasi complicates Funder's second assertion.

In its presentation of characters like Wiesler, his boss Grubitz, and Minister Hempf, *The Lives of Others* captures a range of motivations that drive the state functionaries. Interestingly, Wiesler seems to be more fanatical, more the pure ideologue, than all but one of Bruce's interview subjects. Except for his fateful decision to disobey the orders of his superiors, Wiesler fits Funder's portrait quite nicely. We are made to wonder whether his commitment, his fanaticism, is paradoxically what makes him ripe for dissent. While perhaps there will be no clear resolution in this dispute between the film's critics and defenders on Wiesler's plausibility, Donnersmarck has certainly succeeded in placing the problem of moral corruption at the center of his film.

The Contents of This Volume

The first section of the book contains two essays, each touching on the themes of truth and dissent in communist regimes. Flagg Taylor's essay argues that *The Lives of Others* contains a particularly compelling and accurate portrait of what Václav Havel termed "post-totalitarianism." Such regimes were no longer characterized by the ideological fervor, enthusiasm, violence, and terror so prevalent in communist states from 1917 through the 1950s, but rather by bureaucratic inertia, consumerism, and banality—this pattern was seen in most of the Warsaw Pact regimes of the 1970s and 1980s. Taylor shows how the film captures this atmosphere and argues that the evolution of the central character, the Stasi captain Wiesler, is illuminated by this broader context. His essay underlines how gradual that evolution is, and how it is prompted not simply by a growing attraction to the lives of the artists but also by a growing disgust at the lack of sincere belief and the abuses of power seen in the lives of higher-ups like Grubitz and Hempf.

Lauren Weiner's essay further develops the place of dissent in such societies. Weiner holds that the film provides a worthy portrayal of the life of intellectuals and artists living in communist regimes. She puts characters like Dreyman, Christa-Maria, Jerska, and Hauser in the broader context of a range of real-life figures: from Germans like Reiner Kunze, Erich Loest, Christa Wolf, and Wolf Biermann to Russians such as Osip Mandelstam, Aleksandr Solzhenitsyn, and Dmitri Shostakovich. Though an admirer of the film, Weiner concludes that ultimately Dreyman is portrayed in a more flattering light than his character and actions warrant. The conclusion of the film—focusing on the relation between Wiesler and Dreyman—is "a picture of reconciliation and good feelings that, while highly satisfying as moviemaking, fails to ring true."

The next three essays examine *The Lives of Others'* understanding of art in relation to politics, either through its portrayal of its artist characters' actions or through its own example. Carl Eric Scott casts his gaze across the central characters of the film to reveal several varieties of moral corruption, discussing how these corruptions are related to the larger pattern of "communist moral destruction" analyzed by thinkers such as Aleksandr Solzhenitsyn and Alain Besançon. Scott's close reading of the film demonstrates that it sympathetically conveys a range of human responses to a communist regime's ideology and oppression. He argues that the relationship between Dreyman and Wiesler deserves particularly close attention and can be best described as a "reciprocal rescue"—"as Dreyman is unknowingly saving Wiesler by his art, Wiesler is secretly saving him by his psychological and political cunning." The reciprocal nature of this rescue underlines the way the entire film tempers its presentation of art's potency against the totalitarian spirit, with a recognition that the artistic calling could be held hostage by a communist regime as a way to bind artists, sometimes quite subtly, to its authority and lies.

Paul Cantor's essay grapples with the film's many allusions to the communist playwright Bertolt Brecht and to one play in particular, *Der gute Mensch von Sezuan* (The Good Person of Szechwan). The essay includes an analysis of this play's theme, which concerns the difficulty of being a good person, and illustrates how the entire play utilizes the principles of Brechtian drama. Cantor shows that *Lives* responds to Brecht in two ways. First, it refutes the understanding of human nature displayed in *The Good Person of Szechwan*. Second, it departs from Brecht's dramaturgical approach to character and moral choice. Cantor argues that Donnersmarck's appreciation of and response to Brecht is crucial to his own exploration of the nature and function of art.

For his part, Dirk Johnson argues that despite the film's many allusions to Brecht, its own plot does not follow his dramatic theory but rather the classic Aristotelian understanding of tragedy. The heart of the film is not the tandem transformation of Wiesler and Dreyman; it is the tragedy of Christa-Maria Sieland. Sieland fits the pattern of Aristotle's recommended tragic character: she is an individual of lofty nobility by virtue of being a "great artist," and she has a tragic flaw. But while a number of the specifics of Sieland's fate could only occur in a communist state like the GDR, Johnson argues that it essentially proceeds out of her and the other characters' own choices, in accord with Aristotelian precepts. He notes, however, that a drama in full accord with those precepts would have ended with the scene of her death; further, he calls attention to the film's placement of "bookends" around the main Sieland-centered plot. There thus prove to be aspects of Donnersmarck's drama that in a sense combine Aristotelian and Brechtian principles.

The third section of this volume comprises two essays that compare *The Lives of Others* with another recent film. James Pontuso argues that though Wolfgang Becker's highly successful 2003 film *Good Bye Lenin!* could not seem more different from *Lives* (the former presenting itself as an almost lighthearted comedy), both films point to the success achieved by communist regimes in utilizing "everydayness" as a mechanism of rule. Pontuso examines the thought of Martin Heidegger and Karl Marx to bring out the elements and implications of everydayness and also shows that the East German state sponsored a film genre called *Alltag* specifically to make ordinary life "synonymous with Marxist-Leninist principles." By contrast, in both *Lives* and *Good Bye Lenin!* the actual dreariness and barrenness of everyday existence of the GDR is highlighted, especially by being posed against the longings of the central characters, which point to the perennial need for rich, authentic human experiences.

Marketa Goetz-Stankiewicz's essay compares *Lives* with a highly regarded Czech film from 2000 called *Divided We Fall*. Goetz-Stankiewicz argues that both films examine a quite common and even respectable response to totalitarian oppression: the attempt to withdraw from public life altogether—to live a decent life by isolating oneself from the tentacles of totalitarian power. *Divided We Fall* puts this impulse on display in the midst of the Nazi occupation of Czechoslovakia in World War II by examining the trials of the amiable and entirely ordinary Josef. Goetz-Stankiewicz compares Josef with Dreyman, arguing that "by withdrawing into this gray, seemingly nonpolitical area and claiming rejection of any political stance, they act under an illusion."

The next section of this book contains four chapters that directly address the debate about the film's historical accuracy and the legacy of the GDR. The first of these comes from Manfred Wilke, the primary historical consultant for the film itself. Wilke addresses a number of the issues of historical plausibility, considering how the various characters' actions in the film line up with what we know about Stasi and dissident behavior at the time. He tells us that Donnersmarck consistently sought his advice on historical accuracy for "the purpose of self-enlightenment" and not "to confirm a predetermined verdict." The second comes from Wolf Biermann, a poet, songwriter, essayist, and critic of the GDR who was expelled from the country in 1976. His chapter is partly a report about the film's reception among his fellow dissidents and partly a description of his own reaction to it. Since the decision of artists to engage in dissent or not is a key subject of the film, it is especially valuable to consider his impression and evaluation. We are also honored to be able to provide an interview about the film with Joachim Gauck, the first federal commissioner for the Stasi Archives and the current president of Germany. Of particular note is his explanation of why he expected resistance to the film from three different groups: former dissidents, "part of the old establishment," and "the broad ranks of the conformists." The title of this chapter, "Against Forgetting," reflects both the content of the interview and Gauck's long-fought effort to persuade his fellow Germans never to forget the crimes of the GDR, including his chairmanship of an association called Gegen Vergessen—Für Demokratie (Against Forgetting—For Democracy). The final chapter in this section is by British historian Peter Grieder, author of *The German Democratic Republic* (2012). He provides an overview of the various questions of historical accuracy that have been raised, evaluating each one in turn; whatever his judgments regarding specific issues, he broadly endorses the film's "stylized history," saying it captures the character of the regime and "shed[s] light on certain totalitarian practices in the GDR." He concludes with a timely warning for liberal democracies, particularly that of the United Kingdom, against "sleepwalking into a comprehensive surveillance state by a series of small steps."

We conclude with a chapter from a premier historian of the Stasi, Jens Gieseke, who has worked as a researcher for the federal commissioner for the Stasi Archives. His contribution here describes the development, structure, and typical practices of the Stasi in detail.[40] It provides the reader with a solid factual background to the issues raised by the film and discussed in the essays in this volume.

Perhaps the highest compliment to Donnersmarck and his film has come from Wolf Biermann. It is Biermann—the renowned dissident, tormented by the Stasi for years—who seems ready and willing to let the current generation take the lead in grappling with the vexed legacy of totalitarianism.

> A lot of people in both the East and West are sick to the teeth of the discussions about the Stasi and the GDR dictatorship, and between you and me: I'm just the same. After my Stasi ballads from 1966, my lampoons of the corrupt old men in the Politburo, and my polemical essays after the fall of the GDR, I don't need anymore. But I don't trust myself on this issue. This debut film makes me suspect that the truly deep-reaching confrontation with Germany's second dictatorship is only just beginning.

> And perhaps those who never experienced all the misery should take over now.

It is our hope that Donnersmarck's achievement will inspire other artists to join the "confrontation with Germany's second dictatorship" and humanity's general reckoning with the nature of Marxist socialism as it *really existed*.

Notes

1. The concept of "really existing socialism" (sometimes "actually existing" or simply "real") came to prominence during the Brezhnev era to dismiss the notion that there could be multiple models of socialism. It was a reaction against the Prague Spring and Eurocommunism. For many, the GDR was the emblem of "really existing socialism." Our volume generally uses the English acronym for the GDR throughout, but the German acronym is also quite common (DDR, Deutsche Demokratische Republik).

2. On Donnersmarck's life and background, see Jay Nordlinger, "Florian's World," *National Review,* April 7, 2008, 41–43.

3. Timothy Garton Ash, "The Stasi on Our Minds," *New York Review of Books,* May 31, 2007, http://www.nybooks.com/articles/archives/2007/may/31/the-stasi-on-our-minds/?pagination=false (accessed July 19, 2012).

4. Alan Riding, "Behind the Berlin Wall, Listening to Life," *New York Times,* January 7, 2007, http://www.nytimes.com/2007/01/07/movies/awardsseason/07ridi .html?pagewanted=all (accessed July 19, 2012).

5. John Esther, "Between Principle and Feeling: An Interview with Florian Henckel von Donnersmarck," *Cineaste* 32, no. 2 (2007): 42.

6. John Podhoretz, "Nightmare Come True: Love and Distrust in the East German Police State," *Weekly Standard,* March 12, 2007, http://staging.weeklystandard.com/Content/Public/Articles/000/000/013/360jfrwt.asp (accessed July 19, 2012).

7. Matthew H. Bernstein, *"The Lives of Others," Film Quarterly* 61, no. 1 (2007): 30. Donnersmarck has himself cited *The Conversation* as an important visual inspiration, along with *Three Days of the Condor* (1975), *The French Connection* (1971), *Harold & Maude* (1971), and *M*A*S*H* (1970). See also Rachael K. Bosley, "Under Surveillance," *American Cinematographer* 88, no. 3 (2007): 16–20.

8. Cheryl Dueck, "The Humanization of the Stasi in *Das Leben der Anderen,"* *German Studies Review* 33, no. 1 (2008): 598.

9. See Mary Beth Stein, "Stasi with a Human Face? Ambiguity in *Das Leben der Anderen," German Studies Review* 33, no. 1 (2008): 570.

10. Hubertus Knabe, director of the Berlin-Hohenschönhausen Memorial Museum, refused to let Donnersmarck film on location. See ibid., 570.

11. This also comes out clearly in an interview with Diane Carson. See "Learning from History in *The Lives of Others:* An Interview with Writer/Director Florian Henckel von Donnersmarck," *Journal of Film and Video* 62, nos. 1–2 (2010): 13–22. See also Bosley, "Under Surveillance."

12. Donnersmarck remarked, "The production designer and I spent six months devising the visual world of this film. We saw there were more greens than blues, more orangey brown colors than actual red. We decided to completely eliminate red and blue and just go with all the greens, grays, and browns and not do it in postproduction. We did not want to do anything digitally. Many people in the East felt the film was a complete resurrection of the GDR." See Esther, "Between Principle and Feeling," 43.

13. Prominent films substantially dealing with communism include (in their English titles): *The Tunnel, Good Bye Lenin! Katýn, I Am David, Sunshine, To Live, The Killing Fields,* and *Dr. Zhivago.* This list does not include films primarily about spies or agents, and "prominence" here is being estimated mainly with respect to English-speaking audiences. Lesser-known films include: *12:08 East of Bucharest, Tales from the Golden Age, Bitter Sugar, East-West, The Great Water, The Chekist, Burnt by the Sun, China My Sorrow, Man of Iron, Repentance, Hibiscus Town, One Day in the Life of Ivan Denisovich,* and *Man on a Tightrope.* Those who know foreign cinema, especially East European and Asian, could surely add more titles.

14. Václav Havel, *Open Letters: Selected Writings, 1965–1990* (New York: Vintage, 1992), 135–36.

15. Gary Bruce, *The Firm: The Inside Story of the Stasi* (Oxford: Oxford University Press, 2010), 10, 11, 13.

16. Ibid., 2.

17. For the debate around the concept of totalitarianism, see Flagg Taylor's introduction to his anthology, *The Great Lie: Classic and Recent Appraisals of Ideology and Totalitarianism* (ISI Books, 2011).

18. Havel refers to this as "post-totalitarianism." For more on this concept and its connection to *The Lives of Others,* see Taylor's contribution to this volume.

19. For the debate, see Bruce, *The Firm*, 4–12; Corey Ross, "The GDR as Dictatorship: Totalitarian, Stalinist, Modern, Welfarist?" in *The East German Dictatorship* (London: Arnold, 2002), 19–44; and Peter Grieder, *The German Democratic Republic* (New York: Palgrave MacMillan, 2012), 1–18.

20. Mary Fulbrook, "Putting the People Back In: The Contentious State of GDR History," *German History* 24, no. 4 (2006): 618.

21. Mary Fulbrook, *The People's State: East German Society from Hitler to Honecker* (New Haven: Yale University Press, 1995), ix.

22. Bruce, *The Firm*, 11.

23. Ibid., 12. Or as Bruce puts it: "East German citizens constantly made a judgment about an individual to whom they were speaking and censored their information accordingly" (156; see all of chapter 5, pp. 142–61).

24. Joachim Günter, "Right Life in the Wrong Life: An Interview with Joachim Gauck," originally appeared in German in *Neue Zürcher Zeitung* on May 22, 2010. Translated by Lucy Powell for signandsignt.com: http://www.signandsight.com/features/2039.html (accessed July 19, 2012).

25. Bruce, *The Firm*, 2.

26. John Rodden, *Dialectics, Dogmas, and Dissent: Stories from East German Victims of Human Rights Abuse* (University Park: Pennsylvania State University Press, 2010), 3.

27. Flagg Taylor, *The Great Lie*, x.

28. Jean-François Revel, *Last Exit to Utopia: The Survival of Socialism in a Post-Soviet Era* (New York: Encounter Books, 2009), 109. See also Alain Besançon, *A Century of Horrors* (Wilmington, DE: ISI Books, 2007).

29. Bruce, *The Firm*, 5.

30. Anna Funder, "Tyranny of Terror," *Guardian*, May 5, 2007, http://www.theguardian.com/books/2007/may/05/featuresreviews.guardianreview12 (accessed July 7, 2012).

31. Rodden, *Dialectics, Dogmas, and Dissent*, 4.

32. Stephen Brockmann, *A Critical History of German Film* (Rochester, NY: Camden House, 2010), 498.

33. For a fine treatment of the films of this era, see Mary-Elizabeth O'Brien, *Post-Wall German Cinema and National History: Utopianism and Dissent* (Rochester, NY: Camden House, 2012).

34. Brockmann, *Critical History of German Film*, 428.

35. Quoted in ibid., 428–29.

36. Thomas Lindenberger, "Stasiploitation—Why Not? The Scriptwriter's Historical Creativity in *The Lives of Others*," *German Studies Review* 33, no. 1 (2008): 557.

37. Funder, "Tyranny of Terror."

38. Ibid.

39. Bruce, *The Firm*, 75.

40. Gieseke has criticized *The Lives of Others* for historical inaccuracy and a "Hollywood" treatment. See his "Stasi Goes to Hollywood: Donnersmarck's *The Lives of Others* und die Grenzen der Authentizität," *German Studies Review* 33, no. 1 (2008): 580–87.

Part 1

TRUTH AND DISSENT

Ulrich Tukur (as Lieutenant Colonel Grubitz).

1

POST-TOTALITARIANISM IN
THE LIVES OF OTHERS

F. Flagg Taylor IV

In this essay I will argue that Florian Henckel von Donnersmarck's *The Lives of Others* provides viewers with a striking and deep portrait of a "post-totalitarian" regime. Its depiction of totalitarian tyranny succeeds in particular at revealing the nature and function of ideology and the manner in which one might escape its snares. Its success in this depiction is important for our broader reflection on the nature of totalitarian tyranny.

The concept of totalitarianism has come under criticism for many reasons, and there remains much debate about the regimes that might fall into this category. Hannah Arendt's depiction in her classic work *The Origins of Totalitarianism* and Carl Friedrich and Zbigniew Brzezinski's model applied the concept to Stalin's Soviet Union and to Hitler's Germany. Many critics of the term seized primarily on these portraits and made two noteworthy arguments. First, they argued that totalitarian theorists focused too much on the state and its various instruments and thus also too much on repression. Second, they suggested that the concept was too static—that it could not account for the change that seemed to be occurring, for example, in the Soviet Union after Stalin's death.

Václav Havel's portrait of what he calls "post-totalitarianism" is not susceptible to either of these criticisms. Havel articulates the striking way in which ideology draws everyone into its snares, enabling all citizens to become agents in their own oppression. Havel argues that the simple dichotomies of state and society and rulers and ruled do not fit the reality of totalitarian tyranny. These regimes practiced varied means of seducing the masses and integrating them into approved structures. As Peter Grieder puts it, "Totalitarian polities deployed 'hard' and 'soft' means in their relentless quest for panoptic supervision."[1] Thus, a proper conception of totalitarianism appreciates that terror and violence may wax and wane at various times. "Post-totalitarian regimes did away with the worst aspects of repression but at the same time maintained most mechanisms of control. Although less bloody than under Stalinism, the presence of security services—like the Stasi in the German Democratic Republic (GDR)—sometimes became more pervasive."[2] Havel agrees with Solzhenitsyn that the "Lie"—the enforced participation in the daily ideological distortions of the past and present—is more essential to totalitarian tyranny and more soul crushing than the terror and violence often perpetrated against innocents.

This conception is also then able to account for the evolution of many communist regimes in the latter half of the twentieth century. We are not stuck with an understanding that seems to fit only the Soviet Union under Stalin or Germany under Hitler. While terror and violence certainly declined in the 1970s and 1980s, the ideological universe of Marxist-Leninism (or what Czesław Miłosz called the "New Faith") was perpetuated and hardened in the aftermath of 1968. Havel draws a striking contrast between the atmosphere in Czechoslovakia in the 1950s as opposed to the 1970s and 1980s. The former period was defined by fanaticism, camps, torture, executions, and suffering. In the latter period of "post," "advanced," or "late" totalitarianism, "revolutionary ethos and terror have been replaced by dull inertia, pretext-ridden caution, bureaucratic anonymity, and mindless, stereotypical behavior."[3]

The Lives of Others succeeds in its portrait of this stultifying atmosphere, but I want to suggest this concept is critical for another reason. This distinction between totalitarianism simply and its advanced form is essential in order to make sense of the evolution of the main character, Captain Gerd Wiesler of the Stasi—the central figure of the film. Several critics of the film, though otherwise quite generous in their praise, argue that Wiesler's transformation is either unconvincing or simply pure fantasy. For Timothy Garton Ash, the conversion of Captain Wiesler "seems implausibly rapid and not fully convincing."[4] Garton Ash notes that the historical advisor for the film, Manfred Wilke, who gives his stamp of approval for its accuracy in many areas, offers no example of a Stasi officer who behaves like Wiesler and gets away with it. Even more insistent on this point is Anna Funder, who argues, "No Stasi man ever tried to save his victims, because it was impossible." The movie must fail in its portrait of totalitarianism, according to Funder, insofar as it must provide space for its central figure to "act humanely." For Funder, *The Lives of Others* is thus a "beautiful fiction" that overlies an "uglier truth."[5] Thus, a proper understanding of Wiesler's motives and actions and their very possibility in a regime like the GDR is directly related to our understanding of the nature of totalitarian tyranny. Does the film have something to teach us about such regimes or must it depart from reality in order to provide the dramatic action necessary to make things interesting?

The "Post-totalitarian" Terrain

Scholars have understood both Czechoslovakia and the GDR to have demonstrated the character of a post-totalitarian regime—distinguishing them from both totalitarian and authoritarian regimes.[6] The GDR under Honecker in particular has been described as "neo-Stalinist," "late totalitarian," or "post-totalitarian." Mike Dennis argues that Havel's description of such a regime is applicable to the regimes across the Soviet bloc, and Linz suggests that Czechoslovakia and the GDR share a special kinship as examples of "frozen" post-totalitarian regimes. The mobilization of party members and the masses is routine, lacking in intensity, and not nearly as frequent as under the regime's totalitarian phase. The regime strives to achieve the bare minimum of compliance from the population, and thus the real revolutionary, totalitarian fervor is largely absent. The leadership is lacking in charisma and positions are restricted to those rising from within the party and its technocratic elite. The ideology is still pervasive and dominates the mind and language of the party, yet real commitment to its goals is drastically weakened. Last, the existence of a parallel society where some oppositional activity takes place is fairly common.

Now, let us examine the deepest, most insightful portrait of "post-totalitarianism," that of Havel.[7] In the Czechoslovakia of the 1970s, Havel worried that the surface calm pervading society might give the appearance of broad support for the regime—and thus send precisely the wrong signal both to the rulers and to potential allies in the West. In his first major public letter after his blacklisting in 1969, Havel took great care in describing how below this surface calm, society was plunging into an existential crisis. The crisis was defined by two fundamental causes: fear and apathy or indifference. Havel characterized the fear as a collective anxiety deriving from the recognition of a looming, pervasive presence—the secret police. This organ of the state combined with the myriad of societal collaborators exerted pressure on everyone. Nobody could escape this pressure because everyone had something to lose. Surviving in such an atmosphere of uncertainty and suspicion meant learning to externally adapt oneself to approved language and behaviors. Miłosz famously called this strategy "Ketman," giving the outward appearance of complete orthodoxy while concealing one's true convictions. Miłosz argued that Ketman demands a special sort of mental acuity—a special sensitivity to verbal or facial cues that might help one indicate what might be appropriate in a given situation.[8]

Such a society also provides many opportunities for those with the most pernicious of motives to flourish. As Garton Ash put it, "The most independent, intelligent, and best are at the bottom; the worst, the stupidest, and most servile are at the top. The Party is little more than a union for self-advancement."[9] Those willing to collaborate and inform are guaranteed material prosperity. Thus, it makes no difference whether one truly believes the platitudes of really existing socialism. As long as one behaves as if one does, one will avoid trouble and most likely prosper. Thus does Havel argue that "the number of people who sincerely believe everything that the official propaganda says and who selflessly support the government's authority is smaller than it has ever been. But the number of hypocrites rises steadily: up to a point, every citizen is, in fact, forced to become one."[10] Or, as Miłosz puts it, "If biting dogs can be divided into two main categories, noisy and brutal, or silent and slyly vicious, then the second variety would seem most privileged in the countries of the New Faith."[11]

If this atmosphere gives ample space for those driven by greed and the perverse pleasures of causing others harm, the vast majority of people are moved in another direction. "Work in an office or factory is hard not only because of the amount of labor required, but even more because of the need to be on guard against omnipresent and vigilant eyes and ears. After work one goes to political meetings or special lectures, thus lengthening a day that is without a moment of relaxation or spontaneity."[12] All of this is no doubt quite exhausting for everyone, and sickening for some. Perhaps not surprisingly, especially in the climate of post-totalitarianism, where true revolutionary fervor is minimal, people will seek a life largely outside of state organs and the party. The drive to escape, however, will manifest itself as conformism and routine performance. People will be driven to give the absolute minimum but nonetheless to do what is required, so as to carve out a small space wholly for themselves.[13] And less and less was required as long as one behaved according to the approved code. Havel's example from his most famous and influential essay, "The Power of the Powerless," is the grocer who puts the sign in his window reading, "Workers of the World Unite!" The grocer cares not a whit about the actual content of the slogan. He puts the sign in the window to avoid trouble—to do what the regime asks so that hopefully he will be left alone. By conforming to ideological dictates, the grocer thinks he can escape the pernicious world of politics and secure the private pleasure of family and home and indulge his appetite for material goods and interests. Havel very acutely laid bare the consumerism at the core of a post-totalitarian society. This indifference and general retreat proved quite useful to the regime. Havel concluded, "By fixing a person's whole attention on his mere consumer interests, it is hoped to render him incapable of realizing the increasing extent to which he has been spiritually, politically, and morally violated."[14]

The retreat into the private realm, according to Havel, fails. Because each individual is prevented from relating to a vision of the good and the true in an authentic way, there is a general turning away from the idea of the good and the true. The lifeless and visibly false phantasm of socialism—of universal brotherhood amid plenty—is the only common or public vision permitted. Individuals then succumb to what Havel calls "existence-in-the-world." Here there is no wonder, no longing for meaning, but only a "world of functions, purposes and functioning, a world focused on itself, enclosed within itself, barren in its superficial variety, empty in its illusory richness, ignorant, though awash in information, cold, alienated and ultimately absurd."[15] A general atmosphere of dull uniformity results where nothing distinctive is permitted. Empty, expressionless faces are the outward manifestation of a vague, pervasive anxiety that issues in an aura of unfriendliness. Havel argues, "Standardized life creates standardized citizens with no wills of their own. It begets undifferentiated people with undifferentiated stories. It is a mass producer of banality."[16]

Wiesler in the Post-totalitarian World

Now I want to show why all of this is important for understanding the film as a whole and Wiesler in particular. The sympathetic critics of the film, like Garton Ash and Funder, who argue that there was not nor could there be a Wiesler in real life, focus on Wiesler's observations of Dreyman. Would a Stasi officer really come to respect or admire someone like Dreyman?[17] Critics as well as defenders of the plausibility of Wiesler's transformation, by focusing on Dreyman, also seem to point to his experience of beauty through art as its sole basis. Here the key scene is when Wiesler listens to Dreyman as he plays "Sonata for a Good Man" after Dreyman hears that his friend Albert Jerska has committed suicide. As one critic put it, "Wiesler experiences the mysterious when he encounters beauty, and it changes him."[18] Donnersmarck, to be fair, has given this emphasis some plausibility. The director has said that the genesis for the film is a remark attributed to Lenin by Maxim Gorky— that were Lenin to allow himself to listen to Beethoven's "Appassionata," he doubted he could finish the Bolshevik revolution. Donnersmarck then sought to create a drama where he could, in effect, force a Lenin type to listen to a thing of true beauty. Now, Wiesler's experience of beauty is no doubt part of the story, and a big part at that. Yet I think this interpretation makes Wiesler's change too abrupt and simple. Donnersmarck himself has also said that he wanted the audience to see the change in Wiesler as gradual.[19]

In what follows I want to take a close look at Wiesler and his evolution throughout the film. Wiesler is the pivotal figure in the film, but the basis for the dramatic action lies along two axes—not just his relation to Dreyman. In particular, I want to look at him and his relation to two sets of characters: to Lieutenant Colonel Anton Grubitz of the Stasi and the minister of culture Bruno Hempf (the axis of disgust); and to Dreyman and his girlfriend, the actress Christa-Maria Sieland (the axis of longing).

The opening scenes of the film all introduce this first axis—we see all three of the central characters who work for the state. Our introduction to Wiesler presents him in two contexts: he interrogates a subject who has information about a neighbor's escape to the West, and he conducts a class on interrogation based on that previous success. In Wiesler we see total commitment, self-confidence, and professionalism. His tone and bearing in both cases leave us no doubt that he thinks enemies of the state are quite real and present a threat. This is utterly serious business and Wiesler conducts both the interrogation and the class with scientific precision. He never gets angry nor shows the least bit of emotion, even when encountering resistance by his subject or students. He asks rhetorically, "You think we imprison people on a whim? If you think our humanistic system is capable of such a thing, that alone would justify your arrest." When a student in the class suggests it is inhumane to deprive someone of sleep for such a long time, Wiesler calmly puts a checkmark next to his name on a sheet.

Grubitz, whom we meet at the end of this classroom scene, presents quite a contrast with Wiesler. He enters and starts applauding—"Good, very good"—as if Wiesler was doing some sort of performance. As everyone exits the classroom, Grubitz not so subtly stares at a female student. He tells Wiesler that he has been offered a professorship. He recalls himself and Wiesler sitting in a classroom twenty years earlier and acknowledges that Wiesler enabled him to get good grades (even though life is not about good grades). A trace of ironic knowingness, distance, and lack of seriousness characterizes Grubitz here, and Wiesler looks at him suspiciously, seemingly annoyed that he has to put up with him. Grubitz himself acknowledges Wiesler's attitude toward him when he asks his friend, "Why do you always think I am scheming?" Grubitz has plans to go to the theater to be seen by Minister Hempf. In short, he is an operator who knows what needs to be done to rise in the system. He has used his friend to succeed in school and eventually attain a professorship, and he knows which superiors he must please to rise further.

The following scene at the play introduces the third part of this trio, Minister Hempf. Wiesler and Grubitz differ in their on-the-spot assessments of Dreyman. Grubitz calls him the GDR's "only nonsubversive writer" who is read in the West, while Wiesler detects an arrogance that makes Dreyman worthy of concern. When Wiesler suggests that Dreyman be monitored, Grubitz reasserts his belief in his innocence. Besides, Grubitz says, Hempf likes Dreyman, so they would be sabotaging their own careers by having him monitored. When Grubitz then wanders down from the balcony to speak with Minister Hempf, his assessment changes quickly. Hempf asks Grubitz directly what he thinks of Dreyman and Grubitz replies that perhaps he's not as clean as he seems. Hempf laughs heartily and is glad that Grubitz didn't respond like your average Stasi chump, going on about Dreyman as the GDR's only nonsubversive writer. Here we must ask why Grubitz changed his assessment in the span of a few short minutes. First, we know Grubitz has made his career partly thanks to Wiesler. So he is smart enough to know he is better off following Wiesler's instincts and not his own. But there is something else going on here. Grubitz looks at Hempf carefully and reads him—he figures out exactly what he wants to hear. Donnersmarck has beautifully captured the mental acuity developed in a world dominated by ideology, where appearance is everything and everyone must become an actor. Although lacking in ideological commitment, general intelligence, and knowledge of human nature compared with Wiesler, Grubitz has a well-developed capacity to thrive in the ideological-bureaucratic world of the state.

We should also note here that Hempf is much more like Grubitz than Wiesler. After tasking Grubitz with monitoring Dreyman, Hempf reminds him that success will bring rewards and make him a powerful friend on the Central Committee. And we soon learn just why Hempf has taken an interest in Dreyman—he has his eye on Dreyman's girlfriend, Christa-Maria, and wants to get Dreyman out of the picture completely. So Donnersmarck has captured the reality that Havel and others had noted about the post-totalitarian world: "public and influential positions are occupied, more than ever before, by notorious careerists, opportunists, charlatans, and men of dubious record."[20]

Donnersmarck sets all of this up early in the film to put Wiesler in motion—his evolution is due in part to a growing disgust with the system and the characters he knows have come to dominate it. I think we can even infer that his discontent must have been gnawing at him for some time. He and Grubitz are longtime friends, so Wiesler has witnessed his slow but sure ascent in the Stasi bureaucracy. A less intelligent, less committed, less serious friend has surpassed him—and even done so with his own help! The tension between Wiesler and Grubitz becomes more obvious in another early pivotal scene when the two have lunch in a cafeteria. Wiesler sits down with his tray and when Grubitz objects and suggests they ought to sit with the bosses at another set of tables, Wiesler replies, "Socialism must start somewhere." Thus Wiesler openly acknowledges what is obvious to all but dare not be spoken—the vast gulf between reality and the professed goals of the system. During lunch Grubitz tells Wiesler that the car that dropped Christa-Maria at Dreyman's apartment belongs to Minister Hempf. Since Hempf is a top party official, he cannot be monitored. Grubitz openly admits the operation is in place solely to help Hempf destroy his rival, and that he and Wiesler have much to gain by assisting a member of the Central Committee. Wiesler seems totally unmoved and asks Grubitz if that is why they joined the Stasi. The scene ends with Grubitz tormenting a young Stasi officer he overheard telling a joke about Honecker by asking for his name and rank. He leaves the young officer unsure about whether his indiscretion will actually be catalogued or not. Wiesler looks on with utter disgust. The following scene confirms the steady trajectory of ugliness as we witness Hempf's rape of Christa-Maria in the back of his car.

Disgust, Loneliness, and Longing

The axis of disgust is what drives the early part of the film. Wiesler's sincere attachment to socialism sets him apart from Grubitz and Hempf. Again, I think the allusion to Wiesler's longtime friendship with Grubitz allows us to infer that what Wiesler sees at the beginning of the film of Grubitz and Hempf cannot be a complete surprise. But these early encounters with Grubitz and his motivations and what he learns about Hempf's designs seem to push him to a new level of disaffection. Wiesler's first independent act in the film—that is, an act neither authorized nor dictated by ideology—does not flow from what he observes of Dreyman but from what he knows of Grubitz and Hempf. He knows that it is Hempf's car that drops Christa-Maria off at Dreyman's apartment. He wants Dreyman to see the ugliness that he sees—when he rings the doorbell that brings Dreyman down to the entrance to the building, he utters, "Time for some bitter truths." So it is Wiesler who is the truth teller or the agent of reality. He forces Dreyman to look at the truth in all its naked ugliness. This is far from a full-fledged political rebellion—Wiesler does not seem to have any particular consequences in mind beyond the confirmation by somebody else of this ugly reality.

But this is in itself an extremely important act. For it implies something that will be openly confirmed later—that Dreyman and Christa—the former especially—have each earned their place by blinding themselves to reality. They of course are not agents of the state, and they seem to have carved out a private place for themselves shielded from politics strictly understood. They have the trappings of a normal, decent life. As the other early scenes of the film reveal, Dreyman directs, Christa acts, they attend and throw parties, they have friends, and they are lovers. But as we also see, Dreyman's success—he is the winner of something called the Margot Honecker award—comes at the grace of the state. This "normal" world is infected by the looming presence of the state, its agents, and its ideology. We learn that Dreyman's friend the director Albert Jerska has been blacklisted and so Dreyman must put up with the subpar direction of a lesser talent, Schwalber. And while Dreyman's birthday party is a pleasant gathering of friends, the tension rises to the surface when his friend Paul Hauser accuses Schwalber of being an agent of the Stasi. Jerska cannot participate in the social life of the party. He sits alone on the couch reading Brecht.

The earlier scene where Dreyman makes his weekly visit to Jerska's flat provides further insight into this private world. Jerska is clearly miserable due to his blacklisting. He cannot attend premieres anymore—they fill him with disgust. And what is a director who cannot direct plays? He says that in his next life he will come back merely as an author—then he would not have to depend on the good graces of the state. So Jerska knows two things.

He knows he cannot be who he really is. He is quite literally prevented from directing. But he also knows that even prior to his blacklisting, insofar as his art came with the approval of the state, it was not really his art, an expression of his own mind and heart. During the conversation in Jerska's flat, Dreyman tells him that Minister Hempf has given him "concrete hope" that his blacklisting will come to an end. Though Jerska says he is pleased by the prospect, his look suggests he knows this will not happen. Nor does Dreyman really believe what he is saying. So even in this private world, lies are pervasive, distorting true understanding.

Dreyman, Christa-Maria, Jerska, Hauser, and the other members of this circle seem to have achieved varying degrees of success exempting themselves from the state and its ideological distortions. But the very idea that this retreat could ever really be successful—that one could live a decent life untainted by politics—is itself a lie. And it is a lie that the regime wants its citizens to believe. It offers them a bargain that is difficult to refuse. "Avoid politics if you can; leave it to us! Just do what we tell you, don't try to have deep thoughts, and don't poke your nose into things that don't concern you! Shut up, do your work, look after yourself—and you'll be all right!"[21] It is a bargain that Dreyman has largely accepted. Wiesler's initial act, then, is meant to show Dreyman just how ugly his bargain really is.

Wiesler stands between two groups. Grubitz and Hempf have embraced and flourished in the system because they are moved by nothing but self-interest and appetite. Dreyman and Christa-Maria have remained relatively unharmed by it because they have accepted what the system has offered: work and relative peace in exchange for obedience. Both of these groups have made their peace with the world of appearances for their own purposes. Havel emphasizes how the post-totalitarian system makes everyone an accomplice. He writes: "Everyone . . . is in fact involved and enslaved, not only the greengrocers but also the prime ministers. Differing positions in the hierarchy merely establish differing degrees of involvement: the greengrocer is involved only to a minor extent, but he also has very little power. The prime minister, naturally, has greater power, but in return he is far more deeply involved. Both, however, are unfree, each merely in a somewhat different way. . . . For everyone in his own way is both a victim and a supporter of the system."[22]

This is brought out beautifully in the film when Dreyman tells Christa that he knows about her meetings with Minister Hempf and pleads with her not to go. You don't need him, he tells her. She replies that Dreyman needs the system less than she does, but he gets into bed with the powers that be too. They decide what plays are produced, who acts, and who directs. Here we see what Havel calls the "longing for humanity's rightful dignity, for moral integrity" coupled with the recognition that humanity is also capable "of coming to terms with living within the lie."[23]

Wiesler and Jerska can no longer abide the world of appearances. They are filled with disgust by the yawning gap between ideological pretense and reality. But they are pushed to act for an additional reason. It has long been observed that tyrannies depend for their perpetuation on isolating people from one another. Hannah Arendt has described how totalitarian regimes take this a step further. They do not stop at isolation but attack the integrity of private life as well. "Totalitarian domination . . . bases itself on loneliness, on the experience of not belonging to the world at all, which is among the most radical and desperate experiences of man." Later in this essay she elaborates her conception of loneliness. "What makes loneliness so unbearable is the loss of one's own self which can be realized in solitude, but confirmed in its identity only by the trusting and trustworthy company of my equals. In this situation, man loses trust in himself as the partner of his thoughts and that elementary confidence in the world which is necessary to make experiences at all. Self and world, capacity for thought and experience are lost at the same time."[24]

Wiesler and Jerska each experience this loneliness. For Jerska, it encroaches upon him from the inside out. He no longer has any sense of who he is or that he might find himself by entering a common world. Jerska's response is total despair and eventually suicide. For Wiesler, the self is constituted wholly by his ideological commitments. So once this outside world is revealed to be hollow, he is completely at sea. Wiesler's initial response is to force someone else to see what he sees. Why should he be forced to bear the burden of the false alone?

So it is this world of hypocrisy, pretense, and falsity that sets Wiesler in motion. But it is another world that sets him on a path toward more active rebellion—what I have called the axis of longing. This is the completely foreign world that he discovers as he sits in the attic of Dreyman's flat—the world of love and friendship. Both axes act as catalysts for Wiesler's transformation. Initially he acts to prevent Dreyman from exempting himself from all the ugliness that surrounds him. But he also becomes increasingly fascinated by the beauty that is a part of Dreyman's world. The first thing that really moves Wiesler in this positive way is the love between Dreyman and

Christa-Maria. The strangeness of real human feeling for Wiesler is made perfectly plain in his attempt to mimic what he sees and hears by ordering a prostitute. His intrigue only grows as he listens in on Dreyman's birthday party. Wiesler's second independent act is when he breaks into Dreyman's flat for no other reason than to get a sense of what it might be like to feel what Dreyman feels. He touches and carefully observes his birthday gifts, wondering about the giving and receiving of gifts. He also ends up stealing a Brecht book and we see him in his own apartment reading a poem about a lost love. Wiesler of course does not immediately feel these passions. The episode with the prostitute demonstrates his desire for them, a desire that he does not yet know how to satisfy. What he does feel is the *absence* of these passions. He falls in love not with Dreyman or Christa-Maria but with their love for one another. He also loves their friendships and their dedication to and love of their respective arts.

It is the emergence of this second axis, the axis of longing, that moves Wiesler to a more active rebellion. The content of Christa-Maria's response to Dreyman also seems to move him. It is right after overhearing this conversation that he lies to his coworker, Sergeant Lye, about Christa-Maria's destination. Wiesler then stumbles upon her in a bar and attempts to buttress Dreyman's attempt to restore her faith in herself as an artist. This trajectory continues after he learns of Dreyman's plan to write an essay on suicide in the GDR for publication in the West. He decides not to alert the border guards of what he thinks is an attempt by Hauser to get into West Germany, and he continues not to include anything damning in his written reports. Wiesler also tells his coworker that Dreyman and his friends are writing a play for the GDR's fortieth anniversary (thus repeating the story that Dreyman and his friends had agreed upon).

Yet we ought not to make the mistake of seeing Wiesler's trajectory as easy and steady. This is an error of some critics, who suggest no real Stasi officer could become the "good man" (transformed by beauty) they think Donnersmarck has him become. Another important scene complicates matters and brings the axis of disgust back into play. Wiesler overhears the triumphal meeting between Dreyman, Hauser, and the *Spiegel* editor who plans on publishing Dreyman's suicide essay. Dreyman seems genuinely surprised at how easy his dissident activity is and how incompetent the state security services appear to be. All of this does not sit well with Wiesler—he appears to decide to alert his superiors to Dreyman's essay and the plan for publication. He marches confidently into Grubitz's office with an envelope under his arm. However, Grubitz immediately shows Wiesler a dissertation, "Prison Conditions for Subversive Artists," that he has advised. Grubitz tells him he has given the author a B, so as not to appear too easy. The work puts artists into five categories and suggests the appropriate manner of punishment to ensure the stifling of their artistic impulses. Dreyman is a type 4, the "hysterical anthropocentrist," who hates being alone, loves talking and being around friends. With type 4s, an actual trial should be avoided—temporary detention and complete isolation will provide no material for their writing. As Wiesler listens to Grubitz recount the analysis, we see him glance down at the envelope in his hand. Disgust with Grubitz has made him reconsider his decision to reveal Dreyman's dissident activities. He tells Grubitz he wants to scale back the operation to be more "flexible." From this point forward, Wiesler continues to protect Dreyman by falsifying his reports. And later we learn that Wiesler has even added details about the content of the play that Dreyman is supposedly writing for the anniversary.

Conclusion

It is two axes, not one, that are behind Wiesler's transformation. Some critics who find this character movement unrealistic focus on beauty and the axis of longing but say nothing of the plot elements dealing with what I have termed the axis of disgust. Funder goes even further, arguing that believing a Wiesler to be a real possibility is to misunderstand the "'total' nature of totalitarianism." The system created multiple and minute duties to occupy a variety of individuals in the perpetuation of "real existing socialism." Thus, Funder argues, people could rationalize their involvement by seeing their role as quite small. The individual cogs in the bureaucratic statist machine could just mind their own business and shrink their gaze to their assigned task—and thus not have to face the massive evils being inflicted on much of the population at the hands of the state and its instruments. But later Funder also claims that "most ex-Stasi are still true believers." She argues, "The terrible truth is that the Stasi provide no material for a 'basic expression of belief in humanity.' For expressions of conscience and courage, one would need to look to the resisters. It is this choice, to make the film about the change of heart of a Stasi man, that turns the film, for some, into an inappropriate—if unconscious—plea for absolution of the perpetrators."[25]

There is an interesting tension here between Funder's two points. Her first, regarding the bureaucratized world of state-sponsored mendacity, would seem to enable the system to move largely without "true believers." Her second claim, that even most ex-Stasi remain devoted communists, would have required them to have taken a more global view of their role and its relation to the whole. From the perspective of most scholars and dissidents such as Havel, individuals fervently, sincerely attached to socialism were relatively rare in the 1970s and 1980s. The Grubitzes and Hempfs were the character types who flourished in the system. Somewhat paradoxically, it seems it is Wiesler's sincere attachment to socialism that prods him to reevaluate the state and his role in it.

Yet even my suspicion here about Wiesler's belief is merely an inference—we cannot know this for certain. Yet questions about the level of one's attachment to these ideals are somewhat beside the point. And this I think is where Funder's real mistake lies. She wants to defend the honor of the real dissidents—those who risked their lives to resist the state. She thinks the film does them a disservice in making a Stasi officer the hero and, even further, could lead to a kind of absolution of the evils perpetrated by the Stasi. Her defense of the dissidents is laudable, but I find this second worry unfounded. After all, there is nothing attractive about Grubitz.

But the deeper point brings us back to Havel. Again and again in his writings, Havel emphasizes the need to resist seeing the political landscape in terms of dissidents on the one side and the state and its accomplices on the other. This division would be to misunderstand the nature of the oppression and the possible manner of its ultimate defeat. And the nature of oppression in the post-totalitarian system is defined by ideology—and ideology leaves nobody untouched. Havel argues that one of the main functions of ideology is excusatory. Its purpose "is to provide people, both as victims and pillars of the post-totalitarian system, with the illusion that the system is in harmony with the human order and the order of the universe."[26] This is true from those people in positions of great power and influence down to Havel's greengrocer who merely puts the sign in his window. To paraphrase Alain Besançon, the question is not who really believes in the ideology but who is willing to conform to its demands.[27] "For this reason," argues Havel, "they must live within a lie. They need not accept the lie. It is enough for them to have accepted their life within it and in it. For by this very fact, individuals confirm the system, fulfill the system, make the system, *are* the system."[28]

The great genius of Donnersmarck's film is to illustrate this distinguishing characteristic of ideological tyranny. The fundamental line of conflict is not between social groups or between the oppressive rulers and everyone else. "In the post-totalitarian system, this line runs *de facto* through each person, for everyone in his own way is both a victim and a supporter of the system."[29] This does not mean that Havel or Donnersmarck are in any way excusing those who did exercise real power and used that power for evil ends. They both show the peculiar manner in which ideological tyranny engulfs everyone. This is more troubling than a system put in place by a cadre of greedy souls to oppress the many. Post-totalitarianism "can happen and did happen only because there is obviously in modern humanity a certain tendency toward the creation, or at least the toleration, of such a system."[30] This is the perverse evil of communism—that a system which seems deeply inhuman in so many ways could have survived for so long.

Notes

An earlier version of this essay was published in *Perspectives on Political Science,* April–June 2011, Vol. 40, No. 2. Used by permission.

1. Peter Grieder, "In Defence of Totalitarianism Theory as a Tool of Historical Scholarship," *Totalitarian Movements and Political Religions,* September–December 2007, 578.

2. Juan J. Linz and Alfred Stepan, *Problems of Democratic Transition and Consolidation* (Baltimore: Johns Hopkins University Press, 1996), 50.

3. Václav Havel, "Stories and Totalitarianism," in *Open Letters: Selected Writings, 1965–1990* (New York: Vintage, 1992), 331.

4. Timothy Garton Ash, "The Stasi on Our Minds," *New York Review,* May 31, 2007, http://www.nybooks.com/articles/archives/2007/may/31/the-stasi-on-our-minds/?pagination=false (accessed July 19, 2012).

5. Anna Funder, "Tyranny of Terror," *Guardian,* May 5, 2007, http://www.theguardian.com/books/2007/may/05/featuresreviews.guardianreview12 (accessed July 7, 2012).

6. See Corey Ross, "The GDR as Dictatorship: Totalitarian, Stalinist, Modern, Welfarist?" in *The East German Dictatorship* (London: Arnold, 2002), 24–25; Mike Dennis, *The Rise and Fall of the German Democratic Republic, 1945–1990* (London: Longman, 2000), 185–88; and Linz and Stepan, *Problems of Democratic Transition and Consolidation,* 42–51.

7. In what follows, I am indebted to James Pontuso, *Václav Havel: Civic Responsibility in a Postmodern Age* (Lanham, MD: Rowman and Littlefield, 2004).

8. See Czesław Miłosz, *The Captive Mind,* trans. Jane Zielonko (New York: Random House, 1990), chap. 3.

9. Timothy Garton Ash, "Czechoslovakia under Ice," in *The Uses of Adversity* (New York: Random House, 1989), 63.

10. Václav Havel, "Dear Dr. Husák," in *Open Letters,* 56.

11. Miłosz, *The Captive Mind,* 77.

12. Ibid., 76.

13. Garton Ash noted, "I have never been in a country where politics, and indeed the

whole of public life, is a matter of such supreme indifference." See his "Czechoslovakia under Ice," 63.

14. Havel, "Dear Dr. Husák," 59. The second play in Havel's Vaněk trilogy, "Unveiling," is a biting portrait of a couple who is perfectly emblematic of this naked consumerist retreat. See Marketa Goetz-Stankiewicz, *The Vaněk Plays: Four Authors, One Character* (Vancouver: University of British Columbia Press, 1987); and Pontuso, *Václav Havel*, 85–87.

15. Václav Havel, *Letters to Olga* (London: Faber and Faber, 1988), 341.

16. Havel, "Stories and Totalitarianism," 340.

17. Funder also questions whether a Wiesler could really have kept his activities hidden from his superiors.

18. Santiago Ramos, "Why Dictators Fear Artists," *First Things, On the Square Blog*, July 23, 2007, http://www.firstthings.com/web-exclusives/2007/07/why-dictators-fear-artists (accessed January 23, 2014.)

19. See the interview with Donnersmarck included on the DVD.

20. Havel, "Dear Dr. Husák," 55.

21. Ibid., 61–62.

22. Václav Havel, "The Power of the Powerless," in *Open Letters*, 143–44.

23. Ibid., 145.

24. Hannah Arendt, "Ideology and Terror: A Novel Form of Government," *Review of Politics* 15, no. 3 (1953): 323, 325.

25. Funder, "Tyranny of Terror."

26. Havel, "The Power of the Powerless," 134.

27. See "Language and Power in Soviet Society (Part I): A Conversation between Alain Besançon and George Urban," *Encounter*, May 1987, 11.

28. Havel, "The Power of the Powerless," 136.

29. Ibid., 144.

30. Ibid.

2

WHAT IS A DISSIDENT?

The Travails of the Intellectuals in *The Lives of Others*

Lauren Weiner

During the Soviet era, intellectuals behind the Iron Curtain walked a fine line. We in the West admired those who, like Anna Akhmatova and Vasily Grossman, snatched a measure of liberty by writing "for the desk drawer" (not for publication)[1] or by seeing their work passed from hand to hand in *samizdat* (underground copies) or those who, like Boris Pasternak and Aleksandr Solzhenitsyn, smuggled manuscripts abroad for publication. Viewing the situation from the outside, we tended to consider it a simple matter of rebelling or not rebelling. Often it was not simple. The cultural commissars of the Eastern bloc meted out punishments that differed in severity and kind, and many intellectuals ended up accommodating the commissars to varying degrees.

To Western eyes, the artists and intellectuals portrayed in Florian Henckel von Donnersmarck's *The Lives of Others* offer a puzzling picture. Wending our way through the moral and political subtleties of the East Berlin of this film will show how amply it demonstrates the insidious effects of totalitarianism on those attempting to preserve freedom of thought and expression.

Resisting Soviet power was difficult, and even the proudest resisters bowed at times. The poet Osip Mandelstam, who dared lambaste Josef Stalin in verse, also tried to placate the dictator with a poem of praise. It did not save him from the Gulag. Akhmatova, desperate for her son's release from detention, wrote a few halfhearted odes to Stalin, to no avail.[2] Varlam Shalamov, another great Russian poet, was forced in 1972 to renounce his exposé of the Soviet labor camps, *Kolyma Tales,* in exchange for permission to publish other works.[3] Under official pressure, Pasternak altered his writing style to be more in line with socialist realism. Pasternak felt it prudent to send a condolence telegram to Stalin upon the death of Stalin's wife. With similar prudence, if with greater treachery toward the proletariat, the playwright Bertolt Brecht wrote a supportive letter to Walter Ulbricht, the founder of the German Democratic Republic (GDR), after Ulbricht and the Russians crushed a massive uprising of East German workers in 1953.

As for Brecht's country, East Germany had the least docile population of any of the captive nations if we measure by how many people voted with their feet. Between the GDR's establishment in 1949 and Ulbricht's 1961 closing of the borders lest emigration cause the regime's collapse, one of every six East Germans fled.[4] Yet from those who remained, not much was heard by the outside world. Only rarely did reports surface of an East German writer or artist running afoul of the authorities. One case that stands out, because it received international publicity at the time, was that of the poet-songster Wolf Biermann. Biermann's outspokenness lost him his East German citizenship in 1976. In the 1980s, even as a group of Czechs organized around Charter 77, and Polish workers, intellectuals, and church members nurtured the Solidarity movement, little unrest was visible in the GDR except during a 1987 rock concert on the Western side of the Berlin Wall when youths listening in on the Eastern side clashed with police.[5]

Most of the action of *The Lives of Others* takes place in 1984 in the midst of this political deep freeze. What Donnersmarck has brought to general notice, all these years later, is that there indeed were freethinkers in East Germany, locked in quiet conflict with the largest per capita secret police force in the Soviet empire—the Ministry for State Security, known as the Stasi. How many resisters there were is not easy to say; the subject has thus far received insufficient study. They at least include the lyric poet Reiner Kunze (who was allowed to leave in 1977 and settled in West Germany) and the novelist Erich Loest (resident in West Germany from 1981, many years after he had served a seven-year sentence as a political prisoner). There were also ostensible freethinkers who secretly gave information to the Stasi. The Germanist Julia Hell identified some of "the former GDR's most unsavory authors," meaning paid Stasi collaborators or unpaid Stasi contacts: Fritz Rudolf Fries, Herman Kant, who headed the writers' union, and Sascha Anderson, who led a "strange life as avant-garde artist in the service of the Stasi."[6] No such list would be complete without the prominent dramatist

Heiner Müller. When his assistance to the Stasi came out in the newspapers, the pompous Müller defended it, saying he got valuable literary fodder that way, and also that the secret policemen's contacts with him were "a way of bringing his influence to bear on the Stasi's thinking."[7] Worst of all for the reputation of GDR writers, even the internationally acclaimed novelist Christa Wolf, a dedicated Marxist-Leninist who enjoyed the reputation of a "loyal dissident," had been a secret police informant briefly in the early 1960s.

If *The Lives of Others* has among its characters any who bears comparison with the émigrés Biermann, Kunze, and Loest, it is Paul Hauser. Hauser (played by Hans-Uwe Bauer) is by far the most truculent of the movie's intellectuals and therefore the most admirable. The first line of dialogue we hear from Hauser is an insolent remark he makes to East Germany's minister of culture, Bruno Hempf (played by Thomas Thieme). The rest of Hauser's time on screen is taken up with further mischief, be it publicly unmasking a theater director who works with the Stasi; plotting to outwit the government so he and his friends can expose the bleakness of East Germans' lives; making fun of the state security man who dogs his steps around town; or, most important, encouraging one of the main characters to stand up and oppose the regime.

East bloc writers who forged contacts with the free world and were permitted occasional visits to the West were a privileged group. Hauser is presented as one of these. He is a journalist with a government-granted permit for attendance at conferences abroad. This means he has been trusted not to defect, and indeed the question of this rebel's stance vis-à-vis state socialism as an ideology is an open one. We don't hear him expressing his philosophical or political convictions. The only thing remotely indicative in this regard is his stray comment making fun of his West German uncle "with his big gold Mercedes." We are left to assume that Paul Hauser, like the man he coaches toward subversive action (the illustrious playwright Georg Dreyman, played by Sebastian Koch), holds to Marxism in some fashion—rejecting the corrupt and brutal practices of the regime, not its radically egalitarian aspiration.

That assumption is backed up somewhat by the filmmaker's commentary on the DVD of the film. During the scene where Hauser and Dreyman are in the latter's apartment conspiring with the editor of the West German newspaper *Der Spiegel* (Gregor Hessenstein, played by Herbert Knaup), Donnersmarck notes that the two Easterners react to the visiting Westerner with distrust. They appreciate that he has come to help them publicize the despair that is rampant in their country, but they sense that this outsider does not understand them. Hessenstein brashly pulls out a bottle of champagne and proclaims it "the real stuff," better than the plonk they are used to, and he generally "doesn't stroke them the right way," says Donnersmarck.[8] He meant to show here the estrangement between Germans of the communist East and the capitalist West, though the point is subtle—so subtle that he admits that non-German viewers may have trouble getting it.

It takes a while for the repercussions to arrive, but Hauser's outburst among the theater folk partying in Dreyman's apartment—the occasion where he unmasked the Stasi-assisting theater director —has created quite a stir. And a headache for the secret police, who need discretion. It was fundamental to the workings of the Ministry for State Security to conceal the identities of the legions of ordinary citizens it enlisted to monitor their friends, coworkers, even family members. The targets of the monitoring were suspected of counterrevolution, usually defined as an inclination to emigrate. Discretion, too, entailed a diabolical twist. While the government's helpers were protected with anonymity, anyone it deemed hostile might be falsely tagged as a helper. The Stasi was not above planting slanderous rumors that an individual was one of the *inoffiziellen Mitarbeitern* (informants or "unofficial coworkers")—an accusation, among East Germans, more shameful than being branded an alcoholic or adulterer. This was but one tool used to ruin the reputations of those considered enemies of the people.[9]

The breach by Hauser prompts Hempf, the minister of culture, to cancel the journalist's travel permit. He is being clamped down upon by the authorities—a situation that, in real life, often propelled East Germans toward escape.[10] Hauser, however, only feigns leaving the country. He fakes an escape to test who is and who is not under surveillance, the better to evade state security and help Dreyman compose and transmit his manuscript indicting the GDR as a failed experiment in socialism. In a turn that is funny but also chilling, Hauser's test only seems to work. He and his friends are indeed being tracked by the head of a Stasi operation against Dreyman. This man, Captain Gerd Wiesler (played by Ulrich Mühe), is up in the attic of Dreyman's building listening to the goings-on in the busy director's apartment. (Wiesler's surprise and confusion upon picking up Hauser's voice in his headphones when he understood the journalist to have fled to the West is used for dramatic purposes having to do with the Stasi man's change of heart about the people on whom he is spying.)

Nor is taking away his foreign-travel privilege the worst thing the regime has done to Hauser. The movie had opened with a scene inside Hohenschön-hausen, the Stasi prison and interrogation center, where we saw a hapless citizen being grilled. Hauser is the only recurring character who, we learn, is a Hohenschönhausen veteran. When sympathetic mention is made of this, Hauser blinks and looks down without saying anything. He looks as if it saddens him to pull out those distasteful memories, so he would rather not—indulging in emotion might weaken him. Though hot-tempered and tenacious, Hauser is no he-man; rather, he seems to need to husband his strength for the taking of risks.

The Lives of Others has a martyr to artistic integrity, the stage director Albert Jerska (played by Volkmar Kleinert). Jerska has been sidelined as a director by order of Comrade Minister Hempf for airing at least one criticism of the government. Even though he enjoys a following in the West and could likely get permission to emigrate, he chooses to stay. His plight troubles the movie's main intellectual, the politically reliable, glamorous, and successful Dreyman. Dreyman tries to make Hempf see that this talented man, who "believes in socialism and in this country," never should have been ostra-cized. The average moviegoer may wonder how someone ends up persona non grata when he "believes in socialism and in this country." There is no better place to turn for an explanation than to the Polish émigré poet and former communist Czesław Miłosz, who described "the New Faith" holding sway in the Sovietized part of Europe. For those in power, "the only friend will be the man who accepts the doctrine 100 percent," wrote Miłosz. "If he accepts only 99 percent, he will necessarily have to be considered a foe, for from that remaining one percent a new church can arise."[11]

Jerska is a tragic example of the "captive mind" evoked so well by Miłosz in his classic book of that name. That said, we at the same time can admire this lonely man for not truckling to get back in the government's good graces. As it happens, the East German actor playing Jerska was a prospective *inof-fizieller Mitarbeiter* (IM) in real life. He proved himself a person of extraor-dinary rectitude. According to Donnersmarck (the director's commentary again), a young Volkmar Kleinert was approached repeatedly by the Stasi over the telephone. He summoned the will to shout "No!" into the receiver and hang up. The Stasi never bothered him again, nor did this rebuff hurt his acting career. The experience taught Kleinert that "maybe being upright and honest and courageous, maybe even heroic, didn't always come at a huge price. We always assume that it's going to. . . . Maybe it doesn't." Don-nersmarck's words raise an inevitable and disturbing point: East Germans' acquiescence in—really, complicity with—their own oppression. After all, the Stasi overmastered the people of the GDR without the mass violence committed by Hitler's Gestapo. The Stasi tightened the screws with a velvet hand. Most acquiesced.

The truly excruciating acquiescence in the film is that of its female lead, Dreyman's girlfriend. The action mounts to a height of suspense when Christa-Maria Sieland (played by Martina Gedeck) is brought in for interrogation and threatened with being barred from the acting profession unless she agrees to inform on her lover. Her pliancy in the hands of the Stasi is immediate. The sad common denominator between the man who does not truckle and the woman who does is their desperation. Jerska ends up taking his own life. Sieland dies before our eyes—by suicide or accidentally, it is hard to tell which. This powerful, Anna Karenina–like ending—and the filmmaker confirms that he had Tolstoy's protagonist in mind—arouses more pity than contempt for this weak woman. Who among us is certain that, in her place, we would have been stronger? Moreover, she did nothing political to get in this bind. A star actress of the East German theater, she is apolitical. Her beauty has drawn the attention of a powerful man, Comrade Minister Hempf. He forces her into a sexual relationship behind Dreyman's back. Likewise the playwright, whose work up to the time we meet him is enthusiastically approved by the regime, attracts surveillance not for a political reason but for a personal one. Hempf is fishing for something incriminating that will get his rival arrested and out of the way.

Yes, *The Lives of Others* is a bit of a soap opera. But let no one think that such things did not go on. Ulrich Mühe, the movie's Captain Wiesler, found out years after the fact that his then-wife had been one of several IMs reporting on him to the secret police. Other prominent East Germans who discovered they had spousal spies include Vera Lengsfeld, the Christian Democratic deputy and aide to Chancellor Angela Merkel. Drawing civilians into the security apparatus enhanced the longevity of all the governments behind the Iron Curtain, as we know. Aleksandr Solzhenitsyn pointed out (drawing upon Nadezhda Mandelstam's insight) that the more individuals who got roped in, the better: "Beyond the purpose of weakening ties between people, there was another purpose as well. Any person who had let himself be recruited would, out of fear of public exposure, be very much interested in the continuing stability of the regime."[12]

The struggles of conscience and expediency are many-layered in the human heart—and in this movie. Therein lies its brilliance. Yet when it comes to the character of Dreyman, the layering proves rather maddening. As others have observed, he strangely combines Marxist adherence, humaneness, and careerism.[13] Supposedly this is the story of an apple-polisher who turns from "slactivist" to activist.[14] Dreyman goes from scolding Hauser for calling out the Stasi informant—sympathizing, even, with the authorities when they cancel his feisty friend's travel visa—to standing up for his departed mentor, Jerska, by getting word to the outside about the prevalence of suicide in East Germany.

Should we look from another angle, we might not see much of an evolution. After all, Dreyman's is a charmed life from the movie's beginning to its end. He never has to contend with an ultimatum from the state, as others must. His apartment is bugged but he has no awareness of it until those who were listening in are gone from power. When he secretly puts himself at odds with the regime, his deed stays a secret—until he wants the world to know about it after the collapse of the GDR. The wonderful, if not very plausible, transformation of Captain Wiesler into Dreyman's guardian angel saves the latter from being discovered as the one who wrote in *Der Spiegel* about East Germany's scandalously high suicide rates.

His lover died a sudden and horrible death, and years later when he reads his Stasi file, he finds out that she betrayed him. Because of her, Stasi goons tore up his apartment in search of incriminating evidence. These are bitter realities. Then again, his poring over the Stasi file inspires a roman á clef from his pen, and this book, marking the end of a period of writer's block, is the latest feather in Georg Dreyman's cap and delivers the film's capstone message: that there do exist men of feeling (he means Wiesler) able to rise above terrible times. Donnersmarck asserts that relatively few of the Stasi's millions of victims had the stomach to go to the former East German security directorate and ask to see the file that the Stasi kept on them. Two who did, and who made literary use of their files, were the above-mentioned East German writers Erich Loest and Reiner Kunze.[15] The borrowing of Loest's and Kunze's experience for this fictional character is clever but it is also slightly galling. They triumphed over persecution; Dreyman hardly faces any.

In pondering this matter of the kind and degree of a dissident's dissent, it may help to notice that the spiritual faith of a Solzhenitsyn—also of an Akhmatova, a Miłosz, or a Kunze—was a basis on which to reject communist ideology. Donnersmarck does not deal with God or religion. They are not really present in the East Berlin he gives us, except insofar as a Stasi agent alludes to being ordered to spy on priests. This seems true to the milieu the film is trying to depict. The oppositional artists seem part of a coterie of modern, atheistic bohemians whose politics, if any, are communist or at least Euro-socialist.[16] Paul Hauser's sidekick, the burly and bearded Karl Wallner (played by Matthew Brenner), is the one who most looks the part of the 1960s-style, scruffy academic leftist.

Communism was invented by atheist intellectuals; few intellectuals in East bloc societies were not pulled into its magnetic field. Moreover, there was something else at work that increased this effect. Despite fascism's being as scarce as the Almighty is in *The Lives of Others,* the real versions of Hauser and the rest lived and worked in a place where Nazis were said to be lurking around every corner. The self-presentation of communists everywhere was that they were the people's guardians against fascism (a hardy perennial born in 1935 with the Comintern's "popular front" policy). This had a special meaning and impact in the land of Nazism's birth.

In 1947, Bertolt Brecht wrote in his journal about National Socialism and "the annihilating effects of failure."[17] As these words indicate, in the aftermath of the 1939–1945 conflagration and of the Nuremberg trials, what weighed upon Germans was not only the horror of mass murder committed by the Third Reich but the shame of Germany's losing the war. The German Democratic Republic's leaders deployed both the horror and the shame to put over the idea that their ruling Socialist Unity Party (SED) was, in the words of Julia Hell, "the sole heir of the resistance movement" against Hitler.[18] The country's very raison d'être lay in its "realization of the heritage of the German labor movement and the antifascist struggle."[19] This "founding discourse retained its power until the State imploded in 1989," writes Hell in her book on the centrality of antifascism to the literary imagination of the GDR's writers. In this society, to go against the grain at all was to court association with Adolf Hitler. Hell speaks of "the displaced character of East German politics," in which there was no legitimate political center, let alone a legitimate conservative position.[20]

Another of Bertolt Brecht's journal entries shows this clearly. After the revolt of June 17, 1953, over the state's ratcheting-up of productivity quotas, he had an encounter with a humble workingman—a plumber. Dismay that the "workers' and peasants' state" should be spurned by so many workers and peasants had led Brecht to sound out one of them. He records in his journal that the plumber told him the country needed free elections. And that he, Brecht, rejected the idea. "I said, 'then the Nazis would be elected.'"[21] The hostility to democratic norms was no doubt sincere on his part. But it is not at all clear that he believed the party line—that Nazism was poised for a comeback—that he parroted to this man.[22]

Commentators have noted the incongruity of Bertolt Brecht being the patron saint, so to speak, of an anticommunist film. Paul Cantor, in his contribution to this volume, points out that at any rate, the sentiment in Brecht's lyric poetry is featured more than is the agitprop of his plays—and that even the plays can be good in spite of the dogmatism of their creator. The theatrical performance that the movie shows (from a distance) is unquestionably Brechtian, but it is by the fictional Georg Dreyman, not Bertolt Brecht. The performance occurs early on, and while we don't get to hear much of the dialogue, we see stage décor that conjures up a sleekly stylized version of a factory, the kind of thing Brecht favored. The actors are clad in Brechtian gray, blue-gray, and black—from their heavy work boots to their smocks to the babushka on the head of leading lady Christa-Maria Sieland, who cavorts among her fellow troupers like some Stalinist version of Bizet's Carmen. She plays an assembly-line laborer who has premonitions, and she has a vision of a man who is "crushed by the mighty wheel." The mighty wheel of bourgeois-industrial exploitation, we may be permitted to assume. Her character is named Marta, and this has a subtle and very somber payoff later on. In Dreyman's Stasi file it says that his lover Sieland, upon signing up as an informant, chose "Marta" as her IM cover name.

Since the character of Georg Dreyman is somewhat modeled on Brecht,[23] the latter's life and literary production merit discussion. What Donnersmarck says is that Brecht was "torn between fascination for that ideology [communism] and a full realization of the wrongness that automatically came with it, of the violence of the dictatorship." During the time that the peripatetic Brecht lived in the GDR, some sort of realization did apparently sink in. The fascination was certainly more marked than the realization, though. It shows up often in his poetry and dramas. His 1929 play *The Measure Taken,* about agents secretly dispatched by Moscow to spread revolution in China, justified violence against the innocent if it served the cause. "Sink into dirt, embrace the butcher, but change the world, the world needs change," as the chorus sings in that play.[24] In this same vein is the Brecht poem "Cover Your Tracks," which the critic Walter Benjamin, a friend of the poet's, characterized as "an instruction for the illegal agent."[25]

If a Stasi man ever needed literary inspiration for his conspiratorial work, *The Measure Taken* or "Cover Your Tracks" would have done nicely. But Donnersmarck has other plans for his Captain Gerd Wiesler, placing into his hands a Brecht poem about a cloud, a plum tree, and a kiss. The filmmaker hints that he knows this was self-indulgent. After all, the softening influence on his film character could have been some other canonical German poet—say, Goethe (as Cantor suggests). He describes feeling an irresistible urge to put Brecht in at that point as a tribute to a man who, whatever else he was, was also a fine lyric poet. That most moviegoers would be unaware of the literary/biographical background probably made it seem safe to follow this urge. Really, the unity of it all must have been just too tempting: imitating Brecht's dramaturgy; a dreamy Wiesler on the couch, being swept away by Brecht's words evoking the fleeting joys of nature; Wiesler listening in on the playing of a piano piece whose title is an allusion to Brecht ("A Sonata for a Good Man" after the play *The Good Person of Szechwan*); having this also be the title of Dreyman's novel, which conveys the movie's culminating message; Jerska telling Dreyman his troubles while reciting apt Brecht verses. (The last one was cut from the final version of the film.)

This itemization makes the Brecht obsession seem cruder than it comes across on screen. Furthermore, in all fairness, this film is about the German Democratic Republic, and the figure of Brecht looms large over the arts and culture of that now-defunct nation. Still, it cannot but be seen as a violation of the movie's integrity to have used Brecht in this pervasive way. The movie's very conception bears out this judgment. Donnersmarck's oft-mentioned inspiration in writing his screenplay was an anecdote told by Maxim Gorky, the founder of socialist realism, about Lenin. According to Gorky, Lenin wistfully said that experiencing aesthetic beauty was rewarding but too much of a distraction to the revolutionist, who needed to concentrate on tough tasks—such as certain people needing "to be beaten on the head, beaten mercilessly."[26] The filmmaker created Wiesler as a stand-in for Lenin, and this time around, the exposure to art and culture conquers the ideologue's soul and disabuses him of his rigid ideology.

My point is that Donnersmarck knows Bertolt Brecht would be the last artist to favor a Bolshevik's taking some time off to broaden himself—the last to favor Lenin's tarrying a while with Beethoven (or even with Brecht) when he could be at the office sending more counterrevolutionaries to the firing squad. Brecht would have argued, of course, that his stance was not bloodthirsty. Or at least not simply bloodthirsty. Compassion, which for Donnersmarck flows from works of high art, for Brecht flows from Marx, Engels, and Lenin. These three "were the most compassionate of all men," in Brecht's words.[27] Their dictatorship of the proletariat, however messy in the construction, would bring an end to injustice.

Granted, the poet had his sensitive side—was known to be too sensitive, in fact, to want to live under the system he advocated with such fervor. "The element of playfulness, so important in his work, could not possibly survive in proximity with the very horrors he used to play with," said Hannah Arendt. He knew himself well enough not to spend too much time in the Soviet Union, she pointed out in her 1968 essay on Brecht.[28] Nor did he choose, as many have mistakenly said, to live in the communist half of his native Germany. Brecht's residence in the GDR came about by default. The military administrators in control of West Berlin, where he went after leaving the United States in 1947, did not let him settle in Munich as he wanted.[29] (Anyone that fond of the skullduggery of the communist underground would likely have amassed a security profile that did not smell right to Allied authorities.)

His interwar exile from Germany had begun back when Hitler first took power in 1933. He had criticized the Third Reich from afar, but these antifascist writings were notably flat, according to Arendt, and often inaccurate. The reason: his perceptions were boxed in by the communist equation of capitalism and fascism. For example, in the poem "Burial of the Agitator in the Zinc Coffin," the Nazis' mistreatment of their political adversaries is presented as similar to what other governments did to their political adversaries. Arendt excoriates Brecht for suggesting in this poem that "there was a difference only in degree between countries under capitalist rule. And this was a double lie, for in capitalist countries opponents were not beaten to death and shipped home in sealed coffins, and Germany was not a capitalist country any longer."[30]

The final seven years of Brecht's life (he died in 1956 of a heart attack, aged fifty-eight) were fruitful in terms of mounting plays but not in terms of writing new ones. As a *Staatsdichter* (state poet), he had the use of the grand Schiffbauerdamm theater for productions by his Berliner Ensemble, which became the most distinguished institution in East Germany. Ever mindful that the Schiffbauerdamm could be taken away from his ensemble if he stepped out of line, he paid lip service to the theories of the Russian dramatist Stanislavsky and the socialist realism demanded by Stalin's cultural enforcer, Andrei Zhdanov.[31] Any grumblings against the powerful—such as Brecht's sarcastic (and unpublished) suggestion that if the GDR government was so bent on pushing productivity quotas through the roof, maybe it should dissolve the people and elect a new one—were sotto voce.[32]

The very name of Zhdanov, by the way, was an affliction to the poets and writers mentioned at the outset of this essay. He patrolled all of the arts in the Soviet sphere, music included, scouring everything for signs of imperialist influence that had to be expunged. A famous 1948 decree by this commissar of commissars thrashed Dmitri Shostakovich, Aram Khachaturian, and Sergei Prokofiev, among others, for committing the sin of "formalism." Citing Zhdanov's authority, East German academicians condemned the most ambitious project of Hanns Eisler, an opera based on Goethe's *Faust*. Eisler—Bertolt Brecht's collaborator on *The Measure Taken* and many other works—was denied authorization for his interpretation of Goethe, gave up writing the opera, and retreated in defeat to Austria, where he had been reared. As for Shostakovich, his troubles were so constant that a recent biography of the Russian composer could describe him as "both a celebrated hero and a shivering wreck."[33] Important for our purposes is that an aide to and memorializer of Shostakovich, defending the composer's posthumous reputation, compared him to a traditional Russian figure, that of the *yurodivy*. Apparently it means "bitter jester"—one who entertains the court as is expected of him but finds under-the-radar ways to express his true self. One Shostakovich anecdote has it that, when he wanted to tell visitors a joke, he would take them into the bathroom first so he could turn on the spigot and drown out the surveillance. A scene in *The Lives of Others* has Paul Hauser using the same tactic, only with loud music from his stereo.

The old figure of the yurodivy reminds us that it isn't as if artists and intellectuals were free of intimidation by the powerful before the Bolshevik Revolution of 1917. History is full of willful patrons, from Lorenzo de Medici to England's Charles I to the Duke of Weimar—who, to teach J. S. Bach exactly who was in charge, had him imprisoned in a castle keep for a month. Communism, however, innovated. It did so by being systematic: Zhdanov didn't simply push creative types around; he elevated his whims into the doctrine of "Zhdanovism," the better to impose those whims on all who dared venture into culture and the arts in the Soviet Union or the other "people's democracies." The same was true of scientific socialism's treatment of science—Andrei Zhdanov's counterpart in that field being the famous Trofim Lysenko. The doctrine of "Lysenkoism" held that Mendelian genetics were a capitalist hoax; agronomists and horticulturalists in Russia and the satellite nations were to reject Mendel and build upon Soviet theories exclusively. Bertolt Brecht may be one of the few who, while being subjected to Zhdanovism, also dabbled in Lysenkoism. A ballad for children he composed in 1950 about how to grow millet highlights the wonders emanating from "Lysenko's greenhouse in distant Moscow"; it has Stalin, "the Soviet peoples' great harvest leader," in a cameo role.[34]

The author of "The Rearing of Millet" also wrote many valued works of literature, and for this reason he has defenders (Donnersmarck included) who strain to emphasize whatever qualms about revolutionary coercion Brecht expressed. Hannah Arendt, a fellow German exile and acquaintance of Brecht's, who wishes also to defend him as a great artist, takes a slightly different tack. She shows that he at least paid a price—the highest price— for his in fact nearly uninterrupted Stalinism. When he had to give up his revolutionary cheerleading from a safe distance, Arendt writes, it put him "in infinitely closer contact with a totalitarian state than he had ever been in his life before." And it pricked his conscience to have to "see the sufferings of his own people with his own eyes." The result was that "not a single play and not a single great poem" came from his pen in those seven years. She adds that he "knew that he could not write in East Berlin" and the proof, in her mind, was that at the time of his death he was trying to emigrate to Western Europe.[35] An interesting point of comparison and contrast, then, between Donnersmarck's playwright and Brecht is this: to the degree that Brecht's conscience was awakened, this hurt his muse. The better-late-than- never dissident Dreyman makes out much better—as is his wont!—in that his awakened conscience, rather than stymieing his creative powers, rejuvenates them. We can conclude that just as Wiesler is Donnersmarck's way of using the filmic art to improve the outcome for Lenin, Dreyman is his way of improving the outcome for Brecht.

Here we are led to consider how far the improvement is intended to reach into the realms of political belief and political action. Carl Eric Scott argues persuasively in this volume that the ambivalence displayed by Drey- man implies a political stance—held by the fictional character and his creator alike—of gradualism, expressed as "reform communism" or, most plausibly of all, that ever-elusive "Third Way" between capitalism and communism. This could explain why Donnersmarck—who says he takes the utmost care in naming his characters—made the playwright "Dreyman." Three-Man could be searching for the Third Way. In any case, the ambivalence is frustrating to watch. Dreyman's niceness and lack of guile (which are not Brechtian by any stretch) help drive the drama of *The Lives of Others* forward, to be sure. But when, with furrowed brow, he cautions the *Der Spiegel* editor that the exposé he will write and smuggle out to the newspaper "should remain literature, not political agitation," it seems as though he is stepping on his own heroism. Is it an exposé he is cooking up or a meekly entered demurrer?

Irksomely subtle in much the same way is his behavior when he faces the wrath of the secret police. Stasi agents, acting on Sieland's information, show up at his apartment. As they enter to search it, he gently addresses them as "comrades" to remind them that he would never do anything to harm the state. They ransack the place anyway and find a book by Aleksandr Solzhenitsyn. Again he moves to assure the intruders whose side he is on. Not gently this time, but haughtily, he tells the Stasi goon holding up the copy of Solzhenitsyn's *The First Circle* that this was a gift to him from none other than the wife of East Germany's leader, Erich Honecker. What usually is seditious and suspicious isn't in his case, he is saying.

Stepping on his own heroism and name-dropping as he tries to forestall imprisonment—this, then, is the complicated life of the yurodivy. He is apt to keep onlookers guessing, especially those seeking to judge him in the moral sense. If we don't know quite what to think of Dreyman, his creator has a definite view. He tends to overadmire. He wants us to find the playwright slyly insubordinate rather than compliant, especially in the scene just referred to. One more detail from it will suffice. The goons, before going away, serve notice that Dreyman has the right to file a claim against the government if any property has been damaged in the search. Though his upholstery has been slashed to pieces, he responds, no thanks, he is sure that everything is in perfect order. Anyone who thought—as this viewer did—that he looked and sounded cowed here is corrected by Donnersmarck in his commentary. This is irony from a self-possessed Dreyman, he says. The moment is intended as "a little bow" to Sigmund Freud, who showed a coolly formal sarcasm toward the Gestapo agents who let him leave Nazi-occupied Vienna in 1938. Overadmiration of Dreyman has a serious consequence for *The Lives of Others*. It leads the filmmaker to his ending with Dreyman and Wiesler, a picture of reconciliation and good feelings that, while highly satisfying as moviemaking, fails to ring true. In today's Germany, the former hound dogs of the secret police and their former quarry maintain at best an uneasy coexistence.[36]

Notice, by the way, how Donnersmarck's intended allusion to Freud conflates the GDR's secret police and the secret police of the GDR's oft-invoked nemesis, the Nazis. This is natural enough, and common enough. Yet one of the achievements of this film is that it helps us recognize the difficulty of weighing one form of totalitarianism against the other—the sanguinary nature of the one against the deeper insidiousness of the other. The German Democratic Republic was backed by the quiet presence of Soviet tanks on German soil. The secret police force seldom bashed in heads but its project of achieving *flächendeckend*—blanket coverage—was successful.[37] In East Germany, doctors informed on patients.[38] Secret police went into the high schools and made teachers give students writing assignments that would later be collected as handwriting samples so that anticommunist graffiti artists could be nabbed.[39] And East Germans who had to participate in this degradation of one another were invited to, and did, pick their own cover names.[40] The Stasi did not split open a society blatantly but made in it innumerable hairline cracks.

Christa-Maria Sieland took the very best of herself—"Marta," her role on stage—and made it a sordid secret police pseudonym. It is possible that this character's name—for, again, Donnersmarck wants us to attend to names—alludes to the novelist Christa Wolf, who died at age eighty-two at the time this essay was written. The likelihood of this wanes, however, in light of the significant differences between them. Wolf informed for the Stasi out of commitment to the antifascist cause, for one thing. For another, and to her credit, she made a poor informant. She was taken off the IM roster after some three years, spending far longer as a target of the Stasi's monitoring. A stalwart of the ruling SED Party but a sometime critic of the regime, Wolf did write about the oppressiveness of being watched by state security in an autobiographical novel. It was denigrated as the cri de coeur that came too late, for she waited until it was safe to publish this work, when the Stasi and the entire Honecker regime were on the way out. Most of her fiction explored the legacy of shame left by the German tyranny that ended in 1945. Ultimately she was a captive mind of the German tyranny that ended in 1989. With the GDR in midcollapse, she pleaded with her fellow East Germans not to let it die, to keep persevering in the construction of "a truly democratic society." People ought not flee, she wrote—it was "more difficult but also more honorable to stay in the socialist Fatherland."[41]

A consolation for Wolf and the other SED Party faithful was that the SED was allowed to continue on in the new Germany (though under another name, the Party of Democratic Socialism or PDS). We can assume this leniency would have met with the hearty approval of Bertolt Brecht. In fact it appalled Florian Henckel von Donnersmarck. Just as the Nazi Party was banned in 1945, so should the SED have been banned when the Berlin Wall came down. He offers this opinion in his commentary near the end of the movie in support of a larger point: that ruthless careerists who prospered under communism, like the then–culture minister Hempf, have not been driven from the scene but remain active and successful in the new order.

In one of the epilogue-like sequences that close the film, we catch up with Hempf in the post–cold war period. The former minister is at the theater, and we see him waylay Dreyman in the lobby after the latter has bolted from his seat in the middle of the performance. Seeing and hearing another actress play Marta, the role he created, has overwhelmed the playwright with tragic memories of Sieland. While this distraught reaction is a sign of Dreyman's decency, it is hard not to view him and Hempf as at least somewhat similar—a pair of survivors. For life goes on. One's career does, too, as does one's love life. (The woman next to Dreyman in the audience looks to be his girlfriend.) Of course, Hempf and the playwright still have much that divides them. Hempf dares to challenge Dreyman one last time over "our dear Christa." He also flaunts his lack of repentance for his misdeeds as a GDR official. Dreyman rather wanly pits his indignation at "people like you" against Hempf's brutal thrusts. Only now does Dreyman find out that his home was mined with secret listening devices. And as he takes this in, he does it again—he complicates our notion of the dissident with his dainty shock upon learning that he was not the pet of the regime that he assumed he was.

The mystery of Dreyman is unraveled. To wit, it was possible to have been on both sides in a "participatory dictatorship," as the GDR has been called. And yes, this fictional character does represent an improved version of Bertolt Brecht, because Dreyman sticks more than a baby toe on the side of humanity, truth, and freedom. The "loyal dissident"—that opaque label that some applied to Christa Wolf—is now embodied in an example from which we can learn. We won't necessarily be inspired or uplifted by what we see. Nor should we flinch from drawing conclusions from what we see, as Wolf Biermann reminds us. Biermann, though he was and may still be a Marxist, was no "loyal dissident." His poems and songs mocking East Germany's leaders for failing to live up to his socialist ideals got him kicked out of the GDR in 1976—and in fact one of the leading writers who publicly protested his ejection was Christa Wolf.

Upon seeing *The Lives of Others,* Biermann embraced it. As he says in his contribution to this volume, "The Ghosts Are Leaving the Shadows," he did so despite its having "put a soft pedal on the totalitarian reality." He had initially doubted that a young, upper-class West German like Donnersmarck would be up to tackling this subject. The movie, however, told him something important: that those who have not lived and suffered under a tyranny are nonetheless "obviously quite adequately equipped to judge and even condemn." We for our part must judge that the writer Erich Loest, the poets Reiner Kunze and Wolf Biermann, the actor Volkmar Kleinert,[42] and the politician Vera Lengsfeld are nobler than those who put themselves on both sides. As Biermann says in this volume, the film "shows us what a crazy and complicated mix of good and evil is contained within the human breast, and in what dreadful disarray," yet "despite all the complicated complications in human affairs, what Father God said in the Bible to all his earthly children still holds: 'Let your yes be yes and your no be no.'"

Notes

1. See John Garrard and Carol Garrard, *The Bones of Berdichev: The Life and Fate of Vasily Grossman* (New York: Free Press, 1996), 108, 132.

2. See György Dalos, *The Guest from the Future: Anna Akhmatova and Isaiah Berlin,* trans. Antony Wood (New York: Farrar, Straus, and Giroux, 1999), 88.

3. This account is from the translator's preface. Varlam Shalamov, *Kolyma Tales,* trans. John Glad (London: Penguin Books, 1994).

4. Frederick Kempe, *Berlin 1961: Kennedy, Khrushchev, and the Most Dangerous Place on Earth* (New York: G. P. Putnam's Sons, 2011), xxi.

5. James Mann, *The Rebellion of Ronald Reagan: A History of the End of the Cold War* (New York: Viking, 2009), 190.

6. Julia Hell, "Loyal Dissidents and Stasi Poets: Sascha Anderson, Christa Wolf, and the Incomplete Project of GDR Research," *German Politics and Society* 20, no. 4 (2002): 82.

7. Ian Wallace, "Writers and the Stasi," in *Reassessing the GDR: Papers from a Nottingham Conference,* ed. James Henderson Reid, German Monitor Series (Amsterdam: Rodopi, 1994), 121.

8. These and all subsequent quotations and paraphrases of Florian Henckel von Donnersmarck are from the director's commentary on the Sony Pictures Classics 2007 DVD of *The Lives of Others.*

9. Gary Bruce, *The Firm: The Inside Story of the Stasi* (Oxford: Oxford University Press, 2010), 131.

10. Ibid., 120.

11. Czesław Miłosz, *The Captive Mind* (New York: Vintage Books, 1955), 205.

12. Aleksandr I. Solzhenitsyn, "Our Muzzled Freedom (1975)," in *The Great Lie: Classic and Recent Appraisals of Ideology and Totalitarianism,* ed. F. Flagg Taylor IV (Wilmington, DE: ISI Books, 2011), 151.

13. Paul Cantor, in his contribution to this volume ("Long Day's Journey into Brecht"),

quotes the critic Slavoj Žižek to this effect. Also Carl Eric Scott, in his contribution to this volume ("Communist Moral Corruption and the Redemptive Power of Art"), lays out the clashing elements within Dreyman but argues that these can in some ways be harmonized.

14. Mona Eltahawy, describing mounting political dissent against Hosni Mubarak in Egypt, referred to "the myth of youth 'slactivists' who some alleged were content with organizing on the Internet and speaking out only on social networking sites." *Washington Post,* January 25, 2011.

15. Reiner Kunze produced a memoir, *Codename: Poetry* (1990), as did Erich Loest, *The Stasi Was My Eckermann; or, My Life with the Bedbug* (1991).

16. Scott in this volume delves into "reform communism," speculating that this is where Dreyman sits politically. I am suggesting that the others' politics can be assumed to be roughly similar.

17. *Bertolt Brecht Journals,* trans. Hugh Rorrison, ed. John Willett (New York: Routledge, 1993), 379.

18. Julia Hell, *Post-fascist Fantasies: Psychoanalysis, History, and the Literature of East Germany* (Durham, NC: Duke University Press, 1997), 2.

19. Statement by the GDR government, quoted by Konrad Hugo Jarausch, "Care and Coercion: The GDR as Welfare Dictatorship," in *Dictatorship as Experience: Towards a Sociocultural History of the GDR* (Oxford: Berghahn Books, 2000), 50.

20. Hell, *Post-fascist Fantasies,* 2, 5, 30.

21. *Bertolt Brecht Journals,* 455.

22. Interestingly, it was the political center that the people of East Germany chose when they got the chance, some thirty-five years after Brecht's death. The 1990 vote just after the Berlin Wall fell was a surprise victory for the Christian Democrats, a result that showed unequivocally that the majority of East Germans favored immediate merger with the West.

23. Cantor in this volume shows that those involved in *The Lives of Others,* including the actor playing Dreyman, were encouraged to view him as being in the mold of Brecht. Cantor cites a German-language essay by Sebastian Koch in which Koch says that Dreyman's East Berlin apartment (which figures very prominently in the film) was based on the apartment of Bertolt Brecht.

24. Quoted by Hannah Arendt, *Men in Dark Times* (New York: Harcourt, Brace and World, 1968), 240. She translates *Die Massnahme* as "The Measure Taken"; it is sometimes rendered "The Measures Taken" or "The Decision."

25. Quoted by Eva Horn, "Actors/Agents: Bertolt Brecht and the Politics of Secrecy," *Grey Room* 24 (Summer 2006): 38–55.

26. This part of Maxim Gorky's writings appears on a Web site of the Lenin and Motherland Society, Moscow, http://www.aha.ru/~mausoleu/a_lenin/gorky_e.htm (accessed December 14, 2011).

27. Arendt, *Men in Dark Times,* 236. She got (and apparently translated) this phrase from Brecht's posthumously published work entitled *Me-ti, Buch der Wendungen.*

28. Ibid., 216.

29. Ibid., 208, 216.

30. Ibid., 243.

31. *Bertolt Brecht Journals,* 530.

32. After the Russian playwright Sergei Tretiakov was arrested by the Soviet secret police in 1937 and executed as a spy, Brecht protested his friend's innocence in a poem of commemoration entitled "Are the People Infallible?" This tribute to his friend was, however, written "for an audience consisting of himself alone," said Robert Conquest. Quoted in Sidney Hook, *Out of Step: An Unquiet Life in the 20th Century* (New York: Carrol and Graf, 1987), 494. Not only that, the poem initially had Tretiakov's name in its first line but Brecht later crossed it out. See Joyce Crick, "The Fourth Door: Difficulties with the Truth in the *Svendborg Poems*," in *Brecht's Poetry of Political Exile*, ed. Ronald Speirs (Cambridge: Cambridge University Press, 2000), 133.

33. The words of Wendy Lesser, as quoted by Edward Rothstein in his review of Lesser's *Music for Silent Voices: Shostakovich and His Fifteen Quartets, New York Times Book Review,* May 8, 2011, 16.

34. Bertolt Brecht, "The Rearing of Millet," trans. Robert C. Conard and Ralph Ley, *New German Critique* 9 (Autumn 1976): 146.

35. Arendt, *Men in Dark Times,* 217.

36. Bruce, *The Firm,* 63, 64; Arne Lichtenberg, "Germans Remember 20 Years' Access to Stasi Files," article found on the German public broadcasting Web site Deutsche Welle, February 1, 2012, http:/mobile.dw.de/english/ua.24/mobile.A-15640053–1432.html (accessed February 4, 2012); Biermann, "The Ghosts Are Leaving the Shadows."

37. Bruce, *The Firm,* 45.

38. Ibid., 48, 145, 160.

39. Ibid., 67, 72.

40. Ibid., 81.

41. The two quotations are from an obituary of Christa Wolf in the *London Daily Telegraph,* December 2, 2011.

42. And also his colleague portraying Comrade Minister Hempf, Thomas Thieme, who emigrated from East Germany in 1984 after having been jailed by the regime.

Part 2

ART AND POLITICS

Sebastian Koch (as Georg Dreyman) and Martina Gedeck (as Christa-Maria Sieland).

3

COMMUNIST MORAL CORRUPTION AND THE REDEMPTIVE POWER OF ART

Carl Eric Scott

The Lives of Others, written and directed by Florian Henckel von Donnersmarck, is a masterpiece of filmmaking that shows how pervasively the German Democratic Republic, through its secret police the Stasi, spied upon its own citizens. The film tells the story of the partial moral redemption of a dedicated Stasi captain, Gerd Wiesler, through his unexpected encounter of artistic beauty in the lives of two artists he has been assigned to monitor, the playwright Georg Dreyman and his lover, the actress Christa-Maria Sieland. Through his audio surveillance of Dreyman's apartment, Wiesler becomes intrigued by the friendship, love, and artistry he finds therein. He eventually tries to save these artists from the surveillance operation he is in charge of managing, and he does so even after Dreyman really does engage in antiregime activity.

Why does Wiesler thus risk his life and turn against the East German regime? In a key scene, he is deeply affected when Dreyman plays a beautiful piano composition upon learning of the suicide of his dear friend and artistic collaborator, the director Albert Jerska. Donnersmarck has indicated that this scene was the germ of the entire film: his idea for the story came in reaction to Vladimir Lenin's explanation of why he deliberately avoided listening to music, and especially his favorite Beethoven piano sonata, the "Appassionata," on the grounds that it would make him too soft for his revolutionary duties.[1] What would happen, Donnersmarck wondered, if the situation were in a sense reversed, if a man dedicated to Lenin's ideology were forced by circumstances to truly listen to a powerful piece of music, and more generally to truly encounter art and the artistic way of life? Could art break through the ideological hardening? Donnersmarck obviously believed that, in certain circumstances, it *might* have been able to do so. And so he began work upon a screenplay exploring this possibility.

It would appear, given only this synopsis and these observations, that the film is basically a testament to the redemptive power of art. However, the story concerns not merely Wiesler's transformation but also the possible moral corruption of the artists he is spying upon. While this theme of moral corruption is most vividly portrayed in the character of Christa-Maria, this essay particularly explores how the film considers the theme in Dreyman. I argue that Wiesler and Dreyman come to enact a *reciprocal rescue* of one another from the communist moral corruption peculiar to their particular stations.

Communist Moral Corruption

No serious investigation of communism can neglect considering what Alain Besançon, the author of a book-length essay comparing Nazism and communism, calls communism's "moral destruction." He says the following about how this destruction developed in the Soviet Union:

> At first, a significant portion of the population welcomes the teaching of the lie in good faith. It enters into the new morality, taking along its old moral heritage. . . . Hating the enemies of socialism, they denounce them and approve of having them robbed and killed. . . . Inadvertently, they take part in the crime. Along the way, ignorance, misinformation, and faulty reasoning numb their faculties and they lose their intellectual and moral bearings. . . . Life . . . became grimmer, more dismal. Fear was everywhere and people had to fight to survive. The moral degradation that had been subconscious to that point now crept into consciousness. The socialist people, who had committed evil believing they were doing good, now knew what they were doing. They denounced, stole, and degraded themselves; they became evil and cowardly and they were ashamed.

In comparing Nazism with communism, Besançon concludes that the latter brought about a "more widespread and deeper moral destruction," even if the former probably brought crime to a greater "level of intensity." What is this moral destruction that both ideologies unleashed?

> By moral destruction, I do not mean the breakdown of mores in the sense of the age-old grumbling of the elderly as they examine the mores of youth. Nor do I wish to pass judgment on this century compared to others. There is no philosophical reason to believe that man was either more or less virtuous during this period. Still, communism and Nazism set out to change something more fundamental than mores—that is, the very rule of morality, of our sense of good and evil. And in this, they committed acts unknown in prior human experience.[2]

Among these acts would be convincing a significant portion of a country's population to act as informants against their neighbors, coworkers, friends, and families, such as occurred in East Germany.[3] An image that conveys the vast number of spirits communism corrupted is provided by the film, in its footage of the seemingly endless stacks of the actual Stasi case files. All the despair, fear, and twisted compromise conveyed by the one particular work of fiction that is *The Lives of Others* must, the film visually insists, be multiplied by all those real files it shows accumulated in the former Stasi headquarters. Only such an imaginative multiplication can begin to convey what Besançon is pointing to when he speaks of the depth and the breadth of communism's moral destruction.

This essay considers how communist moral destruction or corruption is presented within the poetic world that is *The Lives of Others* by examining how the three main characters, Gerd Wiesler, Christa-Maria Sieland, and Georg Dreyman, are immersed in or threatened with it, and how they might be rescued from it.

The film also portrays the rather advanced moral corruption of the German equivalents of the *apparatchiki*, the higher-ups like Grubitz and Hempf who do not really believe in the ideology but use it to secure privileged positions. Dreyman appears for much of his life to have hoped that the core of socialism is its humanity. Wiesler affirms this hope in his manner, that is, insofar as it can be expressed in Marxist phraseology.[4] In contrast, the moral corruption of the apparatchiki consists in concluding that the core lesson of the communist system is that "people don't change," as Minister Hempf puts it, but rather are reducible to a fairly limited number of urges, motives, and socio-psychological types. Those who control the organizations that allow one to more scientifically calculate such reduction and act upon it are better able to manipulate people. "Change" does not occur from the inside through persons connecting with one another and their common humanity; it is implemented from the outside by those in power, those enabled to play upon the basic elements of the "person." Men like Hempf secretly conclude that Lenin was wrong about the ultimate end obtainable but correct about the means used to secure power. The film, however, does not dwell upon this far-gone corruption of the apparatchiki, and so this essay will say little more about it.

Wiesler's Partial Redemption from Communism's Moral Degradation

Until Wiesler begins to change, he is a willing agent of an evil regime. He fits a widespread judgment of the Stasi voiced in one scene by a child: he is one of "the bad men who take people off to prison." We see that in interrogation he will employ physical cruelty (sleep deprivation) and will persecute a subject's relatives and loved ones innocent of any official crime. With a quiet intensity that bears witness to his conviction, Wiesler trains students in these and other Stasi arts and exhorts them to remember they will be employing these against "the enemies of socialism." All in all, he is morally corrupt due to his ideology.

Unlike Lenin, he did not come to this ideology as an adult but grew up under it as the official order and morality. This is not to say that as a young man deciding to join the Stasi, he did not have to especially dedicate himself to defending that ideology. In the "Bluecaps" chapter of *The GULAG Archipelago*, Aleksandr Solzhenitsyn recalls how when he and his classmates were encouraged to join the Russian equivalent of the Stasi, something in them balked despite their acceptance of communist doctrine: "It would be hard to identify the exact source of that intuition, not founded on rational argument, which prompted our refusal to enter the NKVD schools. It certainly didn't derive from the lectures on historical materialism we listened to. It was clear from them that the struggle against the internal enemy was a crucial battlefront, and to share in it was an honorable task. . . . It was not our minds that resisted but something inside our breasts."[5]

Philosopher and student of Eastern bloc dissidence Chantal Delsol has called this something "scruples," which in an ideocratic regime are "doubts about the rightness of an action" that by the ideology's lights must merely be irrational.[6] When it becomes plain to Wiesler that the surveillance of Dreyman has been ordered for the sake of removing the minister of culture's romantic rival, he recalls to Grubitz the oath they took to become the party's "shield and sword," thereby suggesting that this mission is not worthy of that charge. We thus see that Wiesler's young trust in the ideals of Marxism was not left at the typical level but became precisely articulated according to its supposedly scientific precepts, and positively sworn to. The Stasi oath was a promise to accept all the necessarily scruple-deaf methods logically justified by those precepts. And like a monastic, the unmarried and unattached Wiesler seems to have denied himself a normal human life just as he seems to have suppressed normal human feelings.[7]

In the earlier portions of the film Wiesler has the *cleaned conscience* of the true-believing Leninist. For him, a moral reality exists. As he begins to see a moral integrity in the lives of the artists directly posed against the corruption of the socialist ideal he is also witnessing, he becomes prepared to reject the Marxist-Leninist articulation of the moral life and his part in upholding it. The film's heart shows us that Wiesler's moral regeneration would not be possible, however, were it simply a matter of his having to admit the apparatchiki corruption of the socialist ideal. Rather, what is crucial is his coming to care for the lives of the artists Dreyman and Sieland. This care to some extent begins with erotic motives, as his professional suspicion of Dreyman seems initially motivated by an attraction to Christa-Maria. But his jealousy becomes overshadowed by his appreciation of the value of their artistic lives, so that eventually, what comes to particularly entangle him with them is his desire to protect their love for one another. In a series of scenes following the early stages of his surveillance, we are shown his newly aroused interest in eros, evidenced by his haplessly yearning employment of a prostitute, as well as his newly aroused interest in art, reflected in his gazing upon the gifts in Dreyman's apartment and in his pilfering the book of Brecht poetry. The most telling scene, of course, is the one in which he is powerfully moved by the sonata he hears Dreyman playing. By that point he knows enough to know what a tragedy Jerska's suicide is for Dreyman, and that the GDR's censorship is implicated in it. He can thus feel the personal import of the art. And unlike Lenin, Wiesler is encountering something he never really has before, something that he had never had to deliberately steel himself against. Dreyman plays a rather stormy composition entitled "Sonata for a Good Man," and after playing it he shares the Lenin quote and asks aloud whether anyone who has "heard this music, I mean really heard it, could be a bad man." Wiesler, evidenced by his shedding a tear, really has heard it. His moral regeneration begins at this scene, as it is immediately followed by his first merciful relaxing of his Stasi code when he decides to avoid pursuing the incriminating information about some parents in his building that their child innocently reveals to him.

What would have happened had Wiesler not been assigned to spy on Dreyman? He would have remained a Stasi captain, interrogator, and teacher. By the time the GDR fell in 1989, he likely would have learned of more apparatchiki abuses of power, but he would have remained dedicated to the ideology. As a former Stasi officer, in 1990 he would have suffered a dramatic demotion of career, a degree of public shunning, and perhaps some measures of official punishment, and he would not have been prepared to understand why this was justified. If a man like Hempf could adjust and make out reasonably well in the new Germany, a man like Wiesler (without the moral regeneration) could only have felt bitter about the whole situation.

Similarly, it is necessary to note that Wiesler's moral redemption can only be partial. The fact that he saved Dreyman and tried to save Sieland cannot alter what his entire career had consisted of up to that point. It is true that in his fake reports about Dreyman's writing of a play about Lenin, he writes that "Lenin, though facing increasing pressure, continues with his revolutionary plans," which actually reveals a certain awareness that it is *he* who is preparing a little "revolution." These "plans" involve working to rescue Dreyman and Sieland, but as they are "revolutionary," the wording likely conveys Wiesler's determination to change his own ways. But here we must ask: where would he have been had his plans succeeded? It is only due to the vengeful action of Minister Hempf that Christa-Maria is interrogated. If Wiesler's maneuvers had worked, and so had left Georg and Christa-Maria in their place, he would have remained in place as well, a place that *requires* him to continue doing Stasi deeds. Would he have then resigned? But doing so would arouse fierce suspicion from his superiors. That is, Wiesler would not have had any easy way to disentangle himself from the regime's ongoing moral destruction. In fact, even the easier way of disentanglement the plot provides him, with his prisonlike demotion to the letter-opening basement, is not totally disentangled. He continues to help the Stasi pry into the lives of others. He does not refuse to do *any* work for the organization. To survive, he must remain engaged in some morally degrading compromise, as most subjects of this regime were forced to at some level. And this does not even begin to delve into the question of how he deals with the guilt he must now feel. The film ends with him as a pitiable figure, now delivering mail in the free but depressingly graffiti-covered East Berlin in his machinelike manner, apparently alone and stunted by his long Stasi training but, as we get a glimmer of in the final and incredibly moving scene, living a life open to art and literature, and perhaps also to love and friendship. In the very last shot, something like a smile, something like contentment, is seen on his face. Here is a man who, damaged as he may be, now has his *own* life to live.

The Moral Corruption of Christa-Maria Sieland

Christa-Maria is killed when she steps in front of a speeding truck after fleeing Georg's apartment. Although the film makes us uncertain about whether she spontaneously decides to commit suicide or is killed by accident while in a suicidal state of mind, for our purposes it is best to regard her death as a suicide. For in this way we can see that she succumbs to the very fate Georg protests against in his *Spiegel* article, that the regime kills off hope and thus drives its subjects to kill themselves. In her case, however, it is not a lack of hope that kills but a presence of guilt. She flees from the apartment when, as she thinks, Georg's incriminating typewriter is about to be found by the Stasi agents due to her treacherous revelation of its location in interrogation. She had expected to be able to feign innocence at this moment, but she proves unable to withstand a furious look from Georg. Wiesler has removed the evidence, but Georg and Christa-Maria do not know this. She flees out into the street and is killed by a truck. Her dying words are, "I can never put right what I've done wrong." Donnersmarck says that in a sense her soul had already died when earlier that day in interrogation she had revealed where the typewriter could be found. There is a level of moral corruption that brings about living death.

The interrogator who convinced her to betray Dreyman was Wiesler, who knew he was being observed by a now-suspicious Grubitz. The film leaves it tantalizingly unclear whether Wiesler meant to signal to her that she should not betray Dreyman by his reprising the "selling oneself for art" theme he had discussed with her in the bar scene or whether he was doing his utmost to get her to reveal the spot, having calculated that only in this way could he buy the time to remove the evidence and thus at least gain Dreyman's safety. In any case, the terms of her betrayal as she understood them were that she would get to remain on the stage. She thus proves willing to facilitate Dreyman's ruin in exchange for being able to live out her life of acclaim on the stage. This is why the resurgent flash of her conscience that led to her suicide/accident may have spared her from an even worse fate, that of total moral corruption.

If suicide or living death are two of the morally degraded possibilities open to Christa-Maria, there were two other possibilities, both having to do with "being in bed with" the regime, that she was deflected from earlier in the film. First, had Wiesler not intervened by manipulating the door buzzer, Dreyman might never have learned about her sexual liaisons with Minister Hempf. She likely would have chosen to keep them a secret, as she tries to do with her drug habit. We have no reason to think Georg would have learned of them anytime soon. Second, had Wiesler not convinced Christa-Maria in the bar scene to stay loyal to Georg, it appears that she was prepared to resign herself to deeply debasing, if not destroying, their love by continuing to service Hempf on the side, in this case with Georg's full knowledge.

There is perhaps no moral degradation so tangible as sexual degradation; the film displays the horrifying preliminaries of Hempf's copulation with Christa-Maria and afterward, we see, she immediately seeks a shower. But the degradation physically manifested in voluntary subservient sex is evoked in a key line by Christa-Maria as the best symbol for what is occurring on a much wider scale: artists like Dreyman and herself "get in bed with them." She gets no denial from Dreyman that the metaphor applies to him. Christa-Maria and he, and many other artists in the film, cooperate with the regime's control over their careers and refrain from presenting anything critical of it.

The price of not cooperating is plain enough: no sanctioned opportunity to develop or share one's art. If the film points out that certain artistic activities, such as writing, are less dependent upon these opportunities than are directing and acting, the basic dependence of all of them remains. After seven years on the blacklist, Jerska decides he cannot go on living without these opportunities, and Christa-Maria decides immediately upon her arrest by the Stasi that not only can she not live without them, but that she is willing to sign up as an informant or to grant sexual favors to Grubitz to keep them. Not only is being an artist integral to the very personality of Jerska, Sieland, and Dreyman but, ironically enough, that artistic life provides the very sanctuary needed to escape from the regime's mechanical, cynical, and crude atmosphere. The artist thus depends upon the regime to allow him or her to rise above its all-around ugliness.

Earlier, at the bar scene, Wiesler could for a time reverse her moral corruption by appealing to the link between her personal integrity and her artistic greatness. Speaking in the name of her audience and echoing Dreyman, he says she is a "great artist" and reasons that since she "already has art" she need not sell herself for it. But this line of reasoning cannot convincingly separate her art from her having an audience, as we see in the later interrogation scenes. Faced with Grubitz's question, "What do actors do when they can no longer act?" Christa-Maria assumes the answer is too terrible to contemplate. She cannot see how she could "have art" on her own. Could she have it as an element of her personality simply shared with her lover? The film does not allow us to confidently feel that such a retreat of her artistic self into private resources would be possible for her or for any serious actor. Wiesler may speak of Christa-Maria "having" art, but he does not necessarily understand what is involved. He has not considered the problem the way Jerska has. Again, this issue is a live one for Dreyman as well, although as an author, and one capable of shifting genres, he can be less directly dependent upon the regime's approval. Of course, regardless of their vulnerabilities, we cannot imagine Dreyman or Jerska winding up actually betraying a friend to the Stasi.

In sum, in Christa-Maria's story we see the full picture of communist moral corruption outside of its ideological (Wiesler-esque) aspect; from metaphorical "getting in bed with them" to the real thing, and from noble efforts at resistance to total capitulation, it is all there. We see narcotics supplied, offers to be an informant given, and a breakdown of the person under interrogation. By the film's vocabulary she was a "good person" pushed by the system into becoming entangled in and accepting of evil deeds. Her story thus fits the classic idea of moral corruption.

Georg Dreyman's Creed and Situation Prior to Writing the *Spiegel* Article

When Hempf speaks with Dreyman in 1991, he says that unlike the new united Germany, the GDR gave one something "to believe in" and something "to rebel against." Had he said this to Wiesler, Wiesler could perhaps have related to a longing for "something to believe in." Had he said this to Dreyman's dissident friend Hauser, Hauser could perhaps have related to a longing for "something to rebel against." But when he says it to Dreyman, both parts of the statement hit their mark. Dreyman was both a believer in and a rebel against the socialist regime. His belief in it is reflected by his plays, his public stance, and his own self-understanding. His political rebellion against the GDR comes to fruition only when he writes the *Spiegel* article, but it was grounded in two ongoing rebellions of his: a humanistic understanding of socialism opposed to the GDR's way of implementing Marxism, and a related yet potentially apolitical emphasis upon the human-izing virtues of art.

Before Dreyman wrote the article, his published work supported the regime—Grubitz's statements about his loyalty indicate that his plays have not included any criticism of the regime evident to the likes of him. Like-wise, there is nothing from his plays that Minister of Culture Hempf can use against him, since otherwise he would not need to order the surveillance measures. The film also suggests that Dreyman really regards himself as a socialist playwright, a role particularly resonant in East Germany, given the famous example of Bertolt Brecht. Hauser and Christa-Maria speak of Dreyman's "idealism" and his "faith," and Hempf characterizes his plays as conveying a "love of mankind" and a belief that "people can change." How might this humanistic faith be connected with his socialism? Or, what do we know of the "socialist" aspect of his art? The action of the one Dreyman play we do see snippets of, *Faces of Love,* does not itself provide evidence of a socialist message, although the main characters are workers. If we consider the example of Brecht and his collaborators,[8] particularly in some of their later plays such as *The Good Person of Szechwan* and *The Caucasian Chalk Circle,* we can see that while classic humanistic questions are presented, they become connected to the impact of a particular socioeconomic system, so that characters are presented as standing for various "types" that make up such a system. The socioeconomic system is very determinative: it is the poverty-causing capitalism of Szechwan and the hardened noble classes of the Caucasian kingdoms that primarily serve to hinder people from doing good or finding justice.[9] Perhaps Dreyman's plays are like these ones, albeit more optimistic about the ability of humans to overcome their circumstances. We don't know, but they must contain some material friendly to socialist ideas, given his reputation. We can see that *Faces of Love* ends with celebra-tory dancing and earlier shows a villain being defeated, but it begins with Christa-Maria's character Marta having a vision of the imminent death of another character's loved one. Thus, the play teaches that people can change and the good can win but also that some people are doomed to their fate. Interestingly, this fate is not obviously bound up in socioeconomic factors, and it is predicted by a vision, a dramatic device perhaps out of place in a drama that ought to be in harmony with historical materialism. Marta says she sees Arthur fall to his death, "crushed by the great wheel," with the wheel evoking a traditional symbol of fate (but also a Marxist symbol for fated history),[10] and then asks, "Why am I not spared these visions?" The darker side of Dreyman's work and character shows up here; indeed, it seems that in writing this play he drew on hazy premonitions of disaster looming over his own life.

In sum, Dreyman's work is identifiably socialist (even if it may contain cloaked criticisms of the regime), is characterized by a Brecht-like acknowledgement of human tragedy, and yet ultimately conveys a hopeful message. This message, I argue, would be in harmony with a conviction that genuine socialism is possible, and that its true form must provide a good deal of personal freedom. Also, this message likely recommends the potentially bridge-building method of imaginatively "putting yourself in the other's place," since on two separate occasions Dreyman uses variants of this phrase, first to defend Jerska to Hempf and second to defend the Stasi's ban of Hauser's travel to Christa. He also prefers to assume the best about others: when Hauser asserts (correctly, as it turns out) that the director Dreyman is currently working with is an informant, Dreyman responds that he does not "know" that he is.

Let us consider more closely Dreyman's faith in the possibility of what can be broadly called "reform communism"[11] or, as it was called in the Prague Spring of 1968, "socialism with a human face." Since "people can change," perhaps *human society* can also change and really achieve socialism. As for the Leninist regimes established in the name of socialism that lamentably developed in such authoritarian ways, it is incorrect to see them as fundamentally tyrannical, so that they would collapse if they granted a real measure of political liberty; rather, what is most fundamental about them is their goal of socialism. If they attempt to moderately reform, we have no reason to think (and we certainly *cannot know*) they will become regimes with market economies and wherein Marxist socialism will be an electoral loser. To assume this would be to assume that the enactment of Marxism absolutely depends on oppression. Such an assumption is heretical by the standards of Marxism and, far worse, it suggests the impossibility of any desirable form of socialism. We are obligated, then, to give reform communism a chance.

Something like this, I hold, is the political creed of Dreyman. While we will see that certain aspects of his stance are "apolitical," I argue that he does have a political view. He does not think the GDR is an adequate attempt at socialism. By 1984, he has read dissident literature like the copy of Solzhenitsyn's *The First Circle* we see on his desk, he has heard the critiques of the regime that persons like Hauser and Wallner can make of it and, like them, he "tremendously admires" Jerska for a "statement" he made ten years earlier that got him blacklisted. He obviously wants a GDR with much greater artistic freedom; he is probably aware that granting this would logically require it to also grant greater freedom of political speech. The suicide article represents a decisive turn in which he says, in effect, *We cannot go on living like this,* but he probably knew for some time about the problem reported therein. He knows that addressing such a problem demands searching criticism of the *entire* GDR way of life. Such criticism would be impossible unless the GDR promoted what Gorbachev eventually did: *glasnost* (publicity). For these reasons, Dreyman's political view, half-baked as it may be, is best described as that of reform communism.[12]

Why does he support the regime in his plays and public persona? And why does he at times object to dissidents like Hauser pushing the authorities too far? Regarding such questions, his appeal to Hempf as a "man of honor" to understand why Jerska cannot "remove his name from that statement" is quite revealing. It reveals how Dreyman thinks the GDR elite must be approached. If the only realistic political hope is to get them to adopt reform communism, this goal can be harmed by insulting them—one must instead understand the position they are in and the honorific need he assumes they have to stand by what they have said. *Arrogant insult* and *going too far too quickly* can bring about a reaction that only makes things worse. Dreyman perhaps wonders if those were the fatal flaws of the Prague Spring of 1968 and the East German artistic dissidence of the 1970s that was apparently a good deal bolder than it is by 1984.[13] One way things could substantially get worse, and not just for the artists, is if the public were cut off from real art altogether.

Dreyman's faith in art we must examine more closely, but it is first necessary to see that the *political* vision Dreyman clings to is a mistaken one. The bottom line, which Donnersmarck may or may not accept, is that the Czechoslovakian reformers and Gorbachev were both wrong to think that a communist system could be reformed and yet remain communist by means of offering *some* political freedoms. Had the Prague Spring reforms gone forward, all indications suggest the Communist Party would have been ousted from power, and the example of the resultant regime would have gravely threatened the authority of all communist states, just as occurred when Gorbachev allowed Poland and Hungary to liberalize in 1989. The truth about the European communist regimes is that they would fall were they not shored up by the party's political monopoly, by the prohibition of market activity, by the closing of borders, by the wide censorship, by the constant activity of security organs like the Stasi, and by the fear of Soviet military intervention. Dreyman, as was the case with many noble dissidents, does not understand this. Wiesler does: the instant the Wall falls, he knows he need no longer obey his Stasi masters. Erich Honecker understood it, going so far as to ban circulation of Soviet pro-glasnost publications. Gorbachev, thank God, did not.

At the shot of Gorbachev in the newspaper, Donnersmarck remarks that "people *can* change." I submit that Dreyman hoped his humanistic message of change might influence up-and-coming party figures *potentially like Gorbachev;* and for Donnersmarck, Dreyman was *right* to never abandon this hope. That particular political hope, of course connected to a broader set of ambitions for art, was not impossible. But reform communism *itself* was impossible; it was a recipe for communism's self-destruction.[14] Thus, the reformist artist might do his part to pull a ruler or an up-and-comer into greater openness toward art and reform, but perhaps he would be able to do so only by himself errantly believing in the viability of reform communism.[15]

Like the tucked-away farm home of Varykino in Boris Pasternak's *Doctor Zhivago,* where in the first deep winters of communism an artist might for a time live apart from political concerns, occupied with his poems, his family, and his lover, Dreyman's apartment and his circle of artistic friends serve as a shelter in the still pretty chilly and seemingly permanent communist society of the GDR. The healing powers of his refuge are undeniable, as the transformation of Wiesler shows. And as it is less obviously threatened by the regime than was Zhivago's hideaway, it provides a sense of stability. Indeed, were it not for the attraction of Minister Hempf to Christa-Maria, one can imagine that Dreyman's life there could continue in its tolerably happy mode: loving Christa, writing plays, seeing them performed, holding parties, exchanging beautiful gifts, reading poetry, and perhaps having, as Pasternak wrote of the family circle at Varykino, "endless discussions about art." True, this life would be buffeted by unwelcome news about artists like Jerska not being able to manage and by accusations from those like Hauser. For those moments, one could turn to dark compositions like "Sonata for a Good Man," thereby supplementing the cheery stride-piano music Dreyman plays in the extended (that is, cut) version of the party scene. At times art would bring about dancing, and at others art would help heal wounds. Is it not so that "every work of art, including tragedy, witnesses to the joy of existence?"[16] One must not let the regime rob you of the sense that living life is itself good; otherwise, one might "wind up like Jerska." Art would let one maintain this sense, and what is more, it would continually remind one of the need to try to be a "good person." In so many ways, it would serve as a refuge from and rebellion against the GDR way of life. One could "champion life itself" as did Pasternak's Zhivago,[17] and one could enter the dissident's "quiet moral transformation [that] involved living life as if the oppressive cope of Marxist-Leninism did not exist, or was moribund."[18] In isolation this quotation might make this sort of dissident stance seem too easily apolitical. For our purposes, however, it brings Dreyman's stance into sharper relief. He wants to live his private life as if the regime did not exist, aided by art, but while also depending upon the regime for many of the accoutrements of this private life and for his very opportunities to try to influence that regime in his public life. That is, he does *not* engage in the enigmatic opposition implicit in publicly acting, most especially in one's art, as if Marxist-Leninism is irrelevant. In a sense, he wants to live like playwright Václav Havel, whose dissidence was obvious but whose dramatic work became confined to *samizdat* publication, *and* to live like playwright Bertolt Brecht, who was granted a state-funded theater and company in exchange for his support of the regime.

While *The Lives of Others* ultimately tends to confirm Solzhenitsyn's belief in the concordance of truth, goodness, and beauty,[19] it shows the difficulties in applying this creed: one can come to rely too much upon beauty, and that reliance might be used to corrupt one. Moreover, the film implies, perhaps contrary to Solzhenitsyn's stance, that beauty might not reliably line up with truth in the final analysis. For example, the film suggests that artistic beauty pervades (1) Brecht's communism-supporting work; (2) Dreyman's evidently loyal but perhaps subtly pro-reformist humanistic plays; and (3) Dreyman's politically devastating work of literary journalism. All are beautiful, but only the last really conveys the political truth. There are other clues. Consider the two gifts besides the "Sonata" opened after the party. One is mistaken by Dreyman as a "backscratcher," but Christa tells him it really is a "salad fork." "Still," he says, "it's beautiful." An artwork's beauty seems to operate free from its function or intention, and what is more, it survives the misinterpretation of intention. The other gift is a beautiful pen, which he implies will help him in writing his next play. But its beauty cannot help him in this. Morally charged actions must occur to break his writer's block, namely, Christa-Maria's abandonment of Hempf and Hauser's kindness to Dreyman at the funeral. It may be good to surround oneself with beautiful objects, but it cannot always suffice. And indeed, Dreyman's surrounding himself with artistic beauty seems to have become blinding. Wiesler says he needs to see some "bitter truths," and upon saying this uses the door buzzer to get him to witness Christa-Maria with Hempf, an action that draws Dreyman *outside* of his art-filled apartment.

Christa-Maria and Georg seem to compound art's power with their love for one another, which obviously involves the love of the artistic qualities of each. And their love is potentially stronger than art itself. After Christa-Maria decides to spurn Hempf, she tells Georg she "will never leave," and shortly before this she tells Wiesler that Georg loves her "above all else." That would include art. Indeed, Georg had just told her that though he was losing his care for his writing and for other people, "now all I fear is losing you." It seems possible that through their love, they could survive losing all else. Alas, Christa-Maria abandons this hope. As Donnersmarck says, she has been deeply wounded by the regime and also suffers from an uncertainty about her personal identity and artistic worth that actors are particularly susceptible to. We must also say that she turns out to love "being herself" in the beauty and lucidity of art more than she loves Dreyman and being with him. Artistic beauty can be posed against the love of persons, the burdens of ordinary life, and the sacrifices of goodness; it can become its own "truth."

We must of course keep in mind that Dreyman's art can potentially influence his society. Again, if he does not experience success in this in any political manner, such success is not impossible, nor is this his art's only way to impact society. His plays can convey to audiences something of the morally regenerating refuge they too might find in art; indeed, in the theater they can together enjoy this private regeneration publicly. A dramatic performance in East Germany, at which such mysterious and rare connections might occur, thus retains something of the ancient aura of a potentially sacred and regime-altering event. Dreyman accordingly feels a great responsibility for his part in such events. In sum, for Dreyman, art nourishes his private life but also grants and burdens him with an important public life.

Dreyman's Path into Moral Corruption

Wiesler saves Dreyman from punishment by the Stasi for the *Spiegel* article. But also, just as Dreyman saves Wiesler from continuing in the morally corrupt Stasi life, Wiesler saves Dreyman from continuing down a path that slowly but surely is morally corrupting him. Additionally, saving him from being caught by the Stasi saves him from another type of moral corruption, the enervating sort in store for any "type 4" artist convicted of political crimes.

Hempf's intrusion into Dreyman's life is necessary for Donnersmarck to illustrate that it is not simply the ideologically determined security needs of the GDR that oppress but the sheer power of its corrupt rulers. Wherever real beauty is created, and especially where this involves displaying the beauty of body and personality, tyrannically empowered rulers like Hempf, of whom there are many lesser versions, will predictably use their power to seize beauty and satisfy their lusts. They might even use their power for merely vindictive whims—sheer jealousy of Dreyman's apparent happiness or hatred of his "arrogance" could bring about actions against him. Thus, the intrusion of the Hempf character is central to the world of *The Lives of Others* and it is pointless to consider Dreyman's situation apart from it.

But the additional intrusion of Wiesler is another matter. A Stasi guardian angel secretly protecting a person is *not* a normal part of a realistic East German "world." Thus, the employment of this plot device pushes us to ask how Dreyman would have developed without Wiesler's actions. As we saw in considering Christa-Maria's corruption, two of these are particularly key: first, his use of the door buzzer trick to get Dreyman to see that Christa is being dropped off by Hempf, and second, his convincing Christa to stick with Dreyman and abandon Hempf. Again, without the first action, Dreyman probably would not have learned of her seeing Hempf for a very long time. And without the second, he would have been faced with the choice of going along with it or breaking it off with her. Even more important, since it is her refusal to continue seeing Hempf that he says gives him "the strength to do something," he would not have written the *Spiegel* article that serves as his political, and really spiritual, break from the regime.

Hauser is right to say to Dreyman that "unless you do something, you're not human!" Certain political situations demand actions of the persons capable of them. Dreyman's position in the GDR has become, by 1984 if not earlier, morally untenable. As there are virtually no signs of reform on the horizon, what justification for his continued support of the GDR can he have? Indeed, Dreyman tells Christa in the conversation about "being in bed with them" that he "so much want[s] to change," even if this statement also indicates he apparently cannot. This felt need for drastic change coexists with a certain contentment with his setup. Dreyman enjoys being "strong" the way Christa needs him to be—his artistic activity allows him to avoid the Jerska-like brooding that is this strength's opposite. He enjoys himself and Christa being a model couple for the artistic community, which can admiringly watch them dance or enjoy their party. Similarly, it is morally important to him to be forgivingly "idealistic," even if someone like Hauser sees this idealism as making him in some way like a "bigwig." In sum, while Jerska puts things too starkly when he speculates that he owed his own once-warm personality entirely to his artistic success, which was made possible only by the "grace of the bigwigs," without question this applies to some degree to Dreyman. As with Christa-Maria, the danger is that he might feel he can "be himself" only within the setup provided by the regime.

If he had continued on his path of partly wanting to change but never acting on it, by the 1989 revolution he might have been without close friends and far more closely associated with the now openly hated GDR. Even if he had been a participant in the 1989 revolts, his reputation as the last significant playwright who still supported the regime would be poor, and it would not be redeemed by any acts of dissidence back when such acts were still quite risky. Moreover, the quality and truthfulness of his art would have diminished—Jerska's death made him unable to write, and were he to simply force himself to overcome that, to essentially *take* Jerska's death without the response of the suicide article, he likely would have harmed the spiritual wellsprings of his art.[20] In sum, without these two interventions of Wiesler, the likelihood of at least several years of compromised decline for Dreyman seems quite high. And at worst, it seems such a post-1989 Dreyman might wind up believing what Jerska did, that his life-affirming and generous personality was all a function of social privilege. That is, the darkest conclusions about his own life derivable from a post-utopian but still determinist reading of Marx and Brecht might come to dominate his self-understanding. Whatever we think of that possibility, the key fact is that Dreyman would have remained "in bed" with the regime even when its full degradations of his loved ones (at the least, of Jerska) had been revealed. Hauser's words accusing him of suppressing his humanity would prove true.

The other possible scenario of Dreyman's moral corruption that Wiesler rescues him from is his being cowed by the "type 4 treatment" had he been proven the author of the *Spiegel* article. This treatment is discussed in the scene when Wiesler goes to Grubitz's office intending to turn Dreyman in. Before he can, Grubitz gleefully shares the contents of a dissertation on Stasi techniques that he has been given credit for supervising. It classifies artists into five types, and Grubitz pegs Dreyman as a type 4, the "hysterical anthropocentric." Stasi experience has shown that punishment for this sort is best administered in what might seem a comparatively cushy manner: good treatment, no trial, total isolation, mysterious release after ten months—in short, "nothing they could write about." But actually, such treatment is calculated to crush the spirit of the type 4 artist, who thrives on social contact. Type 4s subjected to it have almost always refrained from further dissidence upon release, and what is more, they have usually ceased producing *any* art. It is no accident that the two great fears Dreyman confessed to Christa were "being alone" and "not being able to write." So as repellently reductive as this "five types of artists" schema is, we can see that its suggested treatment probably would work against Dreyman. At least to Wiesler, that prospect seems likely enough, and horrifying enough, to spontaneously sway him against his initial resolution to report Dreyman's authorship of the suicide article.

Succumbing to the treatment is a species of moral corruption. It is not simply a passive victimhood. The artist gives up on his morally necessary protest against the regime and worse, he gives up on being his artistic self. Why does he do the latter, when all he has to do to keep from again suffering solitary confinement is to refrain from politically charged activity? This is related to the reason why we are certain that Dreyman's art would weaken if he did not write the *Spiegel* article after Jerska's suicide: there is an inner connection between the inspiration to create beauty and one's trying to do good and portray the truth through this creation. Another aspect of the type 4 treatment is the regime's feigned *indifference* to artistic dissidence. The regime seems to say to artists like Dreyman, "So you've read Solzhenitsyn . . . and so what? Some of us have read him too, and it didn't shake us. The system remains in place. So you've written your 'devastating article.' We don't like it, sure, and we must punish you for it, but it *doesn't really matter to us,* or to anybody, really. Your ten uncertainty-filled months we gave you in solitary confinement show you just how alone you are and just how pointless your activity is." The corruption of the type 4 involves wordlessly getting him to believe this. It is a demoralization in terms of morale but thus necessarily also in terms of morals. Immorality does not consist simply of committing unjust actions like betrayals for gain; it also includes succumbing to certain states of character, such as the type 4's becoming discouraged about his artistic gift.

The key similarity between the moral corruption Dreyman was slipping into on his own and that fostered by the type 4 treatment is just this loss of faith in the worth of one's art and a corresponding inability to produce. While we cannot here explore the film's suggestions about the unexpected problem liberal democratic freedom poses to artists, we must note that both times Dreyman appears to lose confidence in his art correspond to a period in which either by his own timidity or by the deception of others he is living out of kilter with the deepest facts of his life. This occurs first when, despite Jerska's suicide and despite learning of Christa's affair, he attempts to go on writing his pro-socialist dramas. It is a very brief period consisting of the week or so between Jerska's death and funeral. The second occurrence, as we learn from the 1991 theater lobby scene with Hempf, was from late 1989 to late 1991. Until he looks at his file, Dreyman remembers Christa-Maria as a kind of savior. It was she, he thinks, who removed the typewriter. She also symbolizes for him the artistic life, having embodied his quest for beauty and drama. But his actual savior was the representative not of art but of coldly calculating rationality, Wiesler. At least since 1989, art has been failing Dreyman, and his old way of inspiration is not working. His liberating turn to delving into his own private life by way of writing a novel instead of a play is not possible until he is given the means to understand the truth about his private life. He must see beyond the statuesque image of Christa-Maria, a certain "face of love" that his love had created, and realize just how damaged she had been.

So both of Dreyman's cases of writer's block occur during periods in which he is knowingly or unknowingly working against the grain of basic truths about his life. In the second occurrence, the problem of not understanding where one stands, of what one's place in the story is, seems to be the element, in addition to the specter of *indifference,* that links his artistic infertility with that of the "treated" type 4. The type 4 suddenly released after ten months is harrowed by the solitude and fears he is still monitored, but what is more, he doesn't know, nor do his fellow East Germans, why his punishment has been comparatively light. He might not even know what he's being punished for, and being unable to find a solid role for himself in any clear-cut dissident versus regime drama, his powers wane. He is thus a bit like Dreyman having to ask Hempf why he was the only one not under surveillance.

A Typology of Communist Moral Corruption

The types of moral corruption by communism we have found presented by *The Lives of Others* turn out to be basically five. First, there is communism's *ideological* moral corruption, exemplified by Wiesler. It is the success of this Leninist corruption that is the necessary condition of all the others. Second, there is what I have dubbed the *apparatchiki* moral corruption. Third, there is the moral corruption in the *traditional sense* of a good person being seduced or cajoled into doing bad acts that he or she also regards as bad for the sake of personal gain or security, exemplified by Christa-Maria. Obviously, this corruption occurs in all times and everywhere, but communist societies have the unique trait of establishing security services that are driven by a certain ideocratic logic to systematically cultivate it in the widest scope possible.

Fourth, there is the sort of moral corruption that Dreyman takes some steps down the path of but ultimately rejects. What should it be called? It might be called the corruption of the reform communist or of the humanist artist. But there is no reason to think that Christa-Maria is less representative of art than Dreyman is, or that she is somehow opposed to his "love of humanity." Rather, the difference is that her commitment to being a good person, while still integral to who she is, has its weak points, whereas his commitment is "strong." He is a person who cannot be enticed into the acts she is. This difference between them is due to a whole host of reasons but seems to most especially depend upon what she calls his "faith," which we have seen is a faith in humankind, socialism, and the humanizing powers of art. Why isn't such a principled type by his very nature a threat to the regime? The answer is found in what Besançon calls the communist "falsification of the good."[21] Dreyman was brought up under an order that linked the pursuit of goodness with the socialist goal. He strongly identified with that goal. And once he had begun to more fully see the evils of the regime, the question of how to undo those evils without rejecting socialism could only yield the answer of a gradualist reform from within; at least, it could only yield this answer if he were to maintain his idealism. More important, because his idealism was actually fairly vague in political terms and given more manifest expression in the world of art, he would naturally, without the regime doing anything, be drawn into a life centered on *expressing* such idealism. If push came to shove, the regime's rulers would know better than to try to pressure Dreyman into committing deeds whereby he would directly harm others or sell himself for his gain. But they knew they could reasonably expect that his high hopes for the theater's humanistic impact would tend to keep him from speaking out against the regime—and, indeed, could keep him appearing to still be its full supporter. In essence, the regime held the ongoing cultivation and expression of his moral excellence hostage, requiring in exchange that he continually lend the GDR the artistic aura of this high-mindedness. We are thus led to a surprising formulation: this moral corruption is the corruption of the *inadequately political moralist!*

If this corruption is in some senses as old as the world, being the sort of thing we might peg, say, the Harry Truman of the 1920s and 1930s with, vis-à-vis his squeaky-clean image being sponsored by the rotten Prendergast machine (although this would be a gross moral equivalence), the communist version *directly* and *intimately* tempts every idealistic moralist with it, even those trying to evade politics. If one is not willing to tame one's idealism or channel it into the approved path articulated by the ideology but insists on another, necessarily "nonpolitical," path, one will eventually find oneself facing a Dreyman-like situation. In a free society, a person may be at least honorably ignorant about political affairs; in a communist one, everyone, the idealists especially, is pressured into making dishonorable political commitments.

Fifth, there is another way to morally corrupt stoutly principled idealists, and that is to attack their morale so as to deprive them of all hope. This seems to be what the GDR has done to Jerska, and it is scientifically perfected in the other possible path of Dreyman's corruption, the type 4 treatment that snuffs out the desire to make art.

Conclusion

Christa-Maria knows it when she enters the key acts of her moral corruption. Dreyman's slide into corruption, by contrast, happens without his full awareness. He needs to be prodded by others' actions—Jerska's, Christa-Maria's, Hauser's and, most especially, Wiesler's—to get him to resist it. And as has been shown, it is Wiesler's two actions here that are the really decisive ones plot-wise. Moreover, it is Wiesler alone whose actions keep Dreyman from being subjected to the type 4 treatment. Why has Donnersmarck set things up in this manner?

My conclusion is that while Donnersmarck is absolutely serious about the power of art to ultimately overcome communist oppression and to par-tially heal its corruption, he wanted to balance this primary theme of his film with the cautionary theme of the ultimate insufficiency and corrupt-ibility of purely artistic resources. The major insufficiency of art concerns politics. Art's very humanistic potency to both inspire the highest idealisms and to provide healing refuge attracts persons like Dreyman. In a communist society especially, it can thus enable certain forms of denial and escapism. Donnersmarck and Solzhenitsyn stand with Dreyman when he insists that people can change, especially through encountering the power of great and truthful art. But they are not naïve about politics and human failings in the many ways he is. In a particularly shocking instance, Dreyman *looks surprised* when Hauser tells him in the park scene that he can't publish the suicide article under his own name! More understandably and yet none-theless tellingly, Christa's possible weakness and Hempf's possible ferocity simply do not figure into his thinking. These and similar facts point to a real lack in Dreyman and to a real point of weakness found in many artists.

For the key parallel Donnersmarck's film is pointing to, which I call the *reciprocal rescue* from communist moral corruption, is this: as Dreyman is unknowingly saving Wiesler by his art, Wiesler is secretly saving him by his psychological and political cunning. It is a cunning that is systematic and reductive in its calculation of human motives but also able to swiftly move with the interrogator's actorlike instincts. As important, it is a cunning that has inside knowledge about the political regime and an intuitive grasp of its basic realities. It really is, in its stunted, regime-specific way, a form of political prudence. Through a variety of moves and deceptions, including his cowing of Udo, Wiesler shields the *Spiegel* article from surveillance, thereby rescuing Dreyman. His most impressive feat, of course, is removing the typewriter, but we should be as impressed by his placing the red finger-print clue of this removal into his final Stasi report, since this indicates his own calculation that the regime would likely not last, contrary to what most Western political scientists would have guessed in 1985.[22]

Dreyman is a very admirable character and the one closest to Donners-marck himself. The film highlights his strengths and blames him less for his various failings and weaknesses than it does the regime. If tragedy inheres in his "trying to be good" in writing the *Spiegel* article, which is both an act necessary to halt his creeping moral corruption and, plot-wise, one that dooms Christa-Maria to hers, this is the GDR's fault, not his. Nonetheless, the reciprocal nature of the rescue of Wiesler and Dreyman from communism's moral corruption points to an unavoidable conclusion: Dreyman would have been a better man, a better dissident, and perhaps even a better artist if he had had more of Wiesler's cunning in him.

Humanistic art and political acumen need one another. The person best able to do what is good in a quite corrupt society, and probably also in a more typical one of lesser corruptions, is the one taught the fundamental importance of weighing and attending to truth, goodness, and beauty but also taught to acquire knowledge of the regime and of typical human failings and to employ cunning (and often necessarily reductive) calculation whenever necessary to act defensively or offensively against the regime. And this person must also apply all this knowledge to considering his or her own place in that society and what it reveals about his or her own motives. It is a very tall order, and even if obtained, it does not guarantee political success or the avoidance of tragedies.

But it is essentially a quest for moral and political truth to guide one's life, and in undertaking it the artist, or any person, can take solace in the words of the great and at one time greatly damaged man Aleksandr Solzhenitsyn, whose life really exemplified just what these words promised: *Lies can prevail against much in this world, but never against art.*[23] True art will be truthful. It will be truthful about the political lies, even the most powerful ones, and even the ones politics-shunning artists are most drawn to. A wise political thinker is not necessarily very artful; but in certain circumstances the artist may well need to sit at his or her feet or read his or her treatise to produce true art. True art will be truthful even about the lie that art can stand on its own, and even about the lie that one finds truth wherever one finds beauty. For beauty divorced from truth may live for a long time and call itself art, but Solzhenitsyn does not say that lies cannot prevail against *beauty*. Nor does Donnersmarck. Rather, they are agreed that it is *true art* over which lies cannot prevail. *The Lives of Others*, through the story it tells and its own hard-earned excellence, demonstrates how daunting the task of true art can be but also how rewarding and absolutely necessary it is.

Notes

An earlier version of this essay was published in *Perspectives on Political Science*, April–June 2011, Vol. 40, No. 2. Used by permission.

1. Unless otherwise indicated, references to Donnersmarck's statements refer to the "director's commentary" available on the English-language DVD of the film.

2. Alain Besançon, *A Century of Horrors: Communism, Nazism, and the Uniqueness of the Shoah* (Wilmington, DE: ISI Books, 2007), 31–36.

3. John Koehler estimates that 1 out of every 6.5 persons in the population were acting as informants, either as unofficial informers (IMs) or as Stasi personnel. Koehler, *Stasi: The Untold Story of the East German Secret Police* (Boulder, CO: Westview, 1999), 9. Estimation of this is a difficult task, however, requiring one to choose (1) a particular point in time for determining the ratio; (2) how to count those employed by the Stasi in more mundane tasks; and (3) how to count informants seldom utilized, on one hand, and part-time informants (whose numbers we are far from certain about) on the other. Compare Koehler's data with the less sweeping estimates from Gary Bruce, *The Firm: The Inside Story of the Stasi* (New York: Oxford University Press, 2010), 10–11, and from the Jens Gieseke chapter in this volume.

4. Wiesler notably resists sitting in the section of the Stasi lunchroom reserved for "bosses" on the principle that "socialism has to start somewhere."

5. Aleksandr Solzhenitsyn, *The GULAG Archipelago: 1918–1956,* abr. ed. (New York: HarperCollins, 2002), 74.

6. Chantal Delsol, *The Unlearned Lessons of the Twentieth Century: An Essay on Late Modernity* (Wilmington, DE: ISI Books, 2006), 54. On "ideocracy," a term essentially equivalent with "ideological totalitarian regime," see Daniel J. Mahoney, *Aleksandr Solzhenitsyn: The Ascent from Ideology* (Lanham, MD: Rowman and Littlefield, 2001).

7. See Bruce, *The Firm,* 36, for evidence that Wiesler's single status was atypical. The Stasi encouraged marriage, and while its employees' divorce rate mirrored that of the population, "most of the officers who joined the Stasi were already married upon recruitment."

8. John Fuegi's *Brecht and Company: Sex, Politics, and the Making of the Modern Drama* (New York: Grove, 1994) shows that large portions of many of the plays we attribute to Brecht were written by unacknowledged, usually female, collaborators (and lovers).

9. A less Marxism-bound reading of *Caucasian Chalk Circle,* one attuned to communism's own crimes and insufficiencies, may be possible. In any case, the allusions the film makes to *Der gute Mensch von Sezuan* (*Mensch* can be translated as "person" and is represented in the play by a female character) are several and central: it is evoked by the title to the key sonata, Christa-Maria tells Wiesler he is a "good man," and the song used in the montage sequence sings (in a fatalistic tone) of the necessity to "try to be good." The key connection between the film and the play is their shared question of whether humans can be good in a corrupt society. While it would take another essay to explore, my hypothesis is that Donnersmarck alludes to the play to suggest that the path he threads in *The Lives of Others* is between the Scylla of the too-humanist stance of Dreyman and the Charybdis of the too-determinist stance of "Brecht."

10. Marx and Engels refer to the "wheel of history" in Karl Marx and Friedrich Engels, *The Communist Manifesto* (New York: Signet Classic, 1998), 63.

11. My understanding of the term comes from Martin Malia, *The Soviet Tragedy: A History of Socialism in Russia, 1917–1991* (New York: Free Press, 1994) chaps. 9, 11.

12. These reasons are further supported by an allusion. The leader of the Prague Spring reforms was Alexander Dubček, whose autobiography is titled *Hope Dies Last* (New York: Kodansha International, 1993), a phrase Hempf uses when he says, in reference to Dreyman's plea for Jerska's rehabilitation, "Because as you know, Dreyman, hope always dies last."

13. Jerska felt emboldened to make his "statement" around 1974, but 1984 represents a low point for East German artistic dissidence, as Donnersmarck suggests in his commentary and also shows in his film. For example, Grubitz says that Dreyman is the last of the playwrights "still read in the West" to remain loyal, and that Hempf led a "cleaning up" of the "theater scene" several years back.

14. For the full demonstration of this and the above argument, see Malia, *The Soviet Tragedy*, 390–95 esp., and 405–91.

15. What Malia describes as the Prague Spring reformers' "tragic dilemma" to some extent applies to all Dreyman-like dissidents: "Had they been more lucid, either they would have been unable to act at all, in which case they would have given up in despair, or they would have had to attempt a revolution, in which case they would have gone down to defeat. Therefore, they had to take it on faith that the third way did exist, half-fooling themselves into believing they were not destroying the system and hoping they could fool Moscow into believing the same thing" (ibid., 392–93).

16. Boris Pasternak, *Doctor Zhivago*, trans. Manya Harari and Max Hayward (New York: Everyman's Library, 1991), 479.

17. Ibid., from the introduction by John Bayley, xiii.

18. Michael Burleigh, *Sacred Causes: The Clash of Religion and Politics, from the Great War to the War on Terror* (New York: HarperCollins, 2007), 424–25.

19. From his "Nobel Lecture": "Works which have drawn on the truth and which have presented it to us in a concentrated and vibrant form seize us, attract us to themselves powerfully.... So perhaps the old trinity of Truth, Goodness, and Beauty is not simply the decorous and antiquated formula it seemed to us at the time of our self-confident materialistic youth. If the tops of these three trees do converge, as thinkers used to claim, and if the all too obvious shoots of Truth and Goodness have been crushed, cut down, or not permitted to grow, then perhaps the whimsical, unpredictable, and ever surprising shoots of Beauty will force their way through and soar up to *that very spot,* thereby fulfilling the task of all three." Aleksandr Solzhenitsyn, *The Solzhenitsyn Reader,* ed. Edward E. Ericson Jr. and Daniel J. Mahoney (Wilmington, DE: ISI Books, 2006), 515.

20. This proved to be a problem for him anyhow once the Wall fell, but Hempf's indication that Dreyman had written no new plays since then indicates that he had some productivity from 1985 to 1989.

21. Besançon, *A Century of Horrors*, 29.

22. He thought there was a decent chance that Dreyman would someday read his report. Such a chance depends on the regime falling. Were there no or little possibility of this, he would not have taken the (small but high-stakes) risk that his fingerprint clue might be noticed and understood by someone in the Stasi.

23. Solzhenitsyn, "Nobel Lecture," 526.

4

LONG DAY'S JOURNEY INTO BRECHT

The Ambivalent Politics of *The Lives of Others*

Paul A. Cantor

> Once is enough. Didn't we say that everything could be made right again if only one person were found who could stand up against the world, only one?
>
> —Bertolt Brecht, *Der gute Mensch von Sezuan*

Florian Henckel von Donnersmarck's 2006 film *Das Leben der Anderen* (The Lives of Others) was widely, and justifiably, praised as a cinematic masterpiece almost from its first release. The movie was especially celebrated as a political statement, as a scathing indictment of communist tyranny, specifically a long overdue exposé of the horrors of the East German regime, the so-called Deutsche Demokratische Republik (the DDR, the German Democratic Republic). Surprisingly, until *The Lives of Others*, no German film had attempted to portray the brutal nature of the communist regime in East Germany. If anything, by the early twenty-first century, a sort of nostalgia had been developing in German popular culture for the days of the DDR, a tendency epitomized by the success of the film *Good Bye Lenin!* (2003). The cultural acceptance of tyrannies of the Left but not of the Right is always puzzling—one might legitimately wonder whether an equivalent film with the title *Good Bye Goebbels!* would have been tolerated in Germany, or any other country for that matter.

Thus *The Lives of Others* was hailed for its willingness to confront what many Germans seemed content to let slip down the memory hole of history. Using all the power and resources of cinema, above all a remarkable set of performances from his first-rate cast, Donnersmarck told a tale that deeply needed telling. With surgical precision, he anatomizes everything that was wrong with the DDR—the corruption of the regime, the bleakness, sterility, and regimentation of daily existence it brought about, its suppression of political dissent and artistic creativity, and ultimately the spiritual emptiness of life under communism. With the story opening in 1984, the movie inevitably calls to mind George Orwell's great novel, and, indeed, *The Lives of Others* already seems destined to stand with *1984* as one of the most chilling evocations of the nightmare of twentieth-century totalitarianism. As such, many conservative critics welcomed the film and hoped that it might herald the beginning of a new trend of anti-communism in popular culture. Reviewing the film in the *Weekly Standard,* John Podhoretz wrote: "Florian Henckel von Donnersmarck found a great story to tell with a great setting and he told it with peerless skill. . . . Maybe he will be followed by other young filmmakers and writers who can bring fresh eyes and a new perspective to the great struggle of the second half of the 20th century."[1]

But as is usually the case in cultural criticism, praise for *The Lives of Others* was not universal. A number of commentators raised serious doubts about the film. They questioned the historical accuracy of many of its details, and even of its basic take on the East German regime.[2] Given the left-wing political orientation of most cultural critics, it is surprising that the film has frequently been attacked for not being anticommunist enough. Given the enthusiasm of so many conservatives for the film, it comes as a bit of a shock to see *The Lives of Others* condemned for painting too rosy a picture of the DDR. Donnersmarck has been accused of glossing over the true horrors of communist tyranny and in fact creating a sentimental story out of what should have been a more systematic condemnation of East Germany. According to some critics of *The Lives of Others,* Donnersmarck fundamentally erred in supplying a happy ending to what should have been an unrelievedly bleak story. He is criticized for having given a Hollywood treatment—complete with a love story and a tale of personal redemption—to what should have been a chronicle of pure inhumanity and utter despair.

This kind of criticism of *The Lives of Others* focuses on the central figure of Gerd Wiesler (played so perfectly by Ulrich Mühe). Critics charge Donnersmarck with creating too sympathetic a portrait of this captain in the infamous Stasi, the East German secret police. At the beginning of the film, Wiesler seems to stand for everything that was wrong with the East German regime. He is a staunch and committed supporter of the DDR and a cold-blooded, implacable enforcer of its tyranny. Leading a soulless existence in his private life, devoid of love or any human connection, in his public role he is a ruthless interrogator of the enemies of the regime and an expert at surveillance into any subversive activities. His superiors in the Communist Party assign him to spy on a prominent East German playwright, Georg Dreyman, and his girlfriend, the actress Christa-Maria Sieland. At first pursuing his task with heartless efficiency, Wiesler is gradually seduced by what amounts to his voyeuristic glimpse into the emotionally rich "lives of others." A whole new world of aesthetic experience opens up to him, as his spying involves him—perhaps for the first time in his life—in watching a play, reading lyric poetry, listening to classical music and, more generally, sharing in the emotional experience of artistic people. Learning to sympathize with the couple he is spying upon, and perhaps falling in love with the actress himself, Wiesler becomes their protector. He does not report Dreyman's subversive activity when he writes an article for a West German magazine on the high rate of suicide in East Germany and, in a very complicated plot, he becomes involved in covering up the playwright's act of dissent. In a remarkable reversal, the initially villainous Wiesler becomes the quiet hero of *The Lives of Others,* and in the end, he wins a tribute from Dreyman as "ein guter Mensch" (a good man).

Critics of the film condemn Donnersmarck for making a hero out of a Stasi agent and reject his portrait of Wiesler as unrealistic and untrue to history. Anna Funder, for example, writes: "No Stasi agent ever tried to save his victim, because it was impossible. (We'd know if one had, because the files are so comprehensive.) Unlike Wiesler, who runs a nearly solo surveillance operation and can withhold the results from his superior, totalitarian systems rely on thoroughgoing internal surveillance (terror) and division of tasks. The film doesn't accurately portray the way totalitarian systems work, because it needs to leave room for its hero to act humanely (something such systems are designed to prevent)."[3] In a more thoroughgoing indictment of the film, the well-known intellectual Slavoj Žižek argues that "*The Lives of Others* fails to capture the true horror of the GDR." Žižek notes that the film seems to blame the evils of the East German regime on the self-interested actions of a few corrupt officials in the communist hierarchy. "What's lost is that the system would be no less terrifying without the minister's personal corruption, even if it were run by only dedicated and 'honest' bureaucrats."

Žižek extends his critique to Donnersmarck's portrayal of the East German playwright who is a sincere supporter of the communist regime and yet is treated very sympathetically in the movie: "One cannot but recall here a witty formula of life under a hard Communist regime: Of the three features—personal honesty, sincere support of the regime and intelligence—it was possible to combine only two, never all three. If one was honest and supportive, one was not very bright; if one was bright and supportive, one was not honest; if one was honest and bright, one was not supportive. The problem with Dreyman is that he does combine all three features."[4] Žižek raises a serious question: if *The Lives of Others* is such an anticommunist film, why is one of its heroes a pro-communist playwright and the other a reformed agent of the Communist Party? One could try to develop a reading of the movie that would claim that it criticizes not communist ideals but the failure of the East German regime to live up to its communist ideals. Dreyman and Wiesler are shown to be believers in communism, and yet they are also shown to be basically good men, and the problem with the DDR seems to be a few rotten apples in the Marxist barrel. Is the answer a reformed communism, some kind of socialism with a human face?

Despite the cogency of Žižek's observations about *The Lives of Others,* I think that such a reading of the film would be wrong. One should not lose sight completely of surface impressions, and there can be no doubt that the overall impression of Donnersmarck's movie remains strongly anticommunist. The critics of *The Lives of Others* have to a large extent judged it by the wrong standards. They are looking for a documentary, not a feature film.[5] They want a work that would chronicle in great historical detail all the horrors of communist tyranny in East Germany. Such a film would be very valuable, but it is not the kind of work Donnersmarck set out to make. Critics object to the way Donnersmarck has personalized the story and chosen to focus on a few sympathetic and even attractive characters. But this is simply the logic of good drama. Setting his film in what is recognizably the historical East Germany, Donnersmarck created a personal story designed to bring out certain larger truths about human nature. As he succinctly puts it in his DVD commentary: "It's a truthful story, not a true story."[6] One could defend him in terms of Aristotle's distinction in chapter 9 of his *Poetics* between history and poetry (or fiction). History tells us what actually happened; fiction tells us what might have happened in accord with our understanding of human nature. Thus history shows us what human beings are; fiction shows us what they could be in some ideal sense. From that perspective, it does not matter if no actual Stasi agent did what Gerd Wiesler does in *The Lives of Others*.[7] The way Donnersmarck shows him behaving is certainly not impossible and arguably not even implausible. If one believes in the basic decency of human nature, then one would certainly like to think that someone in Wiesler's circumstances might for once do the decent thing and work to save a fellow human being. Anna Funder quotes Donnersmarck as saying: "I didn't want to tell a true story as much as explore how someone might have behaved. The film is more a basic expression of belief in humanity than an account of what actually happened."[8] That seems to be the basic point of *The Lives of Others*, a claim that transcends the details of economic and political history and says something about the permanent ethical potential of humanity.

Nevertheless, the critics of the film have raised some valid points about its meaning and usefully complicated our understanding of its message. They have shown that the film's political sympathies may be more complex than at first appears, and its politics may in fact be ambivalent. In particular, they have reminded us of an important point: just because *The Lives of Others* is anticommunist does not mean that the film is necessarily pro-capitalist. Paying careful attention to its texture reveals that Donnersmarck does not choose to participate in the triumphalism that generally greeted the demise of the East German regime in 1989 and the reunification of Germany under the aegis of the Bundesrepublik Deutschland (the BRD, the Federal Republic of Germany). To be sure, only a brief part of *The Lives of Others* deals with what happened in 1989 and after. Donnersmarck offers a series of codas or epilogues to show the aftermath of Wiesler's decision to come to the aid of Dreyman. But Donnersmarck is a very efficient storyteller and he manages to convey a great deal in the last fifteen minutes of the film.

Consider how Donnersmarck chose to portray what is arguably the most important historical event in his story and one of the greatest moments in German history—the fall of the Berlin Wall. Even on his tight budget, Donnersmarck could easily have used stock newsreel footage to convey a sense of the monumental character of this event—scenes of crowds rejoicing at the Brandenburg Gate or of Beethoven's Ninth Symphony being played to celebrate the return to freedom in the East. But instead of monumentalizing the event in cinematic terms, Donnersmarck chose to mute and minimize it. All we see is Wiesler and some other disgraced Stasi agents working away in the bowels of some building; one of them, listening through a miniature earphone, hears the news of the Wall coming down; they calmly stop working and walk out the door. Although we hear about the momentous event over the radio, we do not see it, and in movies, seeing is everything. Donnersmarck turns what ought to be a climactic moment in his story into a visual anticlimax.[9]

This emblematic moment reflects what appears to be Donnersmarck's conscious decision to downplay the degree to which the "new" Germany has been genuinely transformed. Before the fall of the Wall, Wiesler is shown mechanically steaming open mail for the communists. After the fall, we see him mechanically delivering junk mail for the capitalists. The stage directions in the screenplay stress the parallel by noting that he now delivers commercial flyers with the same care with which he used to do his work as a Stasi officer.[10] Donnersmarck does remarkably little to suggest that things have improved in the new Germany. The most sinister character in the film, Minister Hempf—the man who originally ordered the surveillance of Dreyman—has evidently survived the regime change, unpunished and unharmed. He has become a successful businessman in the reunified Germany and is still part of the in-crowd, attending theatrical premieres, just as we saw him doing in the DDR at the beginning of the film. The original screenplay elaborates upon this point and makes it stronger. Hempf says that he is now doing "richtiges, kapitalistisches Business" (proper capitalist business) and jokes that he is still dealing with the Russians. Although he himself is barred from politics, he has passed the baton to his son, who is already a member of Parliament for the PDS, the Partei des Demokratischen Sozialismus (the Party of Democratic Socialism), the legal successor to the Sozialistische Einheitspartei Deutschland (the German Socialist Unity Party) that had governed East Germany (149).[11]

As for Dreyman, he is still living in the same apartment, and at the prompting of Hempf, he discovers that Wiesler's bugs are still in place, even if they are no longer being used. In the last sequence in the film, we learn that Dreyman has managed to write a new book, *Die Sonate vom guten Mensch* (Sonata for a Good Man), but it is evidently a work of prose, presumably a memoir about the very events we have seen chronicled in the film. What Dreyman has failed to do in the new Germany is to write a new play. When we see him going to a theatrical premiere, it is of a new production of one of his works, but definitely not of a new work. In fact, in what appears to be a pointed gesture, Donnersmarck shows Dreyman attending a staging of the same scene of the same work we saw him watching toward the beginning of the film (the stage directions in the screenplay make it clear that this is taking place in the very same theater, the Gerhart-Hauptmann-Bühne). Back in the

DDR, Dreyman's play was given a heavy-handed socialist realist staging that apparently displeased him. But now, in the new Germany, the play is given a pretentious postmodernist staging that seems to displease Dreyman just as much—he walks out of the production.[12] Whatever else the new Germany may have achieved, it has not restored Dreyman's creativity as a playwright and it has not allowed him to realize his artistic goals—he is still subject to the whims of directors who distort his intentions.

When Dreyman runs into Hempf outside the auditorium, the ex-minister teases him with the fact that the playwright has not written anything since the end of the DDR. But Hempf says that he can understand Dreyman's writer's block: "What should one write in this BRD? There's nothing more to believe in, nothing more to rebel against." In a semi-sinister way, Hempf points to a genuine truth: Dreyman had more motivation to write while living under a tyranny—it turned writing into a heroic act. Donnersmarck allows Hempf to sound the note of nostalgia for the old East Germany: "It was nice in our small republic. Many are beginning to understand that only now" (149). The fact that the villainous Hempf expresses these sentiments suggests that Donnersmarck does not himself share them. Still, he has called attention to a problematic aspect of the change of regime for writers. Dreyman was a hero in the DDR and, although the communist government spied upon him and manipulated his life, at the same time, it took him seriously, honored him and, indeed, in the very act of harassing him, showed that it understood his importance as a writer; in the BRD, Dreyman has become a mere celebrity, dressed, as the stage directions point out, in an Armani suit "for which he is actually too heavy, and perhaps also a bit too old" (147).

We are so used to thinking of the fall of the Berlin Wall as a triumphal moment that we naturally assume that the coda of *The Lives of Others* must be presenting the new Germany in a positive light. Surely, Donnersmarck must prefer the new Germany to the old, but it is nevertheless remarkable how little he does to embody that preference in cinematic terms. He in fact maintains the deliberately drab color scheme of the film in the final scenes— no bright neon lights on Berlin's chic shopping street, the Kurfürstendamm, to illuminate the triumph of capitalism, but instead still the same dull brown, gray, green, and beige we saw characterizing the DDR.[13] As a director, Donnersmarck seems to be doing as much as he can to minimize our sense that conditions have genuinely improved for his central characters with the fall of the Wall. Neither Dreyman nor Wiesler is dancing in the streets of the reunified Berlin.[14]

In sum, although *The Lives of Others* does satisfy the appetite of conservatives for an anticommunist film, it by no means offers them a parable of triumphant capitalism. Every cinematic choice Donnersmarck makes in the coda to his film suggests that he is somehow interested in the continuities between the communist and the capitalist regimes in Germany, not, as his conservative admirers might wish, the discontinuities.

While exploring the factors that complicate any reading of Donnersmarck's film, it is high time that we confront the key figure in any attempt to interpret the politics of *The Lives of Others*—Bertolt Brecht. Anyone offering a straightforward anticommunist reading of the film, especially someone trying to present a pro-capitalist reading, must puzzle over its celebration of Brecht. Brecht is arguably the most famous and successful communist author of the twentieth century. He was about as Marxist and anti-capitalist as an author could be, and moreover was an active partisan of the East German communist regime. He chose to work in East Berlin theater when he returned to Europe after his self-imposed exile from Germany during the Nazi era. His presence in East Germany contributed hugely to the cultural and by extension the political legitimacy of the communist regime. Although Brecht expressed doubts about the DDR in private (in unpublished works),[15] in all his time in East Berlin, he never once publicly defied the communist regime and in fact, in what was far from his finest hour, he openly endorsed the use of Soviet troops to put down the workers' uprising in 1953.[16]

And this is the man Donnersmarck apparently offers as a model of a genuinely great artist in *The Lives of Others*. Dreyman is loosely based on Brecht,[17] who fit the criteria that make Dreyman valuable to his communist masters—a playwright who is loyal to the regime but is nevertheless read and admired in the West. More to the point, Brecht himself functions as a positive figure in the plot of *The Lives of Others*. Wiesler's conversion begins when he sneaks into Dreyman's apartment and steals a volume of Brecht's poetry. Soon we see Wiesler reading the book intently, while we hear Sebastian Koch, the actor who plays Dreyman, giving a moving voice-over reading of Brecht's lyric poem, "Erinnerung an die Marie A.," a poem about the kind of memorable love for a woman that is totally absent from Wiesler's own life. In *The Lives of Others*, Brecht seems to stand for everything that is good and genuine about art. Donnersmarck could easily have substituted any number of German poets for Brecht in the plot. Goethe comes immediately to mind; it would have been just as easy for Wiesler to pick up a volume of Germany's greatest lyric poet, who was still honored in the DDR. Why then did Donnersmarck deliberately choose a communist poet when he wanted to suggest the redemptive power of literature?

As a few commentators have noted, Brecht's presence in *The Lives of Others* actually extends beyond the single lyric poem that is quoted in its script. The film repeatedly echoes the title of one of Brecht's most famous plays, *Der gute Mensch von Sezuan*.[18] This title has been variously translated into English as *The Good Person of Szechwan* and *The Good Woman of Szechwan,* reflecting the ambiguity of the German word *Mensch*—just like the English word "man," *Mensch* can refer either to a "male" or to a "human being" of either sex (the fact that the play involves a woman masquerading as a man explains the different translations of the title). English speakers may easily miss the references to Brecht's title in *The Lives of Others,* but they are unmistakable to Germans (for which reason I will continue to refer to the play by its German title). At a key point in the plot, Dreyman is given the sheet music for a piano work called *Sonate vom guten Menschen* and that later becomes the title of the book he writes after the fall of the Berlin Wall. Early in the film, Minister Hempf says to Dreyman that what "we all love about your plays" is "die Liebe zum Menschen, die guten Menschen"—"your love of humanity, of good human beings" (34). After Wiesler sits down with Christa-Maria Sieland in the bar scene, she calls him "ein guter Mensch" (87). The way this phrase keeps reappearing in various forms throughout the film strongly suggests that Donnersmarck had Brecht's *Der gute Mensch von Sezuan* in mind when creating *The Lives of Others*. I do not claim to understand fully why Donnersmarck decided to present the communist playwright Brecht so positively in his ostensibly anticommunist film.[19] But I believe that a detailed comparison of *The Lives of Others* with *Der gute Mensch von Sezuan* may shed light on the role of Brecht in Donnersmarck's film. Donnersmarck may in fact be engaging with Brecht's play in a serious and meaningful way. *The Lives of Others* might even be regarded as a kind of Brechtian attempt to rewrite and even unwrite Brecht's play. In that sense, Donnersmarck might be said to be using Brecht to undermine Brecht.

Der gute Mensch von Sezuan is set in a semi-mythical China, in what the stage directions describe as a "half-Europeanized city."[20] Three gods, who have evidently seen better days, have come to earth in search of good human beings. They believe that if they can find just one good person who obeys their commandments, it will redeem humanity. Their request for lodging and hospitality is initially rejected by all the ostensibly good citizens of the city. The only one who will take them in for the night is a prostitute named Shen Te. In reward for her goodness, the gods give her the money to buy a little tobacco shop. But before she can get the business going, a crowd of moochers descends upon her, including the former owners of the shop and their many relatives, who proceed to sponge off her and otherwise exploit her good nature. She is too compassionate to refuse any request for a handout.

In order to make ends meet, Shen Te has to invent a masculine cousin named Shui Ta, who comes to her rescue at several crucial moments. Whenever Shen Te adopts the role of Shui Ta, she can do the prudent thing and manage her affairs properly, eventually building her small business up into a factory operation. But whenever Shen Te goes back to being a woman, she loses control of her finances and other aspects of her life. For example, she falls in love with a would-be aviator named Yang Sun, whose unscrupulous dealings threaten to make her default on some loans. As the confusions involving the sexually ambiguous identity of the heroine/hero mount, Shui Ta is eventually accused of having murdered Shen Te. On trial before the three gods, Shen Te is forced to reveal to them the truth about her masquerade and delivers the kind of heavy-handed, didactic speech that is the stock-in-trade of Brecht's Marxist dramaturgy:

> Your order long ago
> to be good and yet to live
> tore me like lightning into two halves. I
> don't know how it happened: I could not
> be good at once to others and myself.
> To help myself and others was too hard for me.
> Ah, your world is hard. Too much poverty, too much despair!
> The hand that is held out to the wretched
> is soon wrenched off! He who helps the lost
> is himself lost! For who can
> long refuse to be wicked when starvation kills?
> Where was I to take all that was needed? Only
> from myself! But then I would die. Good intentions
> crushed me to the ground. But when I did wrong
> I strode in power and ate good meat!
> There must be something wrong with your world. Why
> is wickedness so richly rewarded and why does such hard punishment
> await the good? (100)

As often happens with Brecht, understanding the message of *Der gute Mensch von Sezuan* seems very easy.[21] He has nothing but contempt for the respectable and wealthy citizens of the city, while he offers the poor, the downtrodden, and the outcast as the only possible candidates for true goodness. What makes it difficult if not impossible for the basically decent people to put their goodness into action is the capitalist order. Business is a zero-sum game for Brecht—one person can make a profit only if someone else suffers a loss. Thus Shen Te cannot successfully enter the business world without fundamentally changing her identity. She must repress her natural kindness and adopt the hardheaded, hard-hearted persona of her "cousin," Shui Ta. For Brecht, capitalism brings about a complete disjunction between moral goodness and financial success. One cannot be at one and the same time a good businessman and a good human being.

Brecht's clever theatrical trick for embodying this insight on stage is to split his main character as we have seen into two, Shen Te and Shui Ta. This procedure is typical of his dramaturgy; he would rather have two flat characters than a single complex one.[22] Brecht's drama is never far from social satire, and he had no qualms about putting caricatures on stage. He did not feel compelled, as many other dramatists do, to explore the complexities of human motivation or to suggest profound inner conflicts in his characters. Where another playwright would have shown a Shen Te with mixed feelings about her lover, Yang Sun—torn between her love for him and her realization that he is wrong for her—Brecht just divides her up into a Shen Te, who loves him absolutely, and a Shui Ta, who sees that Yang Sun intends to take her money and leave her in the lurch.

Brecht knew what he was doing; he was not simply incapable of creating fully rounded characters (for example, in Mother Courage, protagonist of one of his greatest plays, *Mutter Courage und ihre Kinder,* he succeeded against his will in creating an emotionally complex figure).[23] Brecht consciously rejected the realism of late nineteenth- and early twentieth-century drama, which he regarded as complicit in the capitalist order and a product of it. For Brecht, dramatists such as Ibsen and Chekhov were too eager, out of commercial motives, to please their audiences, to entertain them with plays about characters with whom they could identify and sympathize, characters placed in familiar settings and recognizably human situations with which the audience felt comfortable. According to Brecht, this kind of realistic drama makes its audience complacent. Even an Ibsen problem play, which seems to expose the contradictions in the social order, leaves its audience passive, accepting the existing state of society as inevitable, simply part of the human condition.[24]

By contrast, Brecht sought to unsettle his audiences by every theatrical means at his disposal, to prevent them from reacting emotionally to his dramas and rather to get them to *think* about each play. Rather than identifying with his characters, the spectators should feel distanced from them and hence more capable of judging them objectively. This is Brecht's famous *Verfremdungseffekt,* often translated as "alienation effect" but more properly rendered as "distancing" or "defamiliarization" or "estrangement effect."[25] Everything about *Der gute Mensch von Sezuan* is calculated to prevent the audience from feeling comfortable with the play, from the exotic setting to the unfamiliar names to the cardboard characters to the absurdity of the young woman masquerading as a man so easily. The epilogue, when one of the actors steps out of character, breaks the dramatic illusion, and addresses the audience directly, is designed to send spectators home dissatisfied, still pondering the significance of what they have seen. Brecht openly admits that his play lacks a satisfactory and satisfying conclusion:

> Ladies and gentlemen, don't be annoyed
> We know this ending leaves you in the void.
> A golden legend we set out to tell
> But then somehow the ending went to hell.
> We're disappointed too, struck with dismay
> All questions open though we've closed our play. . . .
> But what's *your* answer to the situation?
> For love nor money we could find no out:
> Refashion man? Or change the world about?
> Or turn to different gods? Or don't we need
> any? Our bewilderment is great indeed.
> There's only one solution comes to mind:
> that you yourselves should ponder till you find
> the ways and means and measures tending
> to help good people to a happy ending. (103–4)

In this typical Brecht ending, the ball is now in the audience's court; the spectators must find a solution to the problems that baffled the playwright. If the function of drama is to provoke social change, Brecht has come up with an effective approach to writing plays. His theory of the Verfremdungseffekt is also very convenient for him as a playwright. If one accuses his characters of being flat, he can reply that he never intended them to be round. If one accuses his plot of being implausible, he can reply that he never intended it to be realistic. Basically any fault in his play, from clichéd dialogue to stereotypical characters to abrupt plot turns to heavy-handed moralizing can be justified as a Verfremdungseffekt. In the ultimate defense mechanism for Brecht, if the play fails to solve the complex social problems it portrays, it is the fault of the audience, not of the playwright.

Brecht's distinctive conception of drama was remarkably self-serving —he succeeded in erecting a theoretical firewall around his plays that makes them impervious to conventional criticism. If one applies any of the traditional criteria of good drama in evaluating Brecht's work, his answer is always that the problem is with traditional drama, not with his plays. This situation can be frustrating to would-be critics of Brecht—one damns oneself as hopelessly mired in the past if one questions his revolutionary drama. Nevertheless, the temptation to raise doubts about Brecht's plays is irresistible, and *Der gute Mensch von Sezuan* is a case in point. It is very doubtful, for example, that feminists would be pleased by the play.[26] For a revolutionary drama, it seems to buy into traditional sexual stereotypes. In splitting his central figure into male and female halves, Brecht parcels out the human qualities along conventional gender lines. Shen Te is the compassionate one: sensitive, emotional, and capable of deep love. But she is at the same time irrational, weak, incapable of dealing with the difficult issues of life and, above all, she has no mind for business. In short, she is the stereotypical flighty and helpless female. Shui Ta is lacking in fellow feeling and he is tough-minded, if not cruel, in his dealings with others. But he is also rational, clear-headed, and disciplined, fully capable of taking charge of any situation, and a sharp businessman—just the way men like to think of themselves. As a Marxist, Brecht may be progressive on political and economic issues, but on the issue of gender, he is a reactionary sexist. If one focuses on the issue of gender—which is difficult not to do, given the plot—what *Der gute Mensch von Sezuan* teaches is that women are by nature unfit for business and need men to save them from their inherent folly as females.

But Brecht is also vulnerable on the political/economic front—the moment one steps outside of his Marxist framework. In an obvious way, *Der gute Mensch von Sezuan* begs the question on the central issue it raises. If one parcels out all the morally good qualities to one character and all the business acumen to another, then of course one will conclude that it is impossible to be a good human being and a good businessman at the same time. But the real question is whether it is possible to combine the qualities of Shen Te and Shui Ta in a single person, and on that issue, history offers many examples of successful capitalists who behaved morally and compassionately in their dealings with their fellow human beings. One might even argue that decency is the norm in business, which is precisely why we are so struck by the phenomenon of business criminals. We need to check Brecht's portrayal of the capitalist world against historical reality. Although he rejected conventional dramatic realism, he always maintained that his plays were truer to social reality than traditional drama had been. Indeed, he claimed that he broke with the dramatic conventions of the past precisely in order to be able to represent social reality more accurately, to call attention to the hard facts of life that were covered up in traditional drama. It is odd, then, that Brecht chose to set *Der gute Mensch von Sezuan* in the kind of orientalist never-never land one normally associates with German operetta, such as Lehar's *The Land of Smiles* (*Das Land des Lächelns*). Can we really learn anything about the real world from a play that mixes oriental gods incongruously with modern airplanes?[27] In fact, if one sets aside Brecht's ingrained anticapitalist prejudices and looks carefully at what is going on in the play in economic terms, then it seems to teach lessons very different from what the playwright had in mind.

Much of what Shui Ta stands for is in fact simple economic common sense. Brecht wants us to think of the character as hard-hearted, but most of the time he is saying nothing crueler than that human beings need to work for a living: "From now on all this must be managed more sensibly. No more food will be distributed free of charge. Instead, everyone will be given an opportunity to improve his condition by honorable labor. Miss Shen Teh has decided to give you all work" (75–76).[28] Even the parasites come to understand that if Shen Te's business goes under, they will be worse off, and hence they grudgingly welcome the return of the capable and efficient Shui Ta: "He's awfully stingy, but at least he'll save the shop, and then she'll help us" (75). Yang Sun's mother praises what Shui Ta has accomplished by imposing discipline on her son: "I must tell you how my son, thanks to the wisdom and severity of the universally respected Mr. Shui Ta, has been transformed from a depraved young man into a useful citizen. As the whole neighborhood knows, Mr. Shui Ta has opened a small but already thriving tobacco factory near the cattle yard" (79). Mrs. Yang even compares Shui Ta favorably with Shen Te: "He didn't make all sorts of fantastic promises like his widely praised cousin, but forced [Yang Sun] to do honest work" (84).

No doubt Brecht expects us to think of Shui Ta as just another exploitative factory owner, operating a sweatshop, but even in terms of the plot Brecht created, Shui Ta is simply recognizing the facts of economic life. The characters he "mistreats" earn his displeasure only because they are all demanding to be supported at his "cousin's" expense, with no effort on their part. Only a self-styled bohemian artist like Brecht could make a moral principle out of the demand for a free lunch. Brecht himself shows that when Yang Sun refuses to work, he does so out of pride—he thinks that ordinary commerce is beneath his dignity as a potential aviator: "You want me to stand out in the street peddling tobacco to the cement workers, me, Yang Sun, the flier. I'd sooner run through the two hundred [dollars Shen Te gave me] in one night, I'd sooner throw them in the river!" (62). Yang Sun insists on maintaining his dignity, but he does so with Shen Te's borrowed money. Perhaps unwittingly, Brecht exposes the hypocrisy of those who complain about capitalist exploiters while exploiting the generosity of capitalists themselves. As several critics have noted, including admirers such as W. H. Auden, in his last decade Brecht himself led a kind of double life: he did his play producing in communist East Germany but he did his banking in capitalist Switzerland.[29] Indeed, ever since *The Threepenny Opera* Brecht had been preaching anticapitalism all the way to the bank.

As an economic argument, *Der gute Mensch von Sezuan* fails; it is riddled with fallacies and contradictions. Brecht is the kind of person who wants cigars but does not want the cigar factories needed to produce them. All his focus in *Der gute Mensch von Sezuan* seems to be on the process of consumption, not of production, and he is evidently not aware that the two processes are connected. He seems to posit a sort of natural sufficiency of goods, and the only problem is that they are not distributed equally. The capitalist exploiters have grabbed all the wealth and deny goods to the starving masses. Hovering behind *Der gute Mensch von Sezuan* is the Marxist ideal: "From each according to his ability; to each according to his needs." But ironically, in Shui Ta's wisdom, Brecht shows why this formula cannot work in the real world and why communism is always doomed to failure. If people can get what they need through handouts, they will refuse to work, and the result will soon be that nothing gets produced to hand out. Because of the problem of economic incentives, how goods are distributed has a profound effect on how—and even whether—they are produced in the first place. Brecht inadvertently illustrates this basic economic truth in *Der gute Mensch von Sezuan*. Shen Te sets out to run her shop like a communist, but she needs the capitalist Shui Ta to save her from economic disaster—much as the Soviet Union continually needed economic aid and guidance from the capitalist West throughout its catastrophic experiments with communism. Despite all Brecht's efforts to prevent it, economic truth ultimately shines through the Marxist fog of *Der gute Mensch von Sezuan*. As so often happens in his work, Brecht the playwright ends up inadvertently refuting Brecht the Marxist ideologue. If one did not know who wrote *Der gute Mensch von Sezuan,* one might initially assume that it was designed to expose the folly of communism, not the evil of capitalism.[30]

To my knowledge, Donnersmarck has never commented on *Der gute Mensch von Sezuan* or discussed its relation to *The Lives of Others*.[31] We can, therefore, only guess why he chose to make the phrase "guter Mensch" so prominent in his film. There does seem to be a basic similarity between the two works, one that suggests that Donnersmarck may be trying to turn the tables on Brecht. *Der gute Mensch von Sezuan* chronicles the search for a single good human being in the world of capitalism; *The Lives of Others* chronicles the search for a single good human being in the world of social- ism. Donnersmarck seems to be saying in effect to Brecht: "You made it seem so difficult to find a good human being under capitalism; now you have your socialist paradise in the DDR; let's see if it's any easier to find a good human being there." In short, if Donnersmarck goes out of his way to evoke *Der gute Mensch von Sezuan* in *The Lives of Others,* it may be pre- cisely as a challenge to Brecht. Brecht claims that capitalism is incompatible with moral goodness; Donnersmarck counters by showing that socialism is even more incompatible with behaving decently as a human being. His hero, Wiesler, can become "ein guter Mensch" only by turning traitor to the communist regime in East Germany.

Donnersmarck also demonstrates his superiority to Brecht as a drama- tist, at least according to traditional aesthetic criteria. Gerd Wiesler is the kind of complex, sympathetic character Brecht claimed not to want to create (although he did so on numerous occasions). In a Brechtian treatment of *The Lives of Others,* I suppose Wiesler would have to divide into two char- acters, one working for the Stasi and one working against it. Where Brecht typically goes for broad strokes of characterization and sharp contrasts, Donnersmarck seeks out subtle effects. Where Brecht paints in blacks and whites, Donnersmarck employs a palette of grays. Brecht puts a label on a character—"cruel factory owner"—and that is all we need to know about him.[32] Donnersmarck does deal with stereotypes like "Communist Party hack," but his characters are more interesting precisely because they do not always act according to type. Critics of *The Lives of Others* complain that Wiesler's protecting of Dreyman is not sufficiently motivated. But that may be exactly Donnersmarck's point. We never know how a particular human being is going to react in a particular set of circumstances. If one believes in human freedom, then human action is always potentially a mystery, and fictional characters may well surprise us with a seemingly unmotivated change of heart, or at least an enigmatic one.

Much of the criticism of *The Lives of Others* might be characterized as Brechtian in spirit. The critics of the film are asking for greater ideological purity from Donnersmarck, even if they want his film to be more fully anticommunist rather than anticapitalist, as Brecht would have it. Some critics want Wiesler to be the prototypical—perhaps even the stereotypical—Stasi agent, and hence incapable of being the "good man" of Donnersmarck's script. Donnersmarck would answer his critics that he is not interested in being ideologically pure. He is concerned with being true to his vision of human nature rather than to any ideological position on the historical East Germany. Perhaps in anticipation of his critics, Donnersmarck built this defense of his approach into the movie itself. When Dreyman meets with Hessenstein, the representative of the Western magazine that wants to publish the article on suicide in East Germany, the editor presses the writer for more detail and historical background, for example, a clearer explanation of the differences between the circumstances in the DDR in 1967 and those in 1977. Dreyman balks at these instructions: "Es soll ein literarisches Text bleiben. Keine journalistische Hetzschrift"—"It should remain a literary text. Not a piece of journalistic agitation" (100). As a playwright, Dreyman refuses to focus his writing on documentary facts and figures; he wants to keep the spotlight on the human element in the story, the sad tale of the suicide of the director Jerska.

That of course is exactly what Donnersmarck does in the film himself. *The Lives of Others* is at its core an *ethical* drama; it focuses on the possibility of acting humanely in the most inhumane of worlds. Funder quotes Donnersmarck making just this point: "More than anything else, *The Lives of Others* is a human drama about the ability of human beings to do the right thing, no matter how far they have gone down the wrong path."[33] By contrast, in Brecht's dramas, politics/economics trumps ethics. He is first and foremost concerned with the political/economic system under which his characters live, and he believes that it sets inescapable limits upon their ability to act ethically. Donnersmarck's position is just the opposite—in *The Lives of Others,* ethics trumps politics/economics. Donnersmarck's central point is that a human being can act ethically under any circumstances, even in a communist tyranny. Instead of talking about the ambivalence in Donnersmarck's politics, we should probably speak of his ambivalence about politics. He seems by no means certain that any one political system is the simple answer to human problems, and he is interested in the way acting ethically can transcend any political setting.

Thus Donnersmarck remains within the broad outlines of the Western dramatic tradition, which is basically humanistic in nature. From Sophocles to Shakespeare to Ibsen, the premise of traditional drama is that human beings are free to act ethically, to make difficult choices even in the most difficult of circumstances, and thus they can be held responsible for their deeds—even in tragic situations. This is the tradition of drama with which Brecht chose to break. His dramaturgy is designed to deflect interest from character to circumstances. He did not want his audiences to become so obsessed with complexities of character that they would lose sight of the underlying political/economic circumstances that force his characters to act the way they do and eliminate their capacity to make free choices. For Brecht, the problem is not whether human beings want to act ethically, but whether social circumstances allow them to do so. In the famous words of *The Threepenny Opera:* "Wir wären gut—anstatt so roh / Doch die Verhältnisse, sie sind nicht so" (We as human beings want to be good, instead of rough [brutal, coarse], but circumstances [conditions] are not that way [and don't permit it]).[34]

For Brecht, ethical questions are comparatively simple and easily answered: human beings just need to be kind to each other.[35] The real problem is how to reconstitute the social order to make that possible. In Brecht's view, the need to raise ethical issues is already a sign of a defect in the social order. If society were properly ordered, virtue would no longer be necessary. He has Mother Courage make this argument in the course of condemning an army commander:

> If his plan of campaign was any good, why would he need *brave* soldiers, wouldn't plain, ordinary soldiers do? Whenever there are

great virtues, it's a sure sign something's wrong. . . . When a general or a king is stupid and leads his soldiers into a trap, they need the virtue of courage. When he's tightfisted and hasn't enough soldiers, the few he does have need the heroism of Hercules—another virtue. . . . All virtues which a well-regulated country with a good king or a good general wouldn't need. In a good country, virtues wouldn't be necessary. Everybody could be quite ordinary, middling, and, for all I care, cowards.[36]

This attempt to downplay the importance of virtue and to elevate political questions over ethical questions is reminiscent of Žižek's criticism of *The Lives of Others*—his objection that Donnersmarck focuses too much on the moral status of the rulers of the DDR, whether they are corrupt or not—when the real issue is the underlying political system, which would be oppressive even if administered by dedicated public servants. There is a good deal of truth to this argument and, in defense of Donnersmarck, it is unfair to accuse him of ignoring, or even downplaying, the systemic problems of the East German regime. No one can come away from viewing *The Lives of Others* without thinking that there was something fundamentally wrong with political arrangements in the DDR.

Nevertheless, in his quest to create a compelling drama in *The Lives of Others,* Donnersmarck is justified in focusing on ethical issues. Some of his critics seem to wish that he had created a political treatise or a historical analysis instead of the sort of human story audiences expect.[37] Brecht did want to break with the humanistic conception of drama and in effect to turn his plays into political treatises. But to the extent he actually succeeded in doing so, he often made his plays insufferably didactic and barely watchable on stage. In fact, in the Brecht plays that have been theatrically successful, his instincts as a dramatist overrode his agenda as an ideologue, and the human element in the drama survived his attempts to suppress it. By far his most popular work, *The Threepenny Opera,* has enchanted audiences over the years not because of its ham-fisted anticapitalist message but because of its charming and delightful characters, brought to life unforgettably by Kurt Weill's music.[38]

In the history of drama, Brecht is truly the exception that proves the rule. He made every effort to eliminate the traditional emphasis on character in drama, and yet his own plays have succeeded largely because of the incredible rogues' gallery of characters he created—from Mack the Knife to

Mother Courage. At their best, Brecht's morally dubious protagonists win our sympathy even as they send chills down our spines with their villainy. Critics have complained that Donnersmarck sentimentalized *The Lives of Others* by focusing on romance elements in the plot at the expense of ideology. But how would *The Threepenny Opera* play with audiences without Macheath's romances with Polly, Jenny, and assorted other women in the plot? As much as Brecht scorned the romantic sentimentality of traditional drama, he could not do without love scenes in his own works. Even *Der gute Mensch von Sezuan* would be much less dramatic without the romantic involvement of Shen Te and Yang Sun. Contrary to Brecht's theory of drama, the love of Shen Te and Yang Sun gives the audience something to identify with on stage, something to sympathize with.

The issue of sympathy takes us to the heart of the difference between Brecht and Donnersmarck as dramatists. As we have seen, Brecht wanted his audience to feel distanced or alienated or estranged from his characters (even though in practice he often created genuinely sympathetic figures). By contrast, sympathy is at the very center of Donnersmarck's conception of drama and of *The Lives of Others*. That in fact is what the title points to—Wiesler must learn to sympathize with "the lives of others." The film is about observation in all its many meanings: interrogation, viewing a play, espionage, empathizing with others. *The Lives of Others* is reminiscent of Alfred Hitchcock or Fritz Lang in its obsession with spectatorship, the way it invites us to watch people watching other people.[39] At the beginning of the film, Wiesler is the cold, objective observer, wholly distanced from his subjects—the ideal Brechtian spectator. Whether he is interrogating a suspect or watching a play, he keeps his emotions in check because he is trying to spy something out. To become a "good man," he must bridge the gap between himself and "the lives of others" and learn to sympathize with them. He must become the kind of spectator most dramatists crave for their work.

It is perhaps Donnersmarck's joke on Brecht that he gives the prophet of alienation a central role in this plot development. Before the hitherto emotionless Wiesler can shed a tear just listening to a piece of music, he must read a Brecht poem, "Erinnerung an die Marie A." ("Memory of Marie A."). Note that he reads a Brecht lyric, not one of his dramas (which, according to Brecht, would have reinforced his commitment to communism). This nostalgic lament for a lost love is as sentimental as Brecht ever gets, which may be why Donnersmarck chose it. He shows Wiesler turning into a good man not by virtue of any Brechtian alienation effect—after all, the captain is alienated enough already. On the contrary, it is Brecht at his most sentimental who proves to be the force behind Wiesler's conversion to moral goodness. In general, Donnersmarck uses Brecht in a very un-Brechtian manner and for a very un-Brechtian goal—to produce sympathy, not to eliminate it. In *The Lives of Others*, Donnersmarck's use of Brecht creates a de-alienation effect, leading Wiesler back into the fold of humanity, breaking down his ruthless objectivity and awakening his fellow feeling. For Donnersmarck to incorporate Brecht into his movie is, then, just the opposite of an endorsement of his theory of drama, and it does not involve an endorsement of the communist playwright's politics either. Contrary to everything Brecht himself stood for, he functions in *The Lives of Others* as an emblem of the power of art to evoke sympathy.

I do not claim to have solved the riddle of why Donnersmarck gives such a prominent role to the communist playwright Brecht in his ostensibly anticommunist film *The Lives of Others*. But by exploring the movie's subtextual use of Brecht's *Der gute Mensch von Sezuan*, we begin to see that there is at least some irony in Donnersmarck's invocation of his German predecessor. If only by example, *The Lives of Others* refutes Brecht's conception of drama. And by quoting a Brecht romantic lyric, rather than one of his political dramas, Donnersmarck deflects attention from his anticapitalist agenda and reveals the sentimental element that remained a part of Brecht's art, despite all his conscious efforts to suppress it. Thus, in the very process of evoking Brecht, Donnersmarck manages to question his predecessor and establish his difference from Brecht's art and his politics. Above all, Donnersmarck forcefully rejects Brecht's efforts as a dramatist to shift attention from character to circumstances. Donnersmarck understands the antihumanistic implications of Brecht's dramaturgy. By contrast, in his film he works very hard to keep ethical concerns at the center.

At the time and in the circumstances in which *The Lives of Others* was released, it was impossible not to view the film as a political statement, and in what it shows about the East German communist regime, it will always remain a great political film. And yet politics is *not* what is most important in the film—not because of some failure on Donnersmarck's part but because of what he set out to accomplish. *The Lives of Others* takes its place in an older dramatic tradition and is trying to make a statement about human nature. While remaining firmly rooted in a specific historical and political moment, *The Lives of Others* is ultimately about the human capacity to transcend the limitations and constraints of such a moment. It may be historically true that "a good man" was impossible to find in the communist apparatus of East Germany. But it is nevertheless important to Donnersmarck to remind us that it was at least possible that one such man existed—that, contrary to Brecht, human nature is not simply the product of political and economic circumstances. And Donnersmarck has the last laugh on Brecht by choosing his adopted homeland, the socialist paradise of East Germany, as the ultimate test case of whether it is possible to be a good man in an evil state.

Notes

An earlier version of this essay was published in *Perspectives on Political Science,* April–June 2011, Vol. 40, No. 2. Used by permission.

1. John Podhoretz, "Nightmare Come True: Love and Distrust in the East German Police State," *Weekly Standard,* March 12, 2007, 38.

2. See, for example, Timothy Garton Ash, "The Stasi in Our Minds," *New York Review of Books,* May 31, 2007, 3, http://www.nybooks.com/articles /20210 (accessed July 12, 2009). Garton Ash really worries over details: "On everyday duty, Stasi officers would not have worn those smart dress uniforms, with polished knee-length leather boots, leather belts, and cavalry-style trousers. By contrast, the cadets in the Stasi university are shown in ordinary, student-type civilian clothes; they would have been in uniform. A Stasi surveillance team would have been most unlikely to install itself in the attic of the same building—a sure give-away to the residents." I am sure Garton Ash is right about these details, but he reminds me of the sort of critic who complains about the fact that Shakespeare's ordinary Romans anachronistically wear caps.

3. Anna Funder, "Tyranny of Terror," *Guardian,* May 5, 2007, 2, http://www.theguardian .com/books/2007/may/05/featuresreviews.guardianreview12 (accessed May 8, 2008).

4. All three quotations are taken from Slavoj Žižek, "The Dreams of Others," *In These Times,* May 18, 2007, 1, http://www.inthesetimes.com/article/3183/the_dreams_of_others/ (accessed May 9, 2009).

5. Several of the reviews recommend a 2002 Belgian documentary called *The Decomposition of the Soul,* directed by Nina Toussaint and Massimo Ianetta, which deals with Hohenschönhausen, the Stasi prison and interrogation center in Berlin.

6. I cite the director's commentary from the Sony Pictures Classics 2007 DVD of *The Lives of Others.*

7. Since I am not an expert on East German history, I am trying to avoid getting involved in the debate over the historical accuracy of *The Lives of Others.* I will confine myself to pointing out that Donnersmarck did employ a historical consultant on the film, Manfred Wilke of the Free University of Berlin, who is a recognized authority on the communist regime in East Germany. Wilke wrote an essay for the published screenplay of the film called "Wieslers Umkehr"—"Wiesler's Change" (or " Turnaround" or "Conversion"). See Florian Henckel von Donnersmarck, *Das Leben der Anderen: Filmbuch* (Frankfurt: Suhrkampf, 2007), 201–13. While Wilke is unable to cite a case in which a Stasi agent behaved exactly the way Wiesler does, he points to several examples of traitorous behavior within

the official ranks of the Stasi and in particular documents a number of ways in which Stasi agents appeared to lose their nerve during the waning days of the DDR regime. Wiesler's behavior in *The Lives of Others* may seem implausible, but in 1984, the complete collapse of the DDR regime five years later would have seemed far more implausible. Something must have happened to make that collapse possible, and it was not simply the result of external factors; the DDR regime had been rotting away from within for years. Donnersmarck in fact does a brilliant job of showing why supporters of the communist regime gradually lost faith in it and ceased to work for its survival. For what it is worth, one of the skeptics about the film, Garton Ash, writes: "Now I have heard of Stasi informers who ended up protecting those they were informing on. I know of full-time Stasi operatives who became disillusioned, especially during the 1980s. And in many hours of talking to former Stasi officers, I never met a single one who I felt to be, simply and plainly, an evil man. Weak, blinkered, opportunistic, self-deceiving, yes; men who did evil things, most certainly; but always I glimpsed in them the remnants of what might have been, the good that could have grown in other circumstances" ("Stasi in Our Minds," 4).

8. Funder, "Tyranny of Terror," 3.

9. In his commentary on the DVD of the film, Donnersmarck reveals that it is his own voice reporting the news of the fall of the Wall over the radio: "That's me, overjoyed at the end of that dictatorship, as I really was, as everybody was, all over the world. It was a great moment for everybody, of course." I am not trying to question the sincerity of these sentiments, but they make it all the more peculiar that Donnersmarck did nothing in the film to convey this sense of joy visually.

10. Donnersmarck, *Das Leben,* 157. All citations to stage directions will be to this screenplay, and I will also quote the film's dialogue from the screenplay, making it clear when the screenplay differs from the final filmed version; hereinafter page numbers will be incorporated into the body of the essay in parentheses. The translations from the German are my own, sometimes guided by the subtitles on the film.

11. Much, although not all, of this additional dialogue is included as a deleted scene on the DVD of the film. In his DVD commentary, Donnersmarck emphasizes Hempf's links to capitalism: "If this guy had lived in the 1980s, he would have become a big shot on Wall Street or in one of the large corporations."

12. The stage directions at this point (148) say simply that Dreyman finds the situation *unerträglich* ("insufferable" or "intolerable"); it may be that he finds the production distasteful; it may be that it has simply awakened painful memories in him (which is what ex-minister Hempf suggests to him in the next scene). Donnersmarck's commentary on the DVD seems to support this second interpretation: "And here the same play in a new Germany with a new Marta, and that is so painful for Dreyman."

13. In his DVD commentary, Donnersmarck mentions that he considered setting a scene on the Kurfürstendamm (earlier in the film). I do not know Berlin's geography well enough to be sure of this claim, but I believe that all of the post-1989 scenes in the film are set in the former East Berlin. The only visible change is the appearance of graffiti on the buildings, something that could never have happened under the old regime. I am not sure that this development can be regarded as an improvement. In fact, in his DVD commentary Donnersmarck complains that in order to maintain the graffiti-free look he wanted for the old East Berlin, his crew had to repaint the buildings every day to eliminate the graffiti that

always mysteriously appeared overnight. The setting of the concluding sequence of the film in the former East Berlin is emphasized by the fact that the very last scene of *The Lives of Others* is set in Karl-Marx-Allee and takes place in the Karl Marx Bookstore. It does seem odd that an ostensibly anticommunist film ends with the name of Karl Marx still firmly in place in the new Germany. In the DVD commentary, Donnersmarck seems to have an affection for the Karl Marx Bookstore and says rather ruefully that it is "always on the brink of bankruptcy in the West now," perhaps a hint that even for him not everything is better in the new Germany.

14. And of course, although Wiesler and Dreyman come to understand the role that each has played in the other's life, they never actually communicate directly. As Donnersmarck says in his DVD commentary: "It's a buddy movie, this film, only the two buddies never meet." Donnersmarck's explanation in the screenplay for why Dreyman does not speak to Wiesler when he locates him at the end is very interesting: "Das materielle Machtgefälle (und welch eine Rolle spielt das in dem neuen Deutschland!) ist zu gross für eine Begegnung, die auf gleicher menschlicher Ebene stattfinden müsste" (157). Roughly translated: "The difference in the material level of power between them (and what a role that plays in the new Germany!) is too great for a meeting, which must take place on an equal human level." Without making too much of this pointed reference to inequality in the new, capitalist Germany, one might contrast this scene with one of Wiesler's better moments early in the film—when he insists on sitting with the common workers at the Stasi cafeteria, rather than at the officers' table, and says: "Socialism must begin somewhere" (59). Again, however negative a portrayal *The Lives of Others* gives of the DDR, it does not seem simply to champion capitalism over socialism.

15. For Brecht's private criticism of the DDR, see Edward Mendelson, "*The Caucasian Chalk Circle* and *Endgame*," in *Homer to Brecht: The European Epic and Dramatic Traditions*, ed. Michael Seidel and Edward Mendelson (New Haven, CT: Yale University Press, 1977), 341: "Around the time of the Berlin riots of 1953 he wrote (but did not publish) an ironic poem saying that the government had lost the support of the people—it would perhaps be best to dissolve the people and elect a new one."

16. For an account of Brecht's behavior during the workers' uprising of 1953, see Ronald Hayman, *Brecht: A Biography* (New York: Oxford University Press, 1983), 368–69. Here is an excerpt from a letter Brecht published in the official party organ *Neues Deutschland* on June 23, 1953: "Organized fascist elements tried to abuse [the workers'] dissatisfaction for their bloody purpose. . . . It is only thanks to the swift and accurate intervention of Soviet troops that these attempts were frustrated. It was obvious that the intervention of the Soviet troops was in no way directed against the workers' demonstrations. It was perfectly evident that it was directed exclusively against the attempt to start a new holocaust. . . . I now hope that the agitators have been isolated and their network of contacts destroyed" (quoted in Hayman, *Brecht,* 369). For an imaginative and thought-provoking treatment of Brecht's response to the workers' uprising, see Günter Grass's play *Die Plebejer proben den Aufstand.* The English-language edition, *The Plebeians Rehearse the Uprising,* trans. Ralph Manheim (New York: Harcourt, Brace and World, 1966), contains an appendix by Uta Gerhardt, "The Uprising of June 17, 1953" (113–22), which offers a concise but detailed account of the workers' uprising in Berlin and Brecht's response to it. Gerhardt quotes Brecht's infamous endorsement of the communist regime in an open letter to Walter Ulbricht, which concludes: "At this moment I feel the need of expressing my solidarity with the Socialist Unity Party of Germany" (122).

17. Sebastian Koch, the actor who plays Dreyman, suggests in his essay on the film that even Dreyman's apartment was based on Brecht's. See Sebastian Koch, "Warum ich erst jetzt eine Kinohauptrolle in Deutschland spiele," in Donnersmarck, *Das Leben,* 175. Donnersmarck even links the color scheme of the film to Brecht; when commenting on it on the DVD, he says: "Here you can see everything in a Brechtian gray; gray was Brecht's favorite color."

18. See, for example, Anthony Grenville, "A Good Man in East Germany," *AJR [Association of Jewish Refugees] Journal,* September 2007, http://www.ajr.org.uk/journal/issue.Sep07/article.917 (accessed July 28, 2008); and Michael Wood, "At the Movies," *London Review of Books,* March 22, 2007, http://www.lrb.co.uk/v29/n06/wood01_.html (accessed July 12, 2009).

19. For the record, there was to be another use of Brecht in *The Lives of Others.* The DVD includes a deleted scene, placed during the birthday party at Dreyman's apartment, in which his director friend, Jerska, reads out loud a brief poem by Brecht. Evidently copyright problems with the poem prevented Donnersmarck from using it in the film, and the text is not provided on the DVD; it is simply identified as an "animal poem." It turns out to be one of what Brecht called his *Tierverse;* as odd as it may seem, Brecht comes across as a German version of Dr. Seuss in these humorous poems (there are a total of fourteen of them). The text of the first is printed in the German screenplay (52–53):

Es war einmal ein Adler
Der hatte viele Tadler
Die machten ihn herunter
Und haben ihn verdächtigt
Er könne nicht schwimmen in Teich.
Da versuchte er es sogleich
Und ging natürlich unter.
(Der Tadel war also berechtigt).

The poem is about an eagle who had many critics; they made him suspicious that he could not swim in the pond, but he tried it anyway and of course drowned, proving the criticism justified. This "nonsense" verse unfortunately makes a good deal of sense in Jerska's case and prefigures his suicide (his "going under"); in effect, Donnersmarck uses the Brecht poem to show that Jerska has allowed the Communist Party's criticism to get to him and destroy his self-confidence.

20. I cite the English translation by Ralph Manheim, *The Good Person of Szechwan,* in *Brecht: Collected Plays* (New York: Vintage, 1976), 6:2. All future citations to this text will be incorporated into the body of the essay, with page numbers in parentheses.

21. See Eric Bentley, *The Playwright as Thinker: A Study of the Modern Theatre* (New York: Harcourt Brace, 1946), 224: "The theme of *The Good Woman of Setzuan* is not hard to grasp."

22. On Brecht's tendency to split his characters, see Walter H. Sokel, "Brecht's Split Characters and His Sense of the Tragic," in *Brecht: A Collection of Critical Essays,* ed. Peter Demetz (Englewood Cliffs, NJ: Prentice-Hall, 1962), 127–37.

23. See Peter Demetz, introduction to Demetz, *Brecht,* 14; and H. F. Garten, *Modern German Drama* (New York: Grove, 1962), 213.

24. For Brecht's critique of traditional drama, see Mendelson, *"Caucasian Chalk Circle,"* 340.

25. Most of Brecht's theoretical writings about drama and the theater are conveniently available in English in *Brecht on Theatre,* ed. and trans. John Willett (New York: Hill and Wang, 1964). Probably the best overview of his theory is to be found in "The Modern Theatre Is the Epic Theatre" (33–42). Of particular relevance to *Der gute Mensch von Sezuan* is "Alienation Effects in Chinese Acting" (91–99), which, according to Willett, contains the first reference to the Verfremdungseffekt in Brecht's writings. For good overviews of Brecht's theory of drama, see two essays by Eric Bentley, "From Strindberg to Bertolt Brecht" in his *Playwright as Thinker,* 209–31; and "The Stagecraft of Brecht" in his *In Search of Theater* (New York: Vintage, 1957), 134–51.

26. See, for example, Elizabeth Wright, "*The Good Person of Szechwan:* Discourse of a Masquerade," in *The Cambridge Companion to Brecht,* ed. Peter Thomson and Glendyr Sacks (Cambridge: Cambridge University Press, 1994), 117, 122–23. For the contrary view that "Brecht's deconstruction of character is consistent with recent feminist theory of gendered identity," see William E. Gruber, *Missing Persons: Character and Characterization in Modern Drama* (Athens: University of Georgia Press, 1994), 73.

27. Brecht himself was uncertain about the setting of *Der gute Mensch von Sezuan.* When he first got the idea for the play, he planned on setting it in Berlin. Even after he decided upon a Chinese setting, he worried over how oriental the setting should be: "We are still mulling over the problem; bread and milk or rice and tea for the Szechwan parable? Of course there are already airmen and still gods in this Szechwan. I have sedulously avoided any kind of folklore. On the other hand the yellow race eating white French bread is not intended as a joke." Brecht was troubled by the unreality of his Chinese setting and sought to counter it: "The city must be a big, dusty uninhabitable place . . . some attention must be paid to countering the risk of Chinoiserie. The vision is of a Chinese city's outskirts with cement works and so on. There are still gods around but aeroplanes have come in." Both quotations are taken from Stephen Unwin, *A Guide to the Plays of Bertolt Brecht* (London: Methuen, 2005), 202–3. These comments suggest that Brecht never satisfactorily resolved in his own mind how real and how unreal he wanted the setting of the play to be. On the issue of the reality/unreality of the setting, see also John Willett, introduction to *Bertolt Brecht: Collected Plays,* vol. 6, pt. 1, *The Good Person of Szechwan* (London: Methuen, 1985), v–vi, ix–x. Willett quotes Brecht as expressing his concern that the Chinese setting had become a "mere disguise, and a ragged disguise at that" (v).

28. The translation I am quoting uses the name "Shen Teh" for some reason; I have retained the "Shen Te" of Brecht's original German version in my own prose.

29. A. R. Braunmiller reports in his introduction to *The Rise and Fall of the City of Mahagonny,* trans. W. H. Auden and Chester Kallman (Boston: David R. Godine, 1976), 12, that Auden said of Brecht: "You must admire the logic of a man who lives in a Communist country, takes out Austrian citizenship, does his banking in Switzerland, and, like a gambler hedging his bets, sends for the pastor at the end in the event there could be something in that, too." On Brecht's hedging his bets, see also Mendelson, "*Caucasian Chalk Circle,*" 340–41.

30. On the way Brecht's practice as a dramatist often contradicts his theories as a Marxist, see Sokel, "Split Characters," 133; and Demetz, introduction, 8, 13. On problems with Brecht's Marxism, see Sokel, "Split Characters," 137. Brecht always said that he wanted his plays to make people think. The unspoken assumption behind his theory is that they will then think in Marxist terms. But as Demetz points out with regard to *Der gute Mensch von*

Sezuan: "The Epilogue will hardly persuade an audience to reply with the Marxist answer desired by Brecht" (introduction, 13). More generally, Demetz writes: "Alienation effects show relations and events in a new light; they demonstrate that the world is changeable and keep the audience alert for practical political action—why it should be action along Communist lines, Brecht alone knows" (4).

31. The only comment I have been able to find in print from Donnersmarck on Brecht comes in an interview done with Vadim Rizov for the *Reeler,* February 7, 2007, under the title "*Lives* in His Hands: German Director von Donnersmarck on the Art and Politics of *The Lives of Others.*" Donnersmarck shows that he understands the contradictions in Brecht's life and art, and the dualities in his existence: "Brecht first of all is just a great poet. But then he was also someone who lived continuously with this dilemma of somehow theoretically embracing Communism but practically just seeing the awfulness that it was leading to. There's this one beautiful poem of his where he asks forgiveness of the future generations for all the terrible things they did in the name of Communism. And at the same time, he chose to be in the GDR, but then led this strange life between the US and the GDR. There was no one else who had that weird dual existence" (2, http://www.thereeler.com/features/ lives_in_his_hands.php [accessed July 12, 2009]). Donnersmarck makes similar comments about Brecht in the DVD commentary when he gets to the scene of Wiesler reading Brecht: "And here Brecht's beautiful poem. Brecht is really worth learning German for. He is such a master of the perfect word. And that's why I wanted him in here, apart from all his connections to the whole Communism issue. He was someone who was torn between a fascination for that ideology and a full realization of the wrongness that unfortunately came with it, of the violence, of the dictatorship. And that's why I think Brecht had to be in this film. Although maybe I would have put him into any other film too. Because he is just a genius, a forgotten genius, a little bit, outside of Germany, at least I think, forgotten, and even in Germany. But a genius nonetheless." Donnersmarck goes on to talk about giving the keynote address at a Brecht Congress in Augsburg, where he spoke about the importance of Brecht in his life, beginning with his reading of Brecht's play *Baal* when he was twelve years old.

32. See Sokel, "Split Characters," 134: "Brecht, in definite and sharp contrast to traditional Western tragedy, does not begin with the individual but with the problem. . . . Brecht's protagonists . . . are exemplifications of human problems; they are primarily not individuals but dilemmas. They are types." Sokel goes on to show that Brecht's characters are more typical of comedies than of tragedies.

33. Funder, "Tyranny of Terror," 3.

34. *Die Dreigroschenoper, Bertolt Brecht: Werke,* Berliner and Frankfurter Ausgabe (Frankfurt: Suhrkampf, 1988), 2:263 (Erstes Dreigroschen-Finale).

35. See Sokel, "Split Characters," 128, for the view that in Brecht "for human beings it is an easy thing to be good."

36. Bertolt Brecht, *Mother Courage and Her Children,* trans. Eric Bentley (New York: Grove, 1966), 39.

37. In his interview with Rizov, Donnersmarck said: "I didn't want it to turn into some abstract political thing; I just wanted to show the effects with these individuals" (Rizov, *Lives,* 1).

38. See Garten, *Modern German Drama,* 206.

39. One indication of the pervasiveness of observation as a motif in *The Lives of Others*

is the fact that the chief observer, Wiesler, often becomes himself the observed. Consider six scenes: (1) When Wiesler is instructing the Stasi class on the art of interrogation at the beginning of the film, we learn at the end of the scene that he has been observed the whole time by his superior officer Grubitz; (2) When Wiesler is leading the team that bugs Dreyman's apartment, he is observed—through a keyhole—by a neighbor across the hall; (3) Just before entering the bar, Wiesler pauses in the street to observe more of Sieland; we suddenly learn that a drunk has been observing him and he startles Wiesler by asking: "What are you staring at?"; (4) When Wiesler interrogates Sieland, he is being observed the whole time again by Grubitz through a one-way mirror; (5) When Grubitz arrives with his team for the first search of Dreyman's apartment, he winks sarcastically at Wiesler through the surveillance camera, as if to say: "I'm watching you"; (6) At the end of the film, Dreyman, having discovered Wiesler's identity, observes him unseen from a passing car as he walks his delivery route. More generally, the movie repeatedly associates looking at a play with spying into people's lives, and of course throughout, we as audience of the movie are "spying" into the lives of others.

5

THE TRAGIC AMBIGUITY, OR AMBIGUOUS TRAGEDY, OF CHRISTA-MARIA SIELAND

Dirk R. Johnson

To the question of what *The Lives of Others* is *about,* one might answer it is about the oppressiveness of totalitarian societies that monitor and control their citizens' lives and careers. In fact, while *The Lives* seems to be about the machinery of surveillance in one totalitarian society in particular—that of the state secret police, or Stasi, in the former East Germany—it reflects the entire spectrum of totalitarian states that have cast their shadow over Europe's "long twentieth century."[1] Indeed, it does not take a great leap of imagination to envision similar scenarios in Hitler's Germany, Mussolini's Italy, Stalin's Russia, or Ceauşescu's Romania. But what makes this film much more than a snapshot of any one particular society and its oppressive security apparatus is the fact that Director Florian Henckel von Donnersmarck does not focus on the macro picture as such but crafts a classic human tale with a tragic heroine at its center, a tale in which misguided human passions, compounded by unchecked political power, ambition, and corruption, destroy lives.[2] In true Aristotelian fashion, Donnersmarck presents how the lust of a high-ranking East German state minister (Bruno Hempf) for a glamorous stage actress (Christa-Maria Sieland, or "CMS")[3] sets in motion a chain of events that inexorably leads to her death. Despite his nod to Bertolt Brecht,[4] Donnersmarck succeeds in portraying the tragic dimension of this late-twentieth-century reality much more effectively, I will argue, because he adheres to an Aristotelian conception of the tragic.[5]

Brecht's dramatic theory rejects direct audience identification with the central characters and their actions. Brecht expects the audience to think through the main characters' actions and to gain an awareness of the larger historical, political, and social forces that prevent them from escaping their predicament. The audience is not meant to identify with the central characters or their fate but to leave the theater thinking that the tragedy might have been averted if the tragic figures had not been trapped by the larger social and historical conventions of the time. The character of Mother Courage, for example, in Brecht's *Mother Courage and Her Children* (1939) encounters the deprivations and horrors of the Thirty Years' War but does not change her ways and learn from her mistakes because she has internalized the horrible logic of war in order to survive. In the play the *Life of Galileo* (1937–1939), the title character of Galileo, unencumbered by the historical implications of his theories, ushers in a scientific revolution that threatens to topple the power of church and state, but he fails to recognize that scientific knowledge cannot be divorced from social responsibility. Brecht works against the audience being drawn in by the tragedy of these characters and instead uses dramatic effects—most famously, the *V-Effect* (*Verfremdungseffekt,* or alienation effect)—to create an emotional distance between the character and the audience and a dialectic between the individual and larger social forces.

As the founder of "epic theater," Brecht sets himself up in principal opposition to the dramatic theories of Aristotle, the most famous theoretician of ancient tragedy, for whom the natural identification of the audience with the tragic figure on stage was central to tragedy. In his hugely influential aesthetic treatise, the *Poetics,* the philosopher suggests how tragedians should craft their plots to maximize the sensations of "fear and pity" and subsequent "catharsis"—an effect that could best be achieved if the tragic fate of the main character resonated with the audience at some deep emotional level. To achieve this rare form of aesthetic pleasure, the playwright should choose an individual higher than us (in Aristotle's time, this meant someone of noble birth or royal lineage) but also like us; and he should present a figure who was not "perfect" but had some "flaw," a corollary to the first principle.[6] Finally, Aristotle argued that the plot of the tragedy must arise out of the actions of the characters on stage and that this plot should be arranged in such a way that the audience experiences tragic inevitability. Nothing in the plot could be extraneous; every action had to lead directly to another action, all culminating in the final tragic moment.[7] The "goal" here was not to gain greater understanding of the historical and social forces that inhibit progressive change (Brecht) but to gain insight into the fundamental tragic nature of existence. This process of tragic purification and purgation (*catharsis*) would, in a perfect tragedy, ennoble the audience and leave it with a deeper and fuller awareness of the world.

Brecht would have been the more logical inspiration for the director of *The Lives*. By establishing a creative dialectic between the state apparatus and the individual, a Brechtian approach might get us to think about the nature of political power and how the tragic fates of the characters result from an incomplete awareness of their own historical necessity. The fact that Donnersmarck devotes the majority of screen time to behind-the-scenes views of Stasi power structures and surveillance methods further suggests that Brecht might have served as the perfect dramatic model for *The Lives*. Aristotle's emphasis on the lone tragic individual, on the other hand, might not allow the audience to appreciate the role of "the political" in the actions of the characters, and we might lose sight of the larger lesson to be learned from the story of political power and its corruption, specifically, the repressiveness of the Stasi state. But I will argue that Donnersmarck opts for the Aristotelian approach by making the actress Christa-Maria Sieland the film's tragic centerpiece.[8] The director's artistic decision in no way diminishes the role of the "political"; on the contrary, it gives the story an even greater emotional resonance, allowing the audience to reflect on the pervasive cruelty inflicted on individuals in oppressive regimes.[9]

Donnersmarck opens and concludes his film with a framing device. The audience immediately experiences the Stasi's brutal interrogation and training methods in the initial scenes. With a few deft strokes, the director creates a mood of apprehension, terror, and tension. But the actual dramatic narrative first gets under way when Grubitz suggests that he and Wiesler attend a theater production in the evening. Wiesler is skeptical, but Grubitz reveals his self-serving reason for going: "I heard that Minister Bruno Hempf plans to go to the theater tonight. As director of the Department of Culture, I should be there." The film's title, *The Lives of Others*, then appears on the screen. This is followed by the scene in the theater, the actual opening to the narrative. Similarly, the logical conclusion to that narrative is the death of Christa-Maria. However, Donnersmarck chooses not to close his film there, instead following the personal trajectories of those men touched by the actress Christa-Maria—her lover Dreyman, their Stasi protector, Wiesler, and even Bruno Hempf, the man she rejected. Between the bookends of these two events, Donnersmarck presents the dramatic arc of Christa-Maria's story.

In the theater, State Minister Hempf, who desires the actress Christa-Maria, orders his subordinate, Grubitz, to launch a surveillance operation on the playwright Georg Dreyman. Grubitz has just finished telling his own subordinate Wiesler that he believes that Dreyman is "cleaner than clean" and doesn't need to be monitored. But Grubitz is naïve about the nature of power: Hempf will use the levers of the state to dispatch a rival and to gratify his desire. Wiesler, at the bottom rungs, clings with a childlike intensity to the ideals of socialism; the midlevel Grubitz wishes to enjoy the prerogatives of power with minimal exertion; but Hempf believes that he is entitled to the spoils of the system: in this case, what he characterizes as the "most beautiful pearl of the German Democratic Republic," Christa-Maria Sieland. Thus, everything that the GDR has at its disposal is brought into motion by the lust of one man. By revealing the intensely personal nature of this "state action," Donnersmarck not only exposes the venality and corruption of the Stasi regime, he recognizes a very elemental truth about human nature and its relation to absolute political power as such, namely, how political power becomes instrumentalized in order to satisfy basic human desires.[10] Furthermore, by having the lust of one man serve as the dramatic impetus, Donnersmarck reinforces the Aristotelian nature of his narrative: the tragedy emerges directly out of individual motivations and passions.[11]

While the men discuss their plans, we catch a glimpse of the action on the center stage of the theater. Written by Georg Dreyman, Christa-Maria's lover, the play we see has a Brechtian feel. Brecht, who had chosen to live in East Germany during his final years and had established an influential "house theater" in East Berlin (the Berliner Ensemble), was East Germany's most famous author in its early years. But while Donnersmarck presents Dreyman's Brechtian play on center stage, he launches his own Aristotelian narrative in the film. Interestingly, the outlines of the story that he *does* present on stage foreshadow Christa-Maria's eventual tragedy. In the role of the character Marta, she says: "No, sister, believe me. He has fallen. To his death. The great, powerful wheel has crushed him." If one were to substitute "Christa-Maria" for the fallen "Artur," one could recognize her own upcoming fate.

On another level, the Brechtian play in the film suggests a further historical irony. Though the play could suggest itself as the dramaturgical model for the story to come, it would seem to be counterintuitive since that play, according to Brecht's own Marxist principles, would then need to highlight the injustices of a system, but those injustices should already, theoretically, have been overcome (*aufgehoben*). In the "perfect" society of the GDR, the Brechtian play could only focus its attentions outward (for example, toward the unfulfilled promise of historical socialism within Western capitalism) or, selectively, inward (by dramatizing the minor shortcomings of the socialist system on its way to greater perfection). (The glimpses of the play we receive seem to indicate the latter model.) The idea that the "real existing" social-ism in East Germany might itself be the "crushing wheel" would contradict the Brechtian worldview. Just like Wiesler on his own terms, Dreyman has chosen to believe in the "goodness" and the promise of the system, and that is why he can safely write in the Brechtian vein. (Wiesler, too, is safe in the state as long as he fulfills its functions.) But through the personal tragedy of Christa-Maria, Dreyman will come to realize that the Brechtian model cannot do justice to the elemental tragedy and suffering in human existence.

At the post-production party, Minister Hempf closes in on Christa-Maria. In front of Dreyman, Hempf attempts to initiate a dance but is coyly rebuffed. Dreyman is now left with Hempf. In their conversation it becomes clear that Hempf holds the fates and careers of GDR artists in his hands. Dreyman pleads with him to reinstate his friend the director Jerska, who has been blacklisted from cultural life. When Dreyman asks the minister if Jerska can at least hope for reinstatement, Hempf replies cynically: "Of course he can hope! As long as he lives. And even longer. For hope is always the last to die." In this tense scene between a state representative and an intellectual, it is apparent that the "cultural producers"[12] in the GDR are at the mercy of single powerful individuals who can crush the careers of intel-lectuals, writers, directors, or actors at whim. Considering how the GDR controlled the entire work world, it would have been impossible for someone trained in the arts to find any other position in official culture once he or she had fallen from favor. This point is forcibly driven home by the scenes of the broken, bitter Jerska, who must live out the rest of his life in cramped corridors, devoid of hope: "What does a director have who can no longer direct? Not much more than a projectionist without film, a miller without flour. He has nothing."[13] Dreyman attempts to console his friend with false promises: "[Hempf] gave me hope. Concrete, literal hope." That hope dies with Jerska's suicide.

As the Stasi begins its surveillance of Dreyman, Minister Hempf takes up contact with the actress and starts to apply pressure, making appointments to meet her on Thursdays. The director leaves it unclear whether these ini-tial contacts are sexual in nature, but it is more likely that Hempf is trying to "court" her. The scene in the limousine shows a woman so disgusted and resistant to his advances that Christa-Maria probably had to give in to his sexual predation here for the first time. The psychological effects of Hempf's sexual pressure, however, have already taken their toll. In an earlier scene, we see Christa-Maria swallow pills as she prepares for her lover's party. Though she might already have been addicted, Donnersmarck reveals this scene at the moment we know that Christa-Maria is being pressured. Christa-Maria has by now made a "choice": faced with the prospect of being ostracized from the acting profession and ending like Jerska or giving in to Hempf's advances to salvage her career, she has "chosen" to sleep with the minister.

Wiesler decides to make Dreyman aware of the situation: he connects the wiring of their doorbell so that it rings just as Christa-Maria leaves Hempf's limousine. Wiesler thus forces Dreyman to confront Christa-Maria's "betrayal." (Of course, the fundamentally decent Wiesler knows that Christa-Maria is an unwilling participant in this relationship, and by his action he is both testing Dreyman's commitment to her and pushing him to stand up for his lover: "Time for bitter truths," he says as he connects the wires.) After returning to the apartment and showering, Christa-Maria curls up in bed with her back to Dreyman. Though he wants to broach the topic of Hempf at that moment, Dreyman instead remains silent and hugs her. A warm smile slowly appears on Christa-Maria's face.

Clinging to a precarious balance within herself, one that might allow her to save her career, to do what she needs to do to rescue herself, and to keep some dignity and purity intact despite her wretched compromise, Christa-Maria feels that her bond with Dreyman can at least allow her to *believe* in a purer, better world, the possibility of a more whole self. Earlier Christa-Maria told Dreyman: "You are strong and forceful. And that's how I need you, to be whole and pure [*heil*]!" Christa-Maria admires Dreyman's aura of wholeness and moral integrity. As a more fragile human being, she lacks the inner reserves to resist the moral pressures that face her in the form of Hempf. At the same time, she has a deeper awareness of human nature and the corruptive forces that surround her. Whereas Dreyman manages to believe in the purity of the system while still reaping its institutional rewards, Christa-Maria cannot afford that luxury. Her dilemma is stark: compromise or go under. Her beauty and sexual allure are both the keys to her success as an actress and what make her seductive to the forces of corruption. But this is not a woman who decides to sleep with a more powerful person to advance her career. Her life and passion are acting; she has a talent that no one doubts but herself; and yet her career and livelihood will be crushed if she refuses Hempf. Her only other choice is to end up like Jerska.[14]

This brutal reality is emphasized in a later scene. Just before she plans to rendezvous with Hempf, Dreyman tries to stop her. He implores her to believe in herself: "You are a great artist. You don't need him! You don't need him. Stay here. Don't go." Dreyman seems to believe that true love will conquer all. The more worldly-wise Christa-Maria has to spell it out for him: "No? . . . I don't need him? And I don't need this whole system? And you? You don't need it either then? Or not really? Then why do you do it? Why do you sleep with them, too? Why do you? Because they can destroy you just as easily, despite your talent, in which you don't even doubt."[15] Christa-Maria implies that what she is about to do in a literal sense is what they have all been doing metaphorically. But as a beautiful, alluring woman, she is expected to pay the higher price: expose her body to a flesh-and-blood representative of the system. While Dreyman at most makes intellectual compromises, Christa-Maria must become the living spoils of the apparatchiks. What Jerska said earlier about his professional life applies even more to Christa-Maria. Dreyman can continue writing as a dissident within the system even if he can no longer stage plays—as he in fact does after Jerska's death; her career *requires* performance: once she is removed from the stage, her career is over. It is easy for Dreyman to expect Christa-Maria to make a sacrifice, but hers must be complete, whereas his is only partial. At the same time, she confronts Dreyman with the stark reality of their predicament. What difference does it make to "sleep" with the apparatchiks if you have already had to sleep with them all along? Her honesty reveals a higher moral sensitivity to their existence in the GDR.

By deciding to meet with Hempf, Christa-Maria sides with the part of herself that accepts political realities as they are. She jeopardizes her relationship with Dreyman by seeing Hempf, but she will do what she needs to do to preserve herself; she will separate the feelings she has for Dreyman from the more immediate concern for survival. But Donnersmarck then introduces a perfectly situated plot point to test her character. Wiesler, who has just overheard their exchange, enters a bar for a nightcap. Shortly after, Christa-Maria comes in and Wiesler summons the courage to talk with her. Aware of her intention to meet with Hempf but having to keep that information concealed, Wiesler continues with the line of thought that Dreyman had previously introduced. He presents himself as a member of her devoted audience and tells her that she is a great artist who must trust in herself:

"You are a great artist. Don't you know that?" "And you are a good man," Christa-Maria responds. With that, she returns to the apartment and Dreyman's arms. Wiesler appeals to the better side of Christa-Maria's nature—not the side that makes compromise after compromise to save her career, but the one that makes her the great artist others know she is. When she tries to lie to Wiesler, one of the kinds of routine lies that were second nature in the GDR, he responds: "You see, now you weren't at all like yourself." Instead, her higher, more honest self is revealed during live performances on stage, where she is allowed to be who she "is": "I saw you on stage. There you were more like you are than you . . . now are." This is the Christa-Maria her devoted fans can see; it makes her into a great actress;[16] and with the strength of that knowledge she can return to Dreyman.

Christa-Maria's reclaiming of her "true" self is the turning point, or *peripitia,* in the tightly woven plot; for with that decision she has sealed her own fate. In choosing to stand by Dreyman, she must turn her back on Hempf. In a later scene, we see a lonely, dejected Hempf sitting on the edge of a hotel bed after another failed rendezvous with Christa-Maria;[17] this scene transitions in right after Christa-Maria, who has figured out that Dreyman has become an active dissident, tells him: "I am now completely with you, no matter what." Of course, she should realize that a powerful man like Hempf will not take her rejection lightly. Though she might be tempted to repress this awareness, she can be under no illusions.[18] Hempf will come down hard on her for her betrayal; indeed, the tentacles of control now begin to squeeze her ever tighter. ("Whether you break her neck or not is up to you," Hempf later tells Grubitz. "In any case, I don't want to see her playing on a German stage again.")[19] Donnersmarck could simply have shown us the vindictive side of Hempf and let us *assume* that the communist hack would act in such a petty way, but he blends in the short, poignant scene of the dejected Hempf alone in the hotel room. Even this corrupt, despicable human being seeks physical connection—with a beautiful, alluring woman whom he feels he cannot attain by any other means.[20] His corruption lies in his using force and coercion simply because he can. Here, too, Donnersmarck goes against any moralizing impulse and the instinct to see and judge power in terms of black and white; he shows us a world where power serves to conceal as well as compensate for deep-rooted insecurities.[21]

Christa-Maria's decision to return to Dreyman also represents the turning point for her lover. Whereas Christa-Maria tells him that "she will never again leave," Dreyman tells her "that he will now have the strength. I will do something."[22] Indeed, Dreyman will now be motivated to write the incriminating article about hidden suicide statistics in the GDR for the West German newsmagazine *Der Spiegel,* which in turn will enable the Stasi to close in on Dreyman. But what is important is that Dreyman's motivation is brought about by Christa-Maria's renewed commitment. Her love for him and the risks she takes upon herself inspire Dreyman finally to take a principled stand against the regime, something that his dissident friends have long encouraged him to do. Her example and willingness to take on great risk for her lover bring out the moral courage that Dreyman has until now failed to exhibit. The tragic irony is that the very decision that the two lovers make at the height of their passion, a decision that makes them more fully human, is the one that will lead to Christa-Maria's demise.

The events leading up to Christa-Maria's arrest and interrogation follow rapidly. Provided the pretext by Hempf to bring her in for questioning, Grubitz uses the opportunity to discover who is behind the *Spiegel* article. In the scene with Grubitz, Christa-Maria succumbs to fear and pressure, offering to work as a Stasi informant (IM) and even to sleep with Grubitz ("Maybe I can do something that might not be so disagreeable to both of us") if doing so can rescue herself and her career. Though she first thinks she has been taken in for the illegal purchase of drugs, Grubitz informs her of her actual offense: "You have turned a very powerful man into your enemy." Christa-Maria now realizes that she must pay the price for having chosen Dreyman over Hempf. She is even willing to expose her lover as the author of the *Spiegel* article, for in the following scene we see the Stasi appear at Dreyman's doorstep. Christa-Maria has informed on Dreyman, though she has not revealed (yet) the most important incriminating detail: the hiding place of the typewriter, which even for the Stasi is a necessary precondition for arrest.[23] What others say about Christa-Maria, and what she fears about herself, is that she does not have the courage to withstand Stasi pressure.[24] But should we expect that of her? Though under no illusions about the regime (unlike the idealistic Dreyman), Christa-Maria never intended to become a political dissident or to offer moral opposition. She has chosen a form of "inner emigration" in her art that can give her at least a semblance of freedom and sanity. It is a choice made by countless intellectuals and artists within totalitarian societies. It may lack the heroism and the prestige of active resisters, but we should not minimize the suffering and loneliness felt by those who merely seek to survive out of fear for themselves or their loved ones. Individuals with strong moral or ideological convictions may have the stamina to take on great personal risks;[25] but individuals who cling to a sense of their moral self while pressured to compromise their humanity day after day can embody a more profound sense of tragedy.[26]

Christa-Maria is then brought to interrogation with her secret supporter Wiesler. Donnersmarck suggests several possible explanations for their peculiar hedging behavior in this scene. Wiesler gradually turns his swivel chair to face her, fearing that she will recognize him from the bar. He does not want to startle her, since he knows that Grubitz is observing their "performance." Though Christa-Maria clearly recognizes him, she tries to conceal her surprise. But what is going through her mind? Does she think that Wiesler's earlier actions in the bar were just the clever ploy of an ill-intentioned Stasi agent? Was she foolish to trust him then and must now pay the price? Or does she think that Wiesler may actually be on her side (he was, after all, the "good man" who inspired her to return to her lover Dreyman) and may be willing to help her? Why else would he need to conceal his identity now? (Wiesler surely did not reveal enough to her in the bar to incriminate himself.) Donnersmarck further complicates matters by having Wiesler (or so it seems) give Christa-Maria encouraging gestures to trust him and divulge the hiding place of the typewriter.[27] We find out later he intends to use that information to remove the device, but how could *she* know that? Is there enough evidence for her to assume that he will help her? How? These kinds of questions are important as they relate to the nature of her moral complicity, but the director ultimately leaves her motivations unclear. Do Wiesler's interrogation tactics, which play on her fear and vanity, get her to reveal the hiding place? Is it the minuscule hope—her *only* hope—that perhaps this man will rescue her? Or is it resignation and the futility and desperation of the situation? In any case, there can be no doubt (based purely on her actions and not her motivation) that on some level Christa-Maria *betrays* her lover to the Stasi. Whatever the *reason* for her confession—whether she confesses out of a small hope for salvation or out of a mixture of fear and vanity—Christa-Maria falls back on the most basic instinct of survival.[28]

There seems little hope that Christa-Maria will be able to redeem herself. She returns to her apartment and once again takes a shower, her usual response to a feeling of self-defilement. Dreyman comes in and asks her where she's been; she lies to him, prepared to keep up the pretence. Wiesler told her in interrogation that an accomplished actress like her should manage to dissemble in front of her lover, and indeed we would expect Christa-Maria to be able to do so. But then the Stasi appears at their door, demanding a new search. With information provided by her, Grubitz quickly locates the spot in the apartment where the typewriter is supposedly hidden just as Christa-Maria exits the bathroom in her bathrobe.[29] She looks in humiliation over at Dreyman, who realizes her betrayal. Unable to bear the intensity of his glance and the guilt of her decision,[30] she rushes out of the apartment into the street. Though the director leaves it open whether Christa-Maria is so shaken that she is not entirely conscious of what she's doing or whether she intentionally puts herself in the way of the oncoming truck, she becomes one of the many victims of suicide that the "perfect society" of the GDR tries to conceal from the world.[31]

How does Christa-Maria become a tragic figure? What allows her to redeem her humanity and leave the audience with a profound sense of tragedy for her plight? How can we connect with someone who has betrayed the trust of her lover? Christa-Maria is not a "perfect" character, but she must fight to retain her humanity in the face of insurmountable pressures. The fact that she does not always make the best decisions but still remains aware of the morally ambivalent nature of those decisions allows us not to lose faith in her better, more noble nature.[32] Donnersmarck gives us several reasons not to question her essential nobility. First of all, Christa-Maria is incapable of doing exactly what everyone expects the actress to do so easily (and what everyone else in the GDR seems to have mastered), that is, to act "naturally" in a thoroughly duplicitous environment.[33] In moments when she should conceal her intentions and protect herself, she cannot; only when acting on stage can she reveal her true self ("There you were more like you are than you now are"). The reason her audience loves her, Wiesler implies, is because it recognizes her essential sincerity and genuineness as an actress; but that same lack of guile also prevents her from being a successful "actor" on the "stage" of the GDR. Christa-Maria should be able to lie in interrogation; but her interrogators have no problems detecting her lies. She should also be able to feign shock or disbelief when the Stasi uncovers the typewriter in front of Dreyman; but she is incapable of dissembling in a society that demands continual dissimulation.[34]

When Dreyman looks to her in disbelief, Christa-Maria is not able to keep up the pretence. Though she confesses out of weakness and fear, she recognizes now she had betrayed not only her lover but her better self. If the latter is gone, what does she have left? The confession might have seemed the only possible decision for her in that time of psychological duress, but it now reveals its terrible price: she has forfeited that part of her humanity that made her both a great artist and a person worthy of love and respect. On the other hand, Dreyman's reaction, though understandable, is harsh, based on a too simple view of the circumstances. He is quick to judge Christa-Maria without truly understanding her predicament. He has to believe in her absolute moral purity—he disregards his dissident friends' concerns for her reliability—for his worldview can accommodate only absolutes. For Dreyman, there must always be good and bad people; and while his moral certitude is what attracts Christa-Maria to him, it also prevents him from understanding the ambivalent universe she inhabits and in which she fights to survive. While Christa-Maria measures herself against the high standards and expectations that Dreyman sets (and then condemns herself based on them), Dreyman's own moral rectitude prevents him from appreciating the moral complexities she faces.

Suicide becomes the only way out. Though it is impossible for Christa-Maria "to make good again what I have done," as she says in her dying words, her decision to take her life should not be seen as a momentary gesture of desperation or self-loathing but as her final effort to reclaim autonomy. The system has systematically stripped her of dignity and freedom, but what it can't take away from her is the freedom to condemn herself according to her own standards and values. Perhaps the most horrible indictment against totalitarian regimes is that in them suicide can become the last honorable means to express humanity and dignity. Once societies turn behavior patterns such as betrayal, deceit, and duplicity into second nature, into one's "true" nature; once they crush individual hopes and aspirations, then some will choose to opt out of that dehumanizing form of existence. Donnersmarck highlights one such seemingly random suicide and thwarts our expectations of what we tend to think about suicide, namely, that it exhibits moral failure or weakness of character. Instead, he shows us that for people like Christa-Maria, and in repressive societies like the GDR, suicide can become the sole means to reclaim moral autonomy. With Wiesler at her side, the dying Christa-Maria says: "I was too weak." But her life was one not of weakness but of an inner struggle against the worst human instincts that the system both encourages and exploits. Her tragedy resonates with the audience not because it sees her as a pure moral beacon, but rather because she is an all-too-fallible woman who seeks to survive on her own terms but ultimately is crushed by the "great, powerful wheel."[35]

Donnersmarck could have chosen to end his tragic tale with this final scene. His tightly woven Aristotelian narrative followed the tragic heroine from the heights of her fame as an artist in the GDR to her anonymous suicide on the dreary streets of East Berlin. In Aristotelian fashion, the film's ending triggers a "catharsis": the audience feels for the plight of this woman, whose weaknesses certainly contributed to her downfall but whose tragic fate was nonetheless cruel and undeserved.[36] The director has also created, as Aristotle had demanded, a character that, though "higher" than ourselves,[37] is still "like us"—not excessively moral, pure, or righteous, but with shades of both strength and weakness. It would have made sense to end the film here.[38] The audience would have recognized that life is essentially tragic, and the aesthetic pleasure of the film would have resided in experiencing someone of great promise and merit encounter an undeserved fate. But Donnersmarck decides to append a non-Aristotelian conclusion to the film; one could even say that he devises a Brechtian finale. Is the "natural" ending to the film (the death of Christa-Maria) simply too tragic for our modern sensibilities? Would the Aristotelian conclusion perhaps make this film less commercial, less acceptable to audiences that expect Hollywood consolation and reconciliation? Why does the director deprive us of the full cathartic release of his tightly woven plot?

Let me explore first what I have termed Donnersmarck's "Brechtian" solution. By reconnecting his story to the larger historical forces (the rise of Gorbachev; the fall of the Wall; German reunification), the director contextualizes the tragedy of Christa-Maria and redeems it within the larger scope of recent historical events. One could now say: even though she had to die, the greater trajectory of history allows us to learn from her example and to move toward a more informed and humane society. Many of the final scenes of the film take place in former Stasi headquarters, which is now dedicated to education about that period, finding out about Stasi informants and procedures, and contributing to what Germans term *Vergangenheitsbewältigung*—a coming to terms with the past by openly confronting it. This concept is itself "Brechtian": learning from the dialectic of history in order to move toward a more progressive future.

But what if we were to interpret the ending in another way? What if the director has instead taken Aristotle one step further? What if he decided to show us the *effect* of Aristotelian catharsis on the "audience" of his characters? The release and purgation of emotion (catharsis) following tragic performances should, Aristotle suggested, somehow ennoble and refine our awareness of life and the world around us. The effect of tragedy *purifies*—

puts our souls into a forge of emotion to distill out their impurities and to heighten our sensibilities. As the ancient dramatists practiced it, tragedy is, in essence, moral, even if it uses the amoral means of art to achieve its ends. What is original in Donnersmarck's script is that it does not end with the tragic death of the heroine but follows the lives of the three men in Christa-Maria's world *after* the tragic events and shows us how she continues to haunt them. In the case of Hempf, he still thinks about her and reveals perhaps deeper emotions than one would expect, but he can't understand her tragedy as something *he* had caused. He selfishly thinks about how Christa-Maria wounded *him* and the resentment he still feels toward her betrayal. Her tragedy, then, has not changed him one bit, and his life continues to be as miserable as it was before.

Wiesler's life changes fundamentally with Christa-Maria's death. By protecting her from harm, he had put his own career at risk; he must pay the price by losing his position as high-ranking Stasi interrogator. Wiesler's secret devotion to Christa-Maria pushes him to break with his former self but opens him to a warmth and humanity that he had lost. Whereas Christa-Maria struggles to hold onto a humanity that she's always in the danger of losing, Wiesler hopes to recapture a humanity compromised by years of working for a dehumanizing, soulless regime. Christa-Maria's death is, therefore, a truly humbling experience for him, bringing his world of power and status crashing down. We cannot but have the sense that Wiesler's life has been enriched despite this. Wiesler is the only one of the three men who actually *gives up* something because of his commitment to Christa-Maria; but he is also the only one who, despite these sacrifices, reflects an inner peace and a sense of reconciliation with his life and the consequences of his decisions. Donnersmarck's brilliance in showing the humbled Wiesler walking the streets of Berlin as a postman, pulling along his pathetic little bag,[39] reinforces the message that this simple man, who went through the vicissitudes of strong emotions and personal loss and who sacrificed everything to become a "good man," is now richer in soul and awareness than those who do not fully learn the lesson of Christa-Maria's life and death. In the end, he has every right to say that Dreyman's book is "for him," because he's now in the position to *receive* it.

As for Dreyman, the full impact of Christa-Maria's death doesn't hit him at first. In the theater, Dreyman watches his same Brechtian play from the beginning (in the very same scene) being performed in a reunified Berlin, this time in a modern, trendy staging.[40] Dreyman seems to have perfectly adapted to the new requirements of the capitalist theater world and has made the necessary adjustments to succeed in a different system. But he leaves the theater when he is painfully reminded of Christa-Maria. While he still remembers her, her death has not substantially changed him and he has continued in the same paths of his former life. Above all, his art remains unchanged (except for the staging and costuming to reflect different tastes), devoid of passion and immediacy. (It is not surprising that his dramatic art could make the seamless transition from East to West because it remains unthreatening and sterile in both systems.) And his emotional life is built on a fundamental misreading of Christa-Maria's death: he has conveniently made a martyr out of her, perhaps blaming himself for being too hard on her, but probably convinced that she had removed the typewriter for him.[41] Once again, Dreyman can accommodate only simple, uncomplicated truths about people, and he has come to terms with Christa-Maria's death in neat, manageable categories.

Hempf's revelation in the theater lobby changes all that. Sifting through the Stasi records, Dreyman discovers that it wasn't Christa-Maria at all who had removed the typewriter; it was an unknown Stasi agent intervening on their behalf. This discovery has two profound effects on him. For one, he understands that an anonymous man took on great personal risk to help them. His sense of compassion was stronger than his loyalty to the system or concern for his own life and career. When Dreyman later follows Wiesler and witnesses the humbleness of his life and station, he realizes even more how much this man had to sacrifice. But at another level, Dreyman also realizes the truth about his lover Christa-Maria, that his neat picture of her was based on false suppositions and that she was a more complex and conflicted person than he cared to admit. This revelation gives him a fuller picture of her as a human being, and he can now grasp the pressures that she was under. Instead of believing that it was all about *him,* he can see that it really was about *her,* above all, her attempts to navigate an impossible situation. The impact of these discoveries finally allows him to confront the full scope of her tragedy and to achieve catharsis.

Dreyman can now achieve a breakthrough as an artist. He has found a subject matter that actually relates to his life experience, one that emerges from a deeper awareness of individual sacrifice and suffering. By understanding the full extent of Christa-Maria's tragic situation and sacrifice, Dreyman can write a novel that is more than just an exercise in creative writing. Since his fame and reputation had previously depended on tacit support and approval from the East German culture office, Dreyman never really had to risk anything as an artist. His successes fell to him too easily, and they didn't require him to probe his conscience. The death of his friend Jerska and his subsequent decision to write a subversive political piece on suicide in the GDR may have been his first steps in the direction of greater creative awareness and moral reckoning. But even then, his article remained primarily an intellectual exercise—a rationalist's attempt to come to terms with the phenomenon of suicide and the death of a close friend. The discovery of the full story behind Christa-Maria's death and Wiesler's involvement, however, crashes through the convenient inner barrier that he built up around that tragic event. He is now able to take in its full suffering and then to release it in the cauldron of art. The catharsis of Christa-Maria's tragedy has finally changed him at the core of his being and he can move away from his cool, bloodless dramas and produce art truly enriched by personal experience and suffering.[42]

How, then, does Donnersmarck's Aristotelian approach relate to the political dimension of the film? How does it prove superior to what could have been a more Brechtian treatment of power structures? The Brechtian model assumes the corruption of current political structures and a conspiracy of elites against the realization of a humanistic ethic. While Brecht had meant his plays to critique residual capitalist institutions that impeded progress along a Marxist continuum of historical-materialist evolution, his theories could be appropriated by any storyteller intent on pointing out the oppressive nature of institutions—even, ironically, if those institutions happened to be (allegedly) fully realized socialist states. Brecht's most mature dramatic creations, such as Mother Courage and Galileo, were far from being one-dimensional victims of the dominant political realities of their time; they were also complex individuals whose faults, vanities, and weaknesses contributed to their tragic downfalls. However, Brecht's theories and methods of dramaturgy kept the audience's focus on power structures and how they blinded his characters to their full human potential. His characters were immersed in an unfolding historical struggle that was larger than they were and that they could not fully comprehend, but Brecht intended to render this struggle explicit to his audience members through dramatic means so that they could effect progressive change. Brecht's vision, despite his efforts to do justice to the reality of moral complexity and ambiguity, required "victims" and "perpetrators"; it required, in short, a belief in moral absolutes.[43]

If one leaves aside the slightly Brechtian optimism of the final scenes, where the director holds out the hope of a more progressive future through a direct confrontation with the past, the darker heart of Donnersmarck's story is the Aristotelian tragedy of his central heroine, Christa-Maria. Here, the moral lessons to be learned are more ambiguous, more uncertain. Christa-Maria is not a pure "tragic heroine"; nor does her betrayal of her lover seem to correspond to our simple notion of how a "moral" character should behave. Moreover, Donnersmarck shows us other characters who exhibit similar behavior, such as the poor neighbor Frau Meineke, who must suffer in silence while Dreyman's apartment is being bugged due to fear for her daughter's future.[44] Shouldn't a truly moral person try to help her neighbor, we might ask ourselves, even if that means jeopardizing her daughter's university career? Certainly, the director presents several characters who exhibit more traditional "heroic" models of moral courage, such as Dreyman's friend Paul Hauser, a man imprisoned by the system, the film implies, for political resistance. Hauser could have become the moral beacon in a film that otherwise shows its characters in various stages of moral compromise with the regime. But instead, Hauser's intransigence has rendered him slightly inhuman and cold, as though moral righteousness automatically entitles one to feel superior, even toward one's fellow citizens. Does the very fact of Hauser's imprisonment give him that right? And Jerska—are resignation and bitterness the only possible responses to artistic blacklisting? While Donnersmarck in no way intends to whitewash the culpability of the system in its destruction of these human lives, he also does not want to give us one-dimensional, holy victims, making it easy for us to lay the blame.

This returns us to Christa-Maria's tragic situation. What is it in her independent story that gives us a deeper understanding of this regime's moral corruption? What makes Donnersmarck's film such a masterpiece in capturing the essence of late-twentieth-century political oppression?[45] Through the character of Christa-Maria, Donnersmarck can reveal to us the insidiousness of everyday, banal forms of moral corruption. It is not a question of laying the complete burden of blame on a generic system of political governance or oppression, such as on the East German state, or on neatly defined "perpetrators," such as the Stasi and its informants; that would be far too easy and predictable. It is to show how the so-called system as a whole infiltrates the moral fiber of its citizens at a root level and forces them through gradual increments to surrender their personal integrity and autonomy. This is not a classic system "from above," in some pure

Brechtian sense; those systems are long gone and have been superseded by more clever and pervasive mechanisms of control and suasion. It is now a complete "society" of peers and neighbors—of friends, family, and lovers. In short, there are no morally pure figures in this gray universe, for each has been forced to make corrosive moral compromises along the way. But in subtly fleshing out the portrait of one such anonymous figure in this dark period—that of the actress Christa-Maria, or "CMS"—Donnersmarck has allowed us to see how difficult it is for any one person to hold onto a sense of moral self when the pressures to surrender integrity have become all but insurmountable. The "heroes" in Donnersmarck's world, therefore, are not the ones who inhabit an absolute, coherent moral space—such as the Paul Hausers or the Georg Dreymans, for example. The "heroes" are the ones who, while remaining anonymous, fight an uphill battle just to cling to a promise of a better world, the ones who at least have the potential to be redeemed by art. Donnersmarck's film is not about the "political," the high and the mighty, or the morally virtuous; in the end, it is a film about those unsung "lives of others."

Notes

1. I use this term in contrast to Eric Hobsbawm's reference to Europe's "short twentieth century," as I see political totalitarianism as the defining feature of the entire twentieth century (and beyond).

2. There has been much discussion surrounding the historical accuracy of the film and its supposedly fanciful portrayal of the Stasi reality. Here it might be helpful to remember Aristotle's words in the *Poetics* concerning the difference between history and dramatic art: "The poet and historian differ not by writing in verse or in prose. . . . The true difference is that one relates what has happened, the other what may happen. Poetry, therefore, is a more philosophical and a higher thing than history: for poetry tends to express the universal, history the particular" (Aristotle, *Poetics,* trans. Francis Ferguson [New York: Hill and Wang, 1961], 68). While there might not be a single documented case of a Stasi agent who acted like Wiesler, there is also nothing to suggest that there could not have been a Stasi agent who *might* have acted like him.

3. The film puts a human face on the anonymous tragedies of the regime's victims. In the protocols to her case Dreyman later finds Christa-Maria's initials, CMS. But behind these clinical, bureaucratic, and dehumanizing initials resides a human tragedy. This film won't allow Christa-Maria Sieland to remain CMS.

4. Aside from the "Brechtian" play written by Dreyman, we see Wiesler read Brecht's poem "Erinnerung an die Marie A." Unlike Brecht's theater, which had explicitly didactic, political overtones, many of Brecht's poems can be enjoyed on purely lyrical terms. (After Christa-Maria's death, the camera pans over open sky and the tops of trees, an image that

seems to allude to the opening lines of Brecht's poem: "It was a day in that blue month September / Silent beneath the plum trees' slender shade / I held her there / My love, so pale and silent / As if she were a dream that must not fade.") Does this indicate Donnersmarck's greater appreciation for the lyricist than for the Marxist dramatist?

5. The world of theater and drama is central to the film. It is about dramatic performance on many different levels and it is structured like a play. While we the film audience watch the characters perform, they are either watching a dramatic performance (while they are watching each other!) or Wiesler is "watching" (and directing!) the "performance" in the apartment or Grubitz is watching the performance of Christa-Maria and Wiesler (who are, of course, "performing" for each other), etc. The characters are always "on stage"—for each other and for us, the "guilty" onlookers. The similarity of the plot of *The Lives* to that of the German classic *Emilia Galotti*, G. E. Lessing's eighteenth-century "bourgeois tragedy," seems more than coincidental. There a prince asks for the help of his minister to seduce the bourgeois maiden Emilia. The corrupt courtier Marinelli uses the mechanisms of state power to kidnap and hold the girl against her will so that the prince can seduce her. Lessing himself wrote a famous disquisition on Aristotle's aesthetics, and the tightly woven plot of *Emilia Galotti* owes much to Aristotelian principles.

6. "There remains, then, the character between these two extremes—that of a man who is not eminently good and just, yet whose misfortune is brought about not by vice or depravity, but some error or frailty" (Aristotle, *Poetics*, 76).

7. Friedrich Nietzsche understood the difficulty of creating this dramatic necessity: "We know the sort of technical problems that absorb all of a dramatist's energies, often making him sweat blood: how to give *necessity* to the knot and also to the resolution, so that there is only one possible outcome" (Nietzsche, *The Case of Wagner*, section 9, in Friedrich Nietzsche, *The Anti-Christ, Ecce Homo, Twilight of the Idols and Other Writings*, ed. Aaron Ridley and Judith Norman [Cambridge: Cambridge University Press, 2005], 249). Nietzsche's observation is based on an understanding of the underlying *ethical* dimension of tragic art. Dramatic necessity is not merely an arbitrary formulistic principle but rather reflects a subtle awareness of how profound tragic situations could resound in viewers on a subliminal level, thereby effecting a change in their inner being.

8. Surprisingly, most of the studies on the film seem to emphasize the central *male* characters of the film. This reflects a bias against, and a diminishment of, the fascinating female lead, Christa-Maria, and it leads to essential misunderstandings about the film. For example, Thomas Lindenberger suggests that the film is "misogynistic" (!) and then goes on to present dismissive opinions of Christa-Maria ("Stasiploitation—Why Not? The Scriptwriter's Historical Creativity in *The Lives of Others*," *German Studies Review* 31, no. 3 [2011]: 562). Interpretations often write the actress off based on her supposedly negative traits (betrayal, drug addiction, neuroses, vanity, etc.) and then turn to the two male leads, Wiesler and Dreyman, who refract more comforting and traditional aspects of "goodness." But I think that we miss the problematic heart of this film if we do not recognize that Donnersmarck shows us a dominant "man's world" represented by the three main male characters (Dreyman, Wiesler, Hempf) who, in their obsession with the beautiful female object of desire (Christa-Maria), corrupt and destroy an essentially innocent woman.

9. Mary Beth Stein claims that the film's "focus on human motivation makes the plot more universal and universally understandable to foreign audiences, but it leaves the ideo-

logical rigidity and deep-seated paranoia of the SED state largely unexplored. . . . The tragic love story has the effect of blunting the film's political impact" ("Stasi with a Human Face? Ambiguity in *Das Leben der Anderen*," *German Studies Review* 31, no. 3 [2011]: 570). But Stein here reveals a Brechtian sensibility—i.e., that somehow the story would be more effective if it focused on the "political" superstructure. Yet it is Donnersmarck's wise decision to tell an Aristotelian tragedy that allows the story both to transcend its specific Stasi milieu and at the same time to transmit to its audience the corrosive nature of this particular form of twentieth-century totalitarianism.

10. Manfred Wilke claims that dissatisfaction with the regime increased in the final years because people began to realize that members of the all-too-human "clique at the top," the handful of privileged families in the regime, were treating their country like their own "private commissary" (*Selbstbedienungsladen*): "They were only concerned with their privileges, a sybaritic lifestyle and personal power" ("Fiktion oder erlebte Geschichte? Zur Frage der Glaubwürdigkeit des Films *Das Leben der Anderen*," *German Studies Review* 31, no. 3 [2011]: 598). On the other hand, Stein critiques the director for personalizing the motivations of the Stasi power elites, arguing that this was not "realistic" and also detracted from the "political" ("Stasi with a Human Face?" 570–71). I think Donnersmarck's decision to "personalize" the motivations does not arise from his supposed desire to appeal to foreign audiences or to Hollywood but springs from a deep, pessimistic insight into the nature of human passions and political power.

11. The elemental nature of Hempf's drive, his lust for the beautiful Christa-Maria, is similar to the elemental force of Achilles' anger: it triggers the series of events that will lead to Christa-Maria's demise.

12. The term *Kulturproduzenten* is revelatory of the way in which the GDR saw "its" artists only in terms of their production value to the state.

13. Stein accurately, I think, refers to the regime's targeted practice of *Zersetzung* (decomposition) in the way Jerska is shown to be treated in the film, and this practice leads to his thorough isolation and psychological withdrawal and "decomposition": Zersetzung "aimed at the systematic destruction of people by disseminating malicious rumors and creating fear and doubt" ("Stasi with a Human Face?" 574).

14. Jerska is Christa-Maria's negative pole, the horrible "other" that she seeks to banish because he's a living shadow of what she might become. Preparing for the party, she tells Dreyman not to associate with Jerska, that he should not bring that emotional wreck into his life ("Hol dir nicht diese Kaputtheit in dein Leben").

15. The theme of artistic self-doubt reoccurs throughout the film. Whereas Dreyman appears self-confident and never doubts his talent, Christa-Maria questions hers. But self-doubt is an integral part of the creative process and can lead to great artistic production. Great confidence in one's abilities and artistic talent, on the other hand, can yield mediocre, commercial work. It is Christa-Maria's insecurity in this regard that makes her the more human and ultimately more tragic figure.

16. She is a stage actress, not a movie actress, and one is required to reveal much more of oneself in live performance than on film, which in addition allows for numerous takes and final editing.

17. In his description of the scene in the script, Donnersmarck writes: "[Hempf] realizes that she will not come, that she will never come again. That it is over" (*Das Leben*

der Anderen: Filmbuch von Florian Henckel von Donnersmarck [Frankfurt: Suhrkamp, 2006], 113).

18. In the scenes after Christa-Maria sides with Dreyman, she appears to be on a high, seemingly oblivious to the consequences of her decision. She rejoices in her renewed commitment to Dreyman and her sense of liberation from Hempf. (*We* know that she is dancing on the precipice.)

19. Hempf's words reveal Donnersmarck's keen awareness of the differentiated power competencies of the regime: while Hempf supplies the incriminating evidence against Christa-Maria to the Stasi officer Grubitz, letting him decide how to deal with her, he, in his capacity as minister of culture, will blacklist her from cultural life.

20. An interesting parallel is the scene where Wiesler is shown engaging in sexual intercourse with a prostitute to find human connection. Here, too, it is the character of Christa-Maria that triggers this need.

21. Hempf's insecurity is revealed again in a later scene when he tries to project his own failings and frustration onto Dreyman. After Christa-Maria's death, he tells Dreyman: "We knew everything about you. We even knew that you couldn't really satisfy our little Christa." Hempf too cannot shake her lingering memory. (He leaves the theater at the same scene, which for both evokes the memory of the dead actress: "I had the same feeling," he tells Dreyman. "I had to leave too." Despite his audacity in comparing himself to Dreyman, Hempf at least admits to his feelings.)

22. These words, written into the protocol by Wiesler's coworker, are spoken during moments of "intense intimacy."

23. The fact that Christa-Maria refrains from telling him the hiding place of the typewriter may not minimize her guilt in revealing Dreyman as the writer of the *Spiegel* article, but she may hope that Dreyman will manage to escape the Stasi dragnet.

24. When Dreyman is about to tell her about the *Spiegel* piece, Christa-Maria asks him not to: "Perhaps I am really as unreliable as your friends say." Christa-Maria fears her own trustworthiness when put under Stasi pressure.

25. Dreyman's confidant, the journalist Paul Hauser, personifies this type: he is stern and uncompromising and has paid the price for his resistance, but perhaps fails to appreciate the moral complexities of everyday lives in the GDR.

26. This dilemma is portrayed well by the character of Dreyman's neighbor Frau Meineke. Though she would like to tell Dreyman about the surveillance, Wiesler's threat to end her daughter's medical career at the university if she says anything puts her in a horrible predicament. Christa-Maria's situation echoes Lessing's title character in *Emilia Galotti*. There Emilia provokes her death at the hands of her father not to prevent the prince from taking her by force but because she knows that she, as a passionate young woman, might not be able to resist his sexual advances. In both cases, the central tragic heroine is not the simple, resolute figure that others (e.g., Emilia's father in Lessing's drama, Dreyman in *The Lives*) think that she is or want her to be but a more complex, passionate character with conflicting emotions, forced to make difficult choices.

27. Wiesler echoes the words he spoke to her in the bar, that she should consider her audience. (This causes Grubitz to chuckle; he thinks it is a strange interrogation tactic and not a subtle reference.) Is this just another of Wiesler's hints for Christa-Maria to remember him? Is he trying to gain her confidence? Is he just playing to her vanity? Also, Wiesler gives

her an intense, beckoning nod after asking where the typewriter is hidden. Is this a sign that she should trust him to help her?

28. Christa-Maria at first says that she knows nothing about a typewriter and that she had previously lied, but then decides to confess during interrogation. We cannot exclude the possibility that Wiesler's offer that she will be able to return to the stage was the decisive factor in her decision to confess. But is this so terrible? The world of her art is the only thing that Christa-Maria has left to sustain her in this oppressive society.

29. Christa-Maria is wearing a white bathrobe, white being the symbol of purity. Donnersmarck also adds a fascinating little detail: on the upper-right-hand corner of the bathrobe's lapel there is a golden star. For a director like Donnersmarck, so conscious of every cinematic detail and so aware of historical resonances, the golden star must suggest the golden Star of David the Jews were forced to wear in the Third Reich. But what does the director mean by this? Does he give Christa-Maria the ultimate symbol of the victim? Does it refer to the continuity between totalitarian systems on German soil? Or does he want to compare her fate to that of the countless other victims during the Third Reich who suffered similar anonymous tragedies through no fault of their own? Timothy Garton Ash has alluded to the simplistic identification in people's minds of "Stasi" and "Nazi" in his review of the film ("The Stasi on Our Minds," *New York Review of Books,* May 9, 2007), and others have also criticized the historical verisimilitude of showing Grubitz in a "smart" Nazi-style uniform, also likely to suggest totalitarian continuity in Germany. Yet I don't have a problem with Donnersmarck referencing this; on the contrary, I think he is getting us to reflect on the persistence of certain human types despite outward changes in the regime.

30. In the notes to this scene, Donnersmarck writes: "Dreyman now looks at her, full of suspicion and harshness. Her gaze cannot withstand his."

31. Donnersmarck films this scene very suggestively. Christa-Maria runs out of the building, casting a quick sideways glance down the road. We can hear the sound of a truck in the background. She stops at the edge of the pavement and then steps out onto the street, looking forward. As she turns to face the street, she has a blank, stunned look just before the truck hits her. In the notes to this scene, the director makes it a more straightforward suicide.

32. In an Aristotelian sense, Christa-Maria's "tragic flaw" might be her lack of personal self-confidence, which makes her doubt her talent and renders her susceptible to the pressure of others.

33. In the brilliant scene with Wiesler and the young boy in the elevator, even a child's innocent question could lead to terrible repercussions.

34. According to Stein, the "film illustrates how communist dictatorships produced a similar schizophrenia whereby individuals negotiated the tension between state and self through the creation of distinctly public and private faces." I argue that Christa-Maria's greatest vulnerability is that she fails to achieve the "Stasi habitus of studied inscrutability or what Markus Wolf termed '*Die Kunst der Verstellung*'" ("Stasi with a Human Face?" 576).

35. Donnersmarck accentuates her humanity with a symbolic gesture. Dreyman holds the dying Christa-Maria in his arms in the street. Her position in her lover's arms recalls Michelangelo's famous Pietà; there the dying Christ lies in Mary's arms. This reference suggests the Christlike purity of his heroine, whose weaknesses and fallibility and attempt to remain human under difficult circumstances must elicit our compassion. Of course, the

director gives her the only telling name of the characters: she is both Christ(a) *and* Maria, victim *and* consoler. She is the woman into whom all three men (Dreyman, Wiesler, Hempf) project their longings and desires and from whom they await salvation. But none of them take her for the woman she is: complex and ambiguous, weak and strong, talented and ridden with doubts, strongly sensual and strangely aloof. While the men envision her as the figure of purity and perfection, she must fall victim to their unrealistic expectations.

36. "Pity is aroused by unmerited misfortune, fear by the misfortune of a man like ourselves" (Aristotle, *Poetics*, 76).

37. Donnersmarck accentuates Christa-Maria's glamour, particularly in contrast to the drab, depressing reality that surrounds her. In the scene at the seedy bar, she appears with large, dark sunglasses and wears an opulent fur hat. She is aware of her superiority, and she exudes an aura of exclusivity and mystery. As a coveted actress in the regime, she is granted the rare but highly fragile privilege of being exclusive in the otherwise ruthlessly egalitarian society of the GDR.

38. I will disclose here that I was at first disappointed with the film's ending, thinking that its somewhat lengthy historical coda detracted from the visceral power of the original story of Christa-Maria. But after repeated viewings I have come to understand and appreciate Donnersmarck's decision to conclude the film in this way.

39. Wiesler is the only one whose status remains unchanged in the "new" Germany. While those with former prestige manage to keep their standing in the reunified country (Dreymann's plays are still performed and Hempf seems well fed and well clothed), the lowly Wiesler does not experience any upward mobility: he has graduated from opening letters to delivering them!

40. Donnersmarck has an excellent eye for the German theater world: many plays performed in Germany's state-subsidized major theaters are presented in pretentious, artsy productions that appeal only to an elite educated audience. In fact, the current German theater scene shares this in common with the former East Germany and its cultural sponsorship. Rarefied and insular productions are often the result. Is this film Donnersmarck's attempt to write and "stage" a viable, competitive (cinematic) alternative to the state-sponsored theatrical fare?

41. When Grubitz removes the plank from the hiding place and finds it empty, he mutters: "The actress." Dreyman looks up in realization: both of them suspect that Christa-Maria had removed the typewriter.

42. "The literature that transcends the dehumanizing aspects of political repression is also the vehicle through which Dreyman and Wiesler are, in effect, reconciled to one another and their separate pasts" (Stein, "Stasi with a Human Face?" 567).

43. The fact that so many discussions of the film return to the simple moralistic dichotomy of "perpetrators" and "victims" indicates to me that they have fundamentally misunderstood Donnersmarck's film. He shows us a disturbing, morally ambiguous world, one too difficult for many of us to accept, where there are no neat and clear distinctions between victims and perpetrators but where everyone is compromised by various degrees of complicity. It is no coincidence that the dominant shade of color in the film is gray.

44. The film opens with another such character, one who is "forced" to betray his neighbor after extreme physical and psychological duress from the Stasi, even if his only crime might have been friendly association with his neighbor before he attempted to flee to

the West. Lindenberger claims that the director could have made a greater film about such "lesser" characters ("Stasiploitation," 564–55). The fact is: he did.

45. Lindenberger faults the film for being too generic in its portrayal of a totalitarian state, arguing that such a lack of historical specificity renders the film inauthentic (ibid., 565). But here I must agree with Wilke: the question is not the factual accuracy of the historical details as such but rather the overpowering atmosphere of the film itself, which allows the audience to *feel* the pervasiveness of totalitarian control at a subliminal, "gut" level. The director "conveys a feeling of authenticity that goes underneath the skin" (Wilke, "Fiktion oder erlebte Geschichte?" 599). The content may not be applicable only to the Stasi reality, but certainly the GDR state perfected this form of physio-psychological penetration of its subjects to an unprecedented degree.

Part 3

THE LIVES OF OTHERS AND OTHER FILMS

Martina Gedeck (as Christa-Maria Sieland) and Sebastian Koch (as Georg Dreyman).

.

6

THE LIVES OF OTHERS, GOOD BYE LENIN! AND THE POWER OF EVERYDAYNESS

James F. Pontuso

At first viewing, *The Lives of Others* and *Good Bye Lenin!* could not be more different. *Good Bye Lenin!* is a fanciful, lighthearted, and sometimes poignant journey into a world lost forever as the result of the collapse of communism. *The Lives of Others* is a realistic and chilling account of the lengths to which the ruling Communist Party went to keep that world from failing. Although *The Lives of Others* highlights the dark and menacing side of tyranny, both it and *Good Bye Lenin!* reveal a striking feature of post-totalitarian regimes— the Communist Party's dependence on "everydayness" as a mechanism of rule.[1] The movies illustrate the power of everydayness to envelop people so fully in the activities of daily life that they have little time or inclination to object to their political or social system. After all, communism survived long after most people had lost faith in its ideals. As Russian dissident Aleksandr Solzhenitsyn argues, "If no one believes and yet everyone submits, this demonstrates not the weakness" of a political system "but its frightful . . . power."[2] Surprisingly, both films also show the limits of the artificially manufactured and party-manipulated everydayness and highlight the extraordinary influence of a deeper, more subtle, and complex form of interaction that truly governs the relationships between people.

The Problem Raised by *The Lives of Others*

As we know from the various analyses in this book, *The Lives of Others* is about a loyal and effective Stasi operative, Hauptman Gerd Wiesler, who is assigned to spy on Georg Dreyman, a well-known GDR playwright, and his live-in-lover, Christa-Maria Sieland, one of East Germany's foremost actresses. The issue raised by this chapter is why Wiesler comes to identify with the people he is watching. It is not exactly clear why a dedicated state security agent would switch sides and oppose the government he has worked so long and hard to support. Was Wiesler an idealist disgusted by the Communist Party's abuse of power? Was he still a loyal communist who could not stomach the instruments of party rule misused for personal, prurient motives? Had he come to realize that the whole system of communist leadership had been besmirched by egocentric, careerist bureaucrats? Or was his conversion more personal? Perhaps he compared his sterile, soulless life of commitment to the cause with the vibrant, loving relationship of Sieland and Dreyman.

Storyline—*Good Bye Lenin!*

Good Bye Lenin! takes place primarily during the exhilarating and unsettling period in East Germany just as the Berlin Wall falls. It is a story about the high hopes and shattered promises of communism. The movie relates the life of Alex Kerner, who we see initially in 1978 as a Pioneer (the communist version of a Boy Scout), proudly celebrating the first East German astronaut to fly in space. The scene switches to 1989. An older, longhaired, bohemian Alex is in a crowd of street protesters. He has become one of the GDR's discontented and dispirited young persons characteristic of the late communist era. When his mother, Christiane, who is passing by, sees him in a melee between police and demonstrators, she collapses on the street. Alex is arrested but released by the authorities so that he can attend to his critically ill mother. At the hospital he discovers that she is in a coma after suffering a severe heart attack.

Alex is particularly attached to his mother because of the trauma she experienced in 1978 when her husband—Alex's father—abandoned the family. She was so distraught that she fell mute and had to be admitted to a psychiatric hospital. She awakened only to Alex and his sister Ariane's desperate pleadings. Christiane thereafter is a changed person, or at least seems to be. She becomes a loyal communist, throws herself into building socialism, and enlists her children, friends, and coworkers into the ever-present social, cultural, and political activities provided by the party to elicit citizen participation.

Now, in 1989, Christiane remains in a months-long coma while communism collapses in Central Europe, the Berlin Wall is torn down, the GDR disappears, and East and West Germany vote to reunite. Unexpectedly, Christiane awakens, but in a much weakened state. Doctors warn that any shock might kill her. Alex believes that if his mother were to discover the failure of the nation for which she labored so fervently, it would be her demise. He concocts a scheme to fool his bedridden mother into believing that the GDR is alive and well. He redecorates the family apartment with the plain dull furniture that had been relegated to the basement shortly after the end of party rule. He makes everyone who visits Christiane wear their cheaply made, 1970s-style, East German attire—long since gone out of fashion in the West and quickly vanished in the GDR. He rummages around the city to discover jars of foodstuffs no longer produced by now-defunct East German industries and carefully refills the obsolete containers with products from the West. Alex and a friend with ambitions to be a television director fabricate videos that they pass off to Christiane as the daily news. They reverse history so as to make the street protests against the GDR seem to be demonstrations against the capitalist West. In Alex's made-up world, East Germany is not only still alive, it is thriving.

During a trip to their country cottage, Christiane reveals a startling piece of news to her children. Their father, Robert, had not abandoned the family. In fact, he had defected to the West in hopes of building them a better life. The plan called for Christiane and the children to follow soon after. But as the time approached for the escape from East Germany, she had been paralyzed by fear. We can surmise that her attachment to communism was based less on principle than on fear of being uncovered as a would-be traitor to the socialist cause. In one of those odd mental tricks people are prone to as the result of betraying responsibility to a loved one, Christiane throws herself into a cause to hide, even from herself, her guilt and shame.

Although Christiane eventually discovers Alex's deception, she never lets on. Instead, she pretends to believe that an East German hero, astronaut Sigmund Jähn, has become the nation's president. In the alternative universe Alex creates, the Berlin Wall falls but it is communism that prevails in the cold war. It is not, however, the gray, dull, sclerotic communism of party hacks who make inane speeches about the glories of socialism. Nor is the nightly news focused on harvest yields and factory outputs, all delivered in the stylized Soviet-speak that had become the norm wherever communists ruled. Instead, it was the communism of equality, humanity, and solidarity that Marx had envisioned and people like Christiane had dreamed would remake the world. Christiane passes away peacefully, outliving East Germany by a few days.

Backstory

By the 1980s, East Germany was one of the more successful countries in the communist bloc. The effort to build a consensus in the GDR was aided by the traditional discipline and respect for authority of the German people. The unspoken bargain between rulers and ruled rested on the socialist system's ability to provide a safety net for citizens.[3] The party responded to the economic predicament of the 1970s and 1980s by decentralizing the management of industries. This scheme worked no better than Stalinist central planning since the government would not allow any industry to go bankrupt or even worry about making a profit. Managers had little inducement to produce goods that appealed to consumer preferences. Instead, industries became fiefdoms that incentivized hoarding raw materials, equipment, and skilled labor—all the antithesis of efficient business practices. By the late 1980s, the unit price of East German goods was actually higher than those manufactured in West Germany, although GDR workers received one-sixth the real wages of West German workers.[4] "The overall result of these half measures and systematic rigidities," Joseph Rothschild argues, "was to transform both the Soviet Union and east Central Europe into a single 'Greater European Co-Stagnation Sphere.'"[5] Vladimir Tismaneanu explains that "the social contract" between the party and the population "was based on political immobility, widespread apathy, and mass resignation to a status quo perceived as marginally less horrible than the Stalinist period."[6]

Of course, the party still expressed a belief in its ideals and heroes. Wendy Graham Westphal maintains that *Good Bye Lenin!* both highlights the symbols of communist authority and indicates how rapidly East Germans abandoned these once-powerful icons. She explains that "*Good Bye, Lenin!* depicts this shift away from the cultural memory and towards the everyday, communicative memories. . . . The use of the English term 'Good Bye' informs the audience that the cultural memories of the East . . . will be replaced by a westernized (or even Americanized) identity." Of course, Lenin was the pivotal figure "of socialist or Communist states and their ideology" and became a key element in the "state's efforts to create a cultural memory of itself." To say good-bye to this "mythical" idol of "East German propaganda," Westphal concludes, "represents the farewell to the cultural memories for which they [dedicated East Germans] stood."[7]

The party even tried to make its ever-present network of secret police and informers a routine part of daily life. As Václav Havel points out in his analysis of the greengrocer, people became so used to being watched that they simply ceased thinking about an alternative to party rule or to the way of life that it had created for them.[8] The secret police methodically isolated and manipulated those who deviated from the established line into supinely accepting the status quo. Stefan Sperling explains that "the Stasi employed what was called *Zersetzung*, a form of psychological warfare that proceeded by person-specific anonymous manipulations intended to dissolve its victims' interpersonal and intimate relationships. The Stasi University at Potsdam even offered a doctorate in the subject."[9]

When the founding ideology lost its luster, communist rulers were stuck. They did not have the resources to adapt to the economic challenges of the West, and they certainly could not tolerate a cultural norm that urged individualism over collective action. Instead of adapting to a changed world, they attempted to create an alternate reality, one in which 1960s technology and 1970s style became the everyday norm. In economists' terms, the authorities defended their sunk costs by making it a monopoly. Marxism promised to fulfill people's needs, but it could not match the real material progress of the market system. Instead, ruling elites relied on the power of convention, ordinariness, and conformity to control people. The party enforced a system in which everything was planned, organized, and unchanging. Apartments, clothes, food, transportation, education, entertainment, art, and music were all made to correspond not so much to the Marxist ideal but to the era in which communism had enjoyed its greatest economic advancement. The goal was to fully enmesh people in a particular way of life so that they unthinkingly accepted it as natural, normal, and commonsensical.

This communist alternative reality is wonderfully and comically expressed in *Good Bye Lenin!* when its lead character Alex Kerner has to go to such elaborate and arduous lengths to re-create the everyday life of East Germany, "a country," he remarks, "that never existed in that form."

Everydayness

Every strategy communists employed—force, ideology, and the effort to provide economic security—failed to justify their continued predominance.

Whether by design or default, communists attempted to use the inertia of everyday life to maintain their authority. As Martin Heidegger explains, everyday life has a certain power. *Everydayness,* a term Heidegger coined, is the ordinary, commonplace routine way in which human beings encounter, understand, and deal with the world. We hardly ever wonder about everyday occurrences; not much reflection goes into brushing our teeth, tying our shoes, or drinking coffee. We rarely ponder why the sky is blue or the sun comes up in the east. We expend little effort worrying about why we should drive on the right-hand side of the road—unless, of course, we visit England. We take the things ready at hand to be natural, reasonable, and the way they should be. "Because average everydayness constitutes the ontic immediacy of this being [*Dasein*]," Heidegger explains, "it was and will be *passed over* again and again. . . . That which is ontically nearest and familiar is . . . farthest, unrecognizable and constantly overlooked." Everyday life enframes us in the familiar such that we almost never distinguish what is truly natural from what is culturally derived. It is as if some distant, anonymous "they" established a set of rules that we all are compelled to follow. Heidegger explains, "We enjoy ourselves and have fun the way they enjoy themselves. We read, see, and judge literature and art the way they see and judge. But we also withdraw from the 'great mass' the way they withdraw, we find 'shocking' what they find shocking. The they, which is nothing definite and which all are, though not as a sum, prescribes the kind of being of everydayness."[10]

Because our consciousness, what Heidegger terms *Dasein,* takes its bearing from the they, "it is insensitive to every difference of level and genuineness. Publicness obscures everything, and then claims that what has been thus covered over is what is familiar and accessible to everybody." This covering over of different ways of life is what communists hoped would support their status quo. Moreover, Heidegger explains, everydayness can overpower ingenuity, complexity, and diversity since "every mystery loses its power. The care of averageness reveals, in turn, an essential tendency of Da-sein, which we call *leveling* down of all possibilities of being."[11] Everydayness is the background on which consciousness rests. In every time and place everydayness has been the manner in which people relate themselves to reality. Communist rulers seemed to intuitively apply Heidegger's analysis; they hoped people would forget to question the life around them because it had become so common.

For Heidegger, authenticity is the alternative to everydayness. To be authentic entails living beyond mere existence, questioning conventions, and pondering Being—the fathomless source of existence. Authentic people reject the comforts of everydayness and do not let "them" decide their actions. To be authentic we must stalwartly face the uncertainty of living without the guidance of "them" and embrace the angst-filled existence that the awareness of our own demise entails. The authentic life is preferable since everydayness can become a kind of social tyranny in which the human spirit loses its dignity. Heidegger claims that "this being-with-one-another dissolves one's own Da-sein completely into the kind of being of 'the others.'" In a sense, identification with "others" is so total it becomes "inconspicuousness" and "unascertainability." It is at the point in which the authority of others is not perceived that "it unfolds its true dictatorship."[12]

In many ways Heidegger's criticism of everydayness was a response to the technology-grounded direction of the modern world and especially Karl Marx's economic-based theory of life. Marx argues that the most fundamental human activity is to provide for one's physical needs, and all that comes after is influenced by this endeavor. He explains, "Life involves above all eating and drinking, shelter, clothing. . . . This is the first historical act . . . which must be fulfilled . . . today as well as a thousand years ago." From this premise Marx postulates that the way in which people gain their livelihood affects everything else they do. In a real sense, he claims, people are what they produce and the way they produce it. He reasons: "The way in which a man produces his food . . . his mode of production . . . is . . . a definite way of expressing . . . life. As individuals express their life, so they are. What they are, therefore, coincides with what they produce and how they produce. The nature of individuals thus depends on the material conditions which determine their production."[13]

Marx claims that we are "species beings" and that our individual destiny is significant only as part of the masses. The metaphysical questions that give rise to philosophic inquiry are irrelevant because investigations into the origin, purpose, or end of life are not fruitful. He advises: "Give up your abstractions and you will give up your questions. . . . Do not think, do not question me, for as soon as you think and question, your abstraction from the existence of nature and man makes no sense. Or are you such an egoist that you assert everything as nothing and yet want yourself to exist."[14] To put it bluntly, Marx would consider Heidegger's authentic life a ridiculous waste of time. Angst is foolish for Marx since death is best overcome by not thinking about it. Furthermore, the purpose of life is readily known—humans obtain the material necessities that make life possible. One could go so far as to say that for Marx everydayness is all that exists.

What does everydayness have to do with *Good Bye Lenin!* and *The Lives of Others*? These films show that communist governments did not, as many scholars suggest, deviate from Marx's principle.[15] They stressed economic progress as the most important activity of human society. It is no coincidence that in communist countries the corn or wheat harvest and factory output became the central topic on the closely controlled nightly news. Occasionally the monotony of everydayness was broken by some innovation, as is shown by excitement of the young Alex Kerner for East Germany's entry into the space program or by the consummate theatrical performances of Christa-Maria Sieland.

When manipulated by a group desperate to maintain power, everydayness became a tool of oppression. "Society was petrified," Havel explains, "into the fiction of everlasting harmony."[16] *The Lives of Others* accurately portrays the Stasi seeking to know and manipulate everything so that the communist mirage of a normal society could not be breached. The high point of everydayness occurred in the late 1970s and 1980s, a time "of apathy and widespread demoralization," Havel explains, "an era of gray, everyday totalitarian consumerism."[17] The system succeeded in creating peace and calm but, Havel quips, it was "calm as a morgue or a grave."[18]

Everydayness and *Alltag* Films in the GDR

There is evidence that East German authorities used a strategy of everydayness to control the population. The state-sponsored film industry, always a propaganda tool of the party, created a genre called *Alltag*—everyday life. Daniela Berghahn explains that the GDP's 1950s socialist realism movies, which were intended to make the everyday labor of ordinary workers heroic, were transformed by East German filmmakers in the 1960s into a way of highlighting the gap between socialist ideals and the grinding mediocrity of everyday life. However, the GDR's unadventurous leadership balked at this bleak realism. At its plenum held in 1965, the party banned films known as *Gegenwartsfilme* (contemporary films) that "examined socialist society more critically and more honestly."[19]

Artists loyal to the party adapted to the limitations on creativity by creating a new genre: Alltag. Alltag movies presented everyday life in the GDR but presented it as neither dreary nor heroic. Alltag films made ordinary life synonymous with Marxist-Leninist principles. GDR film director Lothar Warneke explained his use of Alltag while justifying it with an ideological credo: "Every moment is endlessly rich, . . . boredom is the most superficial reaction to everydayness." The routine behavior of ordinary people "has political meaning; the individual becomes a conscious subject." Thus Alltag films show "to what degree Communist principles have become inner human requirements, what, as Lenin put it, has become habit."[20]

Alltag movies became a propaganda tool of communists highlighting the legitimacy of the East German way of life. Indeed, Kurt Hager, chief ideologist for the East German Communist Party, declared in 1972 that "today the great, the historically, and personally meaningful grows precisely in *Alltag*."[21] Guenther K. Lehmann, a professor of aesthetics at Leipzig University known for his adherence to the party line, explained that everydayness, while critical of the overblown heroes of socialist realism, had became a way of orientating people favorably to the experience of their daily lives.

> Everydayness seems to have always been identical with the boring and monotonous. For this reason, genuine, meaningful human existence has never seemed accessible in the prose of *Alltag*. Now, however, literature and art compete to uncover the poetry of "ordinary *Alltag*." The interest in everyday subjects and processes is general. We often find headlines in papers and illustrated magazines such as "Out of the *Alltag* of the Republic," "Passing the Test in *Alltag*," "The Arts in Socialist *Alltag*," "From the *Alltag* of Socialist Jurisprudence," etc. . . . In concern for everyday activity, a healthy skepticism toward idealized exceptions combines itself with a decisive orientation toward that which animates millions of people every day and everywhere.[22]

Joshua Feinstein's book-length study of East German films, *The Triumph of the Ordinary*, raises the key paradox of the Alltag genre. How could the progressive character of Marxist philosophy be squared with the inert makeup of communist East Germany? Feinstein holds that

> a distinct image of East Germany gradually emerged in the GDR cinema, but it was not the one that the regime had originally sought. Instead of a heroic, future-oriented vision of socialism, a largely static society came into focus. . . . How was it possible to depict a

society as simultaneously dynamic and subject to an authority that was unimpeachable and thus timeless? The articulation of properties associated with *Alltag,* or everydayness, occurred in film as well as in other media both as a means of resistance and as an avenue of accommodation. . . . Positing the existence of a preexisting essentially timeless community satisfied the regime's need for legitimacy while also providing refuge from the Party's forced march toward the future.[23]

Nature's Everydayness

We are now in a better position to understand *The Lives of Others* and *Good Bye Lenin!* Both movies were a reaction to Alltag films and disclose the artificiality, conformity, repression, and mind-numbing self-deceit of the everyday life created to keep communist regimes in power. We also see, ironically, that the comedy *Good Bye Lenin!* is in some ways more heartbreaking than *The Lives of Others.* While *The Lives of Others* has a tragic moment when Christa-Maria's disloyalty is disclosed and she meets a horrible end, much of Christiane's adult life is a betrayal and a lie. She threw herself into party activities not because she cared about the GDR's brand of socialism but because she was frightened that her untrustworthiness would be revealed and her attempt to defect punished. In choosing to stay in East Germany, not only did she leave the husband she loved, she also cut her children off from their father and deceived them into believing that they had been abandoned.

These films also show us that party-constructed everydayness turned out to be a poor mechanism of control. It forced people to follow a specific set of doctrines and to sustain a static, never-altering society. Life is too complex to follow one path; the lives of most people are full of mysterious twists and turns—loves, hatreds, and longings—that can never be calculated or controlled at the central planning office. Havel explains: "Between the aims of the post-totalitarian system and the aims of life there is a yawning abyss: while life, in its essence, moves toward plurality, diversity, independent self-constitution, and self-organization, in short, toward the fulfillment of its own freedom, the post-totalitarian system demands conformity, uniformity, and discipline. While life ever strives to create new and improbable structures, the post-totalitarian system contrives to force life into its most probable states . . . a movement toward being ever more completely and unreservedly itself."[24]

The Lives of Others sharply contrasts the barren everydayness of existence in the GDR with the more spontaneous authentic lives of Dreyman, Sieland, and their friends. The movie has been attacked because Stasi agent Wiesler suddenly dedicates himself to protecting the subjects of his surveillance—something, critics maintain, that would never occur to a hardened veteran of the East German state security system. But perhaps Wiesler felt as if he could live fully only by involving himself in the lives of others. This seemingly incongruous plot twist reveals much about communism's collapse. The artificial, managed, rigid, and sterile everydayness that communism used to maintain control was undermined by a truer, more multifarious reality of people's everyday existence. Sieland and Dreyman have complex and interesting lives, full of music, creativity, art, and passion. Wiesler, on the other hand, inhabits the artificial world of late communist tyranny. His apartment is functional but dull and monotonous. The art on his walls is pedestrian, in line with the egalitarian principles of the regime. He eats packaged, precooked food, an efficient way to deliver calories but hardly an appealing experience for the senses. Even Wiesler's sexual encounters are perfunctory—undertaken with an inexpensive prostitute for the gratification of the most rudimentary erotic urges.

The Lives of Others' creator, Florian Henckel von Donnersmarck, makes an odd and perhaps revealing comment about the inspiration for the film: "And, so, the original idea came from this quote by Lenin who said that he didn't want to listen to a certain type of music anymore because it made him feel so soft inside that he couldn't commit all the atrocities he [felt] he had to commit to finish his revolution. So, basically, my film took that literally and tried to find a way of forcing Lenin to listen to that music."[25] On the surface von Donnersmarck's remark seems to wish for a more humane, less brutal, path to socialism than the one inspired by Lenin. But perhaps Donnersmarck is indicating that the boredom, tedium, and rigidity of late totalitarianism were an inevitable outcome of Lenin's revolution.

Why did Donnersmarck compare the Marxist revolution with art? Lenin's goal was to transform the human condition. He hoped to institute a social system that resolved life's existential uncertainty, a project that gave meaning to his life and guidance to his adherents. Lenin was supremely confident, perhaps to overcompensate for the doubt and uncertainty that surrounded every choice he made. He believed that Marxist philosophy had resolved the ambiguity of being; once people enjoyed material well-being equally, all their longings would be fulfilled and their lives made whole.

However, despite what Marx claimed, existence is always shrouded in mystery. Humans would be content with satisfying their everyday material needs if they weren't aware of the fragility and contingency of their lives. If, as Marx suggests, they could forget death, they might be happy to exist in the moment as species beings.[26] But we are finite creatures who can imagine the infinite and we are never fully satisfied or at home even in the most lush of material circumstances.

In order to master the elusive character of being, Lenin asserted his will against other people to make them obey, against nature to make it bountiful, and against being to make it orderly. Lenin allowed no inner doubts to check his ambition or ameliorate his cruelty. His Marxist doctrines made him believe that he could conquer chance. Acting on these principles, Lenin hoped to make individuals free from contingency, anxiety, and material shortages. He wanted to put people in full control of their destiny. Such an endeavor turns out to be impossible since the beginning, end, and purpose of our lives are not fully comprehensible. So long as the mystery surrounding human life persists, the totalitarian temptation will be attractive because it seeks to stamp out mystery. By the 1980s the revolutionary optimism of communism was gone, lost decades earlier in the brutality of Stalin's Gulag. Communism's only mechanism for maintaining power was to make rigid, structured, and controlled existence seem normal. But because people wonder about their existence, the artificially created everydayness of late communism inevitably became surreal to those living under its grip.

But even if Lenin could have created a Marxist utopia, would it resolve all human problems? What, for example, could the best-ordered society do to fix poor choices, the kind that Christa-Maria or Christiane made? Would infidelity and misfortune disappear simply because society had become more equitable? How could even the most just regime repair the heartbreak of having neglected one's responsibilities? Even the most productive societies cannot fully stem people's baser passions. It is hard to imagine, for instance, that Hempf would be less obsessive and jealous because there was a higher gross domestic product. Even a just government could not cure the sorrow Alex's sister Ariane felt when she discovered letters from her father hidden by her fearful mother. True, a decent and prosperous society can resolve some human problems. But because we have inner lives independent of our environment, society can only be a necessary but not a sufficient source of our happiness.

People are shaken from the assurance of everydayness by natural disasters, political upheavals, economic reversals, or personal crises. Of course, humans are self-conscious as well as conscious of their surroundings. They contemplate ways of life different from their own sometimes boring and ordinary existence—which is why art and artists gave the communist authorities such trouble. In order to be entertaining, even the simplest art cannot merely reflect ordinary life. Art would be boring if it only re-created what we ordinarily do. Art must present something new, different, and unexpected. The eternal need for art exists because we are not fully at home or satisfied with our lives. We are beings who can imagine perfect wisdom, beauty, harmony, and happiness, but never fully attain it. Art exists because we have a longing for something we can never quite reach. At its best, art presents an alternative to everydayness and makes us ponder the meaning of our lives. It is little wonder, then, that even pliant and loyal artists such as Dreyman in *The Lives of Others* were always under suspicion and often culpable of challenging the party-enforced status quo.

The revolution to bring about a perfect world defined Lenin's life. Revolutions are exciting and interesting for the revolutionaries. For Lenin's revolution to succeed, people would have to be happy to become species beings and content with everyday life. Had Lenin listened to music, he would have realized that human beings are never content with mere materialism and that art engages the imagination in such a way as to provide a glimpse of the beautiful and eternal, while at the same time demonstrating that these moments of delight are fleeting.

Marx was incorrect because he thought a life dedicated to material well-being both for oneself and the species would make us happy. But we are far too complex to be content with mere life. We seek love, companionship, beauty, and fun besides the satisfaction of our physical desires. Despite all of his mother's indoctrination and devotion to the cause of socialism, the young adult Alex Kerner is far more interested in the affections of a pretty girl than he is in the fate of the masses. As we have seen, his mother, Christiane, was not as dedicated to building socialism as she seemed; she turned to it as an alternative to a lost love and a marriage broken by the division of Germany.

Marx was even wrong about materialism. Consumers seek more than having goods that meet their bare needs. They want new, innovative, and stylish products. As *Good Bye Lenin!* delightfully shows, within a short time after the collapse of communism, the whole centrally planned way of life in East Germany vanished, visible only as heaps of rubbish left for the trash collector. "I can't believe what crap we used to wear," Ariane comments when

Alex coaxes her into wearing a pre-1989 outfit. Producers of those Western goods were, of course, driven by the profit motive, just as Marx contended. But they also sought to create something new and interesting. They wanted their innovations to be popular and attractive. Besides wealth they sought honor and distinction, as shown by as Alex's friend Denis, who longs to become an important filmmaker.

Heidegger was wrong as well. Everydayness does not overwhelm our ability to live authentic lives. Wiesler is converted by the authentic relationship between Sieland and Dreyman. Their passion is not merely physical; it grows out of the realization of their vulnerability. They understand the fragility of existence, as indeed most lovers do. It is, after all, awareness of our own mortality that makes us say, "I'll love you forever," even and perhaps exactly because we understand that nothing is forever.

Because of our contingency and fragility we have empathy; occasionally we relate to other people's problems. While Heidegger dismisses empathy as little more than a primordial awareness of the they, a distant, ever-present foundation of consciousness of the way the world works, it is more likely that empathy is possible because we can put ourselves in the place of others.[27] When we see other people's fears, hopes, tensions, and pains, we readily understand their feelings and sometimes make them our own.

We usually learn about virtue when we are children, a time when we are weak, dependent, and needy. Our vulnerability at such times makes us aware of the need for standards of conduct since we are the ones most likely to be hurt by their absence. Alex is particularly empathetic because, at a time when he needed them, he almost lost both parents in his youth; his father seemingly abandoned the family and his mother suffered a nervous collapse. It should not be surprising, then, that teenagers—feeling less at risk—throw off the lessons of youth to test their independence or power. Alex, of course, rebelled against the regime his mother was so devoted to. People not treated well as children often spend their lives confused and anxious, as if they do not know how to live well. They seem always to be searching for some formula—as does Ariane—that will guide them through life. It seems, then, that humans want to be trained in morality.

Empathy is the basis of all the metaphysical experiences that are particularly human. Empathy is the reason that we comprehend general categories of such things as love, friendship, courage, good, and evil. We have empathy because in our everyday lives we were taught about the world by particular people. Our families, teachers, elders, and neighbors instructed us in how to behave. We were not thrown into a world controlled by some anonymous distant they, as Heidegger's phenomenological analysis insists; more likely we were first carried around the world by our mothers.

Part of our everyday experience is a consideration of the ethical and moral consequences of our actions. All morality begins with an awareness of how our actions might affect others. We can put ourselves in the place of others and feel—or imagine we feel—their joys and sorrows. A moral sense arises from envisaging how others perceive our behavior. Perhaps it is not so odd that even a grizzled Stasi veteran such as Wiesler could experience compassion for people caught in a difficult situation; perhaps he was acting like a human being.

It is astonishing that works of popular culture—*The Lives of Others* and *Good Bye Lenin!*—show that two of the most influential philosophers of the twentieth century were wrong about the human condition. The real power of everydayness was not, as communist leaders had hoped, its ability to make us satisfied with a mundane existence. Nor is everydayness characterized by inauthentic, thoughtless activity, as Heidegger argued. Real everyday life, as these two movies show, is more complex, mysterious, full, and rich than Heidegger or Marx maintain. Everyday life is governed by the nature of human longings, and the nature of human beings is to wonder about their individual fate. We are beings who love and hate, who act nobly and wickedly, who desire more than mere life, who seek fulfillment as well as longevity. It could be argued that nature's everydayness proved not only that the most influential philosopher of the twentieth century was wrong, it was also the true conqueror of communism.

Notes

1. The post-totalitarian system was one in which show trials, torture, mass deportations, and executions were things of the past. Josef Stalin and his henchmen had murdered so many people and destroyed so many lives that even the most ardent communists had doubts about returning to terror as a method of political control. By the 1970s and 1980s the Communist Party had developed less fearsome but more subtle and selective methods of maintaining its self-appointed leading role in society. Post-totalitarian communists were not reticent about using power to maintain their position. Those caught deviating from the party line could lose their job, not be able to work at their chosen profession, and forego any possibility of advancement in their career. Those considered a real threat were forced to relocate to a part of the country where they could find "suitable work." They were denied passports and could not travel. Their families suffered. Spouses could not obtain work, elderly parents were harassed and (by far the most effective threat), children were not allowed to

receive a good education. For a lengthy treatment of post-totalitarianism, see James F. Pontuso, *Václav Havel: Civic Responsibility in the Postmodern Age* (Lanham, MD: Rowman and Littlefield, 2004), chap. 3.

2. Aleksandr Solzhenitsyn, "Sakharov i kritika Pisma vozhdyam," *Kontinent* 2 (1975): 352–53, quoted in John Dunlop, "Solzhenitsyn in Exile," *Survey* 21 (Summer 1975): 135–36.

3. Marc Fisher, *After the Wall: Germany, Germans and the Burdens of History* (New York: Simon and Schuster, 1995), 114–16.

4. Lonnie R. Johnson, *Central Europe: Enemies, Neighbors, Friends* (Oxford: Oxford University Press, 2002), 258–59.

5. Joseph Rothschild, *Return to Diversity* (Oxford: Oxford University Press, 1993), 219.

6. Vladimir Tismaneanu, *Reinventing Politics: Eastern Europe from Stain to Havel* (New York: Free Press, 1992), 87.

7. Wendy Graham Westphal, "Dis-membering and Re-membering the GDR: Material Culture and East Germany's Self-Reflexive Memory in *Good Bye, Lenin!*" in *Germany and the Imagined East*, ed. Lee M. Roberts (Newcastle, UK: Cambridge Scholars, 2005), 8.

8. Václav Havel, "The Power of the Powerless," in *Open Letters: Selected Writings, 1965–1990*, ed. Paul Wilson (New York: Knopf, 1991), 131–55.

9. Stefan Sperling, "The Politics of Transparency and Surveillance in Post-reunification Germany," *Surveillance and Society* 8, no. 4 (2011): 400n6.

10. Martin Heidegger, *Being and Time*, trans. Joan Stambaugh (Albany: State University of New York Press, 1996), 41, 119.

11. Ibid., 119.

12. Ibid.

13. Robert C. Tucker, ed., *Marx-Engels Reader* (New York: Norton, 1978), 53, 136; Arthur Mendel, ed., *Essential Works of Marxism* (New York: Bantam, 1965), 104; Karl Marx, *Writings of the Young Marx on Philosophy and History*, ed. and trans. Lloyd Easton and Kurt Guddat (Garden City, NY: Doubleday, 1976), 19, 149, 409, 458.

14. Karl Marx, *The German Ideology*, ed. R. Pascal (New York: International, 1933), 14–15; Marx, *Writings of the Young Marx*, 313–14.

15. See, for example, Shlomo Avineri, *The Social and Political Thought of Karl Marx* (Cambridge: Cambridge University Press, 1968).

16. Václav Havel, "Stories of Totalitarianism," in *Open Letters*, 336.

17. Václav Havel, *Disturbing the Peace: A Conversation with Karel Hvížďala*, trans. Paul Wilson (New York: Knopf, 1990), 119–20.

18. Václav Havel, "Dear Dr. Husák," in *Open Letters*, 72.

19. Daniela Berghahn, *Hollywood behind the Wall: The Cinema of East Germany* (Manchester, UK: Manchester University Press, 2005), 142; Andrew Gaskievicz, "A History of Film in the GDR: Review of Daniela Berghahn, *Hollywood behind the Wall*," *Humanities and Social Sciences*, March 2007, http://www.het.org/reviews/showrev.php?id=12971 (accessed January 20, 2014).

20. Quoted in Joshua Feinstein, *The Triumph of the Ordinary: Depictions of Daily Life in the East German Cinema, 1949–1989* (Chapel Hill: University of North Carolina Press, 2002), 200.

21. Quoted in ibid., 202.

22. Guenther K. Lehmann, "Poesie des Alltäglichen, Bemerkungen zu äesthetischen Fragen der Arbeit," *Sonntag* 50 (1973), quoted in Feinstein, *The Triumph of the Ordinary*, 202.

23. Feinstein, *The Triumph of the Ordinary*, 229.

24. Václav Havel, "The Power of the Powerless," in *Open Letters*, 134–35.

25. "The Lives of Others," interview with Florian Henckel von Donnersmarck, *Movie Interview,* February 6, 2007, http://www.moviefreak.com/artman/publish/interviews_florianhenckelvondonnersmarck.shtml.

26. Marx, *The German Ideology*, 14–15; Marx, *Writings of the Young Marx*, 313–14.

27. Heidegger, *Being and Time*, 116.

7

ON THE IMPOSSIBILITY OF WITHDRAWAL

Life in the Gray Zone

Marketa Goetz-Stankiewicz

> Wretchedness was the lot of those who, under any circumstances, remained
> in the middle.
>
> —Ivan Klíma

Among the Polish writer Sławomir Mrożek's delightful fables there is one
entitled "The Lion." The scene is a Roman amphitheater where the Roman
citizens as well as the emperor are watching an entertainment. I retell it here
in abbreviated form.

A group of Christians is huddling at the center of the arena. A roaring
group of lions emerges from the tunnel. Gayus, the keeper of the lions, is
checking whether all the beasts have come into the arena when he notices
one lion has stopped at the entrance and is calmly chewing a carrot. Gayus
prods him with his long pole. After all, it is his duty to see that none of the
lions remains idle. Repeated prodding does not help. The lion merely turns
his head and says, "Oh, leave me alone." Gayus gets worried. If the supervisor catches him neglecting his duties he will soon find himself among the
victims in the arena.

A discussion ensues during which Gayus pleads with the lion to at least
run around in the arena and roar without jumping on any of those wretches
there. "I'm no fool," the lion says finally. "Hasn't it occurred to you that one
of these days the Christians might come to power?" Fixing his wise gaze on
the stunned Gayus, he continues: "And then what? Investigations, rehabili-

tations, and those up there in the amphitheatre will say, 'It wasn't us, it was the lions.' And I want to save my skin. There will be witnesses to say that all I did was eat a carrot. Mind you, it's filthy stuff, this carrot."

Gayus hesitantly manages to object: "But all your colleagues in there, they're all gobbling up the Christians with gusto."

"Stupid beasts, shortsighted opportunists," is the lion's curt answer.

After some intense thought and a good deal of stutter Gayus finally manages to ask the lion a key question: "And . . . should they, those Christians, come to power . . . will you then testify that I didn't force you to do anything?"[1]

The ironic wisdom of this brief fable reaches directly and deeply into the atmosphere permeating two Central European films that deal with societies under a totalitarian dictatorship: Czechoslovakia under Nazi occupation and East Germany under communism. The films are multileveled explorations of human nature under coercive political circumstances. The Czech film *Musíme si pomáhat,* circulating in English under the somewhat confusing title *Divided We Fall,* was made in 2000 by the Czech director Jan Hřebejk (film script by Petr Jarchovský), with the well-known comic actor Boleslav Polívka in the main role.[2] Seven years later, in 2007, the German film *Das Leben der Anderen* (The Lives of Others) was debuted by first-time writer and director Florian Henckel von Donnersmarck.

I will explore how the films portray the lives of people, "normal" citizens trying to live decent and ordinary lives, who get sucked into a murderous political system and become its tools, even collaborators. Basic, perennial human qualities that could be regarded as innocuous in themselves—ambitions, desires, fears, lassitude, or indifference—appear as the main drives that propel the protagonists into a moral and existential quicksand from which there is no return, unless it comes from a drastic reversal of the situation: the downfall of the ruling regime. This is the case in both films as the filmmakers use the reversal, each in his own unique way, as a harmonizing coda to the often-discordant symphony of the characters' lives. Although ideology as such (National Socialism in the former film, communism in the latter) is not explicitly mentioned but is recognizable only by its visual iconic signs—uniforms, helmets, flags, and the use of certain typical phrases—it is obvious that it exists everywhere. Like Ibsen's Boyg, it is shown to penetrate the entire atmosphere and the characters' very lives.

My main concern is the films' dealing with the so-called gray zone—a kind of ethical no-man's-land—in which the characters find themselves and try to maintain an uneasy balance, consciously or unconsciously. Living under what Aleksandr Solzhenitsyn simply called "the Lie," the protagonists of the films tried to create their own secret laws and values in contrast to the "laws" of the system. When Georg Dreyman in *The Lives of Others* shrugs and turns to his piano, when Josef in *Divided We Fall* constantly speaks of the system as "they," each works on the assumption that he feels he does not belong to the alien realm that "they" own and command. But by withdrawing into this gray, seemingly nonpolitical area and claiming rejection of any political stance, they act under an illusion. Both films explore why this attempt at withdrawal fails, but they also force viewers to face the reality of the success of totalitarian power. A seemingly simple question has been asked in many variations since the totalitarian regimes held millions in their sway: how could people endure these regimes? Manès Sperber—perhaps a typical "Central European" who was born in Galicia and lived in Vienna and later taught in Berlin—offers an interesting answer that comes to the fore in both of these films. Totalitarian power is possible because "it succeeds in forcing those whom it endangers into a state of alienation from themselves, and by permitting the powers to enter their own souls, they can, without realizing it, end up on their side."[3]

Balancing Acts

Divided We Fall is set in a small town in Czechoslovakia that in 1939 had become a German protectorate under Nazi occupation. The film's first images show an episode in the year 1937: three friends jump out of a rickety old car and relieve themselves, with their backs to the camera, against the lovely vista of the peaceful Czech countryside. Merrily pretending that one of them is to be left behind, they engage in a boisterous game. We are faced with an idyllic scene of carefree youth. Within a couple of years the three will have to face radically different fates: one, David, is a Jew destined with his family for the concentration camp and likely death; the second, Horst, German by birth, will benefit from his nationality to become an ally of the occupying Nazi forces; the third, Josef, is just trying to live a quiet life with his wife, stay out of trouble, and not rock any boat. Allowing the film's concrete scenes to become transparent, we could lightly regard these figures as an archetypal threesome reflecting basic patterns of human nature: man the thinker, who becomes a victim; man the player, indulging in any game that is to be played; and man submerged in the multitude, holding still under the waves of life.

It is this third one who turns out to be the film's uneasy protagonist. He is an ordinary guy, basically decent but a little lazy, easily frightened, perhaps a bit of a yes-man who wants to get by, make the best of things the way they are, and be left in peace. The Czech filmmaker, true to the ironic tradition of his nation that cringes at displaying "heroism" of any sort, goes to some length to stress the nonheroic nature of his "hero." He reveals him as a grouchy fellow who is nursing the "disabled" status that was granted to him after an accident on his job some years ago, seemingly impotent, and even unable to control his bowels in a dangerous situation. Yet, as if despite himself, and despite being constantly seen in a comic light, Josef rises to the occasion, and an extremely dangerous occasion at that. In his cellar and with his wife's support he hides their Jewish neighbor David, who has managed to escape from the concentration camp where his family has perished. It all happened as if by chance, not by a conscious rebellious decision on Josef's part but rather during a tense yet hilarious rain-soaked scene involving German officers stuck on a country road. Josef, with David packed into the trunk of his car, advises them in faulty-accented German—adding to the mixture of comedy and horror—how to change a switch in their engine. As the German car takes off, Josef, staring at the empty misty country road, can't bear to see David walk off into darkness and most likely death. So he takes him home, hides him in his cellar for two years, and manages, under great danger and at times very precariously, to save his life until the end of the war and the Nazi occupation.

Absurd political systems require varieties of balancing acts on the part of their citizens. Josef's balancing act means coping with the constant fear of being discovered. And it also means facing difficult ethical choices. By hiding David, Josef must consider engaging in some distasteful behavior. The audience is led with Josef into the gray area of moral ambiguity since Josef has realized that he must collaborate in order to save not only his wife but also his secret Jew in the cellar. Josef's collaboration with the enemy includes becoming a drinking partner of the town's Nazi commander and even acting as confiscator of Jewish property. When the regime changes near the end of the film, Josef barely escapes being shot by the revengeful militia that considers him a traitor.

In *The Lives of Others* Georg Dreyman, a playwright, is also involved in a balancing act. However, this is only implied and is likely to go unnoticed by someone not tuned into the atmosphere. The year is 1984. Dreyman, whose plays run successfully in official theaters, reads in the privacy of his home

Western journals that have been spirited into the country but does not use in any subversive way the information he gleans from them. We might ask: has ambition drawn Dreyman into being a quasi-tool of the system? We know, after all, that he is the winner of something called the Margot Honecker Award. But then we might argue that his ambition is no more than the healthy wish of a writer/dramatist to see his plays performed. There is a clear contrast here with Dreyman's blacklisted friend, the once-prominent director Albert Jerska.

Later on we find out that the balancing act of his lover Christa-Maria Sieland, a well-known actress, has darker colors. Up to now, the film implies, Dreyman is not even aware of balancing his existence, and there is no inkling of a price he has to pay for adapting himself to the demands of the system. In his naïveté, which allows him still to harbor some hope in the system's fairness, he approaches the powerful minister of culture with a question regarding his colleague and friend Jerska (a talented director whose "subversive" political attitude resulted in his being banned from his professional work in the theater). When Dreyman asks the minister whether there is hope for his friend to be permitted to work again, the answer is given with a paternalistic smile close to a smirk: "Hope? Of course! One can always hope, even after death!" This ironic and obliquely religious reference would have pleased the shrewd old devil of C. S. Lewis's *Screwtape Letters* who advises his nephew to keep the person to be seduced by evil "well fed on hazy ideas."[4] Dreyman's question has been answered ostensibly positively. The pleader stands there, seemingly rewarded but strangely shaken. The moment of his hitherto avoided enlightenment comes soon afterward when he receives the news of his friend's suicide. It is only now that he becomes aware of his own previous balancing act and realizes that up to this moment he had internalized the absurd situation he was part of and accepted it as "normal." Does Aldous Huxley provide another, admittedly cryptic, yet implicitly political view of the situation? "Everything that happens is intrinsically like the man it happens to . . . but in some indescribable way the event is modified, qualitatively modified, so as to suit the character of each person involved in it."[5]

The figure who has aroused most interest among critics and commentators is Gerd Wiesler, the Stasi captain, ice-cold interrogator and stern lecturer at the Stasi academy who moves from monitoring Dreyman's bugged apartment in order to find incriminating information to protecting Dreyman from his superiors. His change from Saul to Paul, if you wish, resulted in Wiesler's actually saving the playwright, whose subversive activities undertaken after the death of Jerska would surely have landed him in prison. The filmmaker Donnersmarck explained in an interview that the basis of Wiesler's change is his lost faith in ideology. But this comment in no way affected the excited discussions that the film unleashed. Their focal thought could be reduced to the following question: could a brief perception of the beauty of poetry (Wiesler reads a Brecht poem in a volume he had lifted from Dreyman's apartment) and the mysterious wonder of music (Dreyman's friend had composed a piece of music, the "Sonata for a Good Man"—"Die Sonate vom guten Menschen") that Wiesler hears (ironically) through his earphones really result in so drastic a change? Debates ensued among commentators, scholars, and the media whether it is at all possible for a man hardened by ideology to undergo a change of this sort. For example, an internationally rather prominent voice, that of Timothy Garton Ash, claimed that "it would take more than the odd sonata and a Brecht poem to thaw the driven puritan we are shown at the beginning."[6] Of course there is a point to this, but the debates seem to have overlooked the subtly indicated previous cracks in the ideological armor of Wiesler's mind. When, for instance, he is shown pleading with the business-minded call girl whom he had booked (who consults her watch when she has done her job) to "please stay a little longer"(a request she cheerfully denies because other customers are waiting), he is reduced—the filmmaker makes sure that we realize this—to a pathetic, aging man, aware of his own loneliness and the paucity of his life. The film does not imply Wiesler's realization that this paucity is due to the system he serves, but his longing touch of the lovers' bed during one of his hurried secret visits to their apartment suggests a yearning far beyond the erotic and the political. Later, when he experiences the beauty of poetry and the mystery of music—both of which have been denied to him (the party ideology rejects mystery, goodness is dictated as adherence to this ideology, and beauty must conform to the ideology's prescription)—we might be led to the question: is Captain Wiesler's "conversion" (underacted admirably by Ulrich Mühe), culminating in his new refusal to accept an absurd system as "normal," really an impossible dream?

Thinking of the duo Dreyman/Wiesler, whose absurd relationship appears as the main theme of *The Lives of Others,* one might call to mind a text that provides a surprising inverted view of their connection. It is by Wolf Biermann, the German poet and *Liedermacher* (song maker), as he calls himself, who wrote the "Stasi Ballad," which he performed during his 1992 tour of North America. Some verses will give a taste of the provocative text:

In human terms I feel close to
those poor Stasi-dogs
who in snow and thundershowers
tiresomely have to keep up with me
who installed the microphone
songs, jokes, quiet curses,
in the john and in the kitchen,
brothers from security
you know all my misery
You alone can bear witness
how all my human striving
passionately tender and wild
is linked to our great endeavor
Words that else were lost
you capture on spools of tape
and I know! Now and then
in your bed you sing my songs.[7]

Gerd Wiesler did not sing a Biermann song but he was carried away by the "Sonata for a Good Man." Wiesler too is thus lured away from his envelopment of normality and forced to confront questions and longings from which he had heretofore been shielded. He and Dreyman move along similar arcs.

The focal point, then, of both films is the illusion of "normality" that emerges as perhaps the most deadly weapon of totalitarian and also post-totalitarian systems. The dissident writers were acutely aware of this. The Czech writer Ivan Klíma captures how this illusion of normality comes to dominate the personalities of citizens of these nations: "Totalitarian power does not allow differing opinions and therefore does not allow debates or even meaningful conversation. . . . Every individual, regardless of his inner make-up has to adapt to the official model; the development of his personality is restrained; the space in which the human mind and spirit moves becomes continually narrower."[8]

Yet another question arises: what enables some individuals to burst through these confines of the human spirit but not others? Why do some people seemingly surrender to the Lie and flourish under the system while others are crushed and tossed aside? Here is another area where the two films are of use. For in each case there are secondary characters who illuminate the range of human possibility under these regimes.

In *The Lives of Others* there is Georg Dreyman's lover, the beautiful, high-strung, renowned actress Christa-Maria Sieland, constantly reassured by her friends as well as by her adoring audience that she is a great actress. She harbors the ambition to keep her position in the theater and realize herself as the artist she hopes she might be. In the film this eventually comes at a price: it means admitting the sexual advances of a very powerful man, Hempf, the minister of culture in the GDR. Could she therefore be considered selling herself? A hesitant "yes" seems to be the only answer here. But—to stretch a point—in the tradition of the noble century prostitutes who appear in literature from Dostoevsky to Brecht she sells only her body, not her soul. And yet, we know she sells more than her body. Her anguish when confronted by Dreyman suggests Christa knows this as well. Eventually, under extreme pressure and the threat of losing her stage career, she betrays her lover's by now illicit activity by revealing the hiding place of Dreyman's typewriter. Not realizing that he was saved by another source, she later runs out of the house and is killed by a truck. Was this an accident or suicide, the ultimate example of self-censorship? The film does not tell us. Her life, balancing in the morally gray zone, has collapsed.

Consider then Josef's friend Horst in *Divided We Fall,* who is caught up in the web of the German/Czech conundrum. Born in Czech lands to a German-speaking family and saddled with the unfortunate German name Horst, very difficult for Czechs to stomach (the Nazi Horst Wessel song rings in their ears), he is married to a German and from all we hear an enthusiastic adherent of Hitler. Under the German occupation this means that Horst is in good stead with the authorities and thus finds a way to flourish—materially, that is—under the Nazi occupation. He brings food and drink to his friends, but they have to listen to his impassioned lectures about the victorious German army encircling Moscow, which he demonstrates graphically on the dining-room table with the sausages he brought, while his hosts worry about their good china.

Now, is Horst merely a cheap opportunist who wants to show off as his friends' benevolent helper? He is both more and less than that. The moral ambiguity of his character comes to the fore in various ways: for example, he does not let anyone know that Josef and his wife illicitly have a slaughtered pig hanging in the cellar. The fact that Horst benefits from his silence by way of several excellent pork chop dinners weighs lightly on the moral scale if compared with his silence when he suspects that there is something "subversive" going on in the cellar—much more dangerous than the illicit pig. There are French lessons going on there; indeed, it is David, the hidden Jew, who teaches French to Josef's wife. But Horst's obvious willingness to shelter his friend whom he suspects of harboring a secret is almost deleted in the audience's mind when he makes rather brutish but unsuccessful erotic advances on Josef's pretty wife. Some years later, in 1945, when the war has ended and the regime changes, we find him, obviously beaten up, huddled in a cellar under the guns of the newly formed local Czech militia. Now it is his turn to be "saved" by Josef, who identifies him (falsely) as a physician. For all his moral murkiness, viewers are likely to be glad that he is saved from brutal revenge by the irate Czech militia, not only because throughout the film they have been amused by his antics but also because he, having helped at the birth of his own children, could assist at the birth of the half-Jewish baby of Josef's wife. The moral ambiguity of the character rubs off on the audience which, at this point, is likely to leave ethical considerations aside and adopt purely utilitarian principles in view of the urgent situation. Again, the audience imperceptibly is made to emulate the character's dubious ethics, although the sustained humor of the action seems to let viewers morally off the hook—a brilliant touch. One more word about the "half-Jewish" baby: Josef, frantic because circumstances force him to announce that his wife is pregnant, urgently pleads with David to "help" him out of the dilemma, believing this to be the only possible salvation (since Josef himself is impotent). David does help.

There are other portraits in *The Lives of Others* that provide us with different views of souls who appear to have surrendered themselves to totalitarian power. Colonel Grubitz assigns his inferior Captain Wiesler to the watchdog job above Dreyman's apartment. His restless spirit flits through the action, busy trying to realize his ambition to pull his weight in the system. He emulates the system itself by his contradictory treatment of a student whom he overhears telling an antigovernment joke. In quick succession he frightens and then jovially reassures the student—and with him the audience. Only in the last minutes of the film do we find out that the reassurance was a sham and the student was expelled and punished. However, as becomes obvious in brief flashes, Grubitz himself is constantly plagued by fears. He, too, is caught in the web of power. In the end, after he has made a threatening but at that point impotent gesture against his inferior Wiesler because he realizes that he has been outwitted, we lose sight of him. He is likely, one is made to feel, to continue his rat's dance under the new system.

An interesting example that provides another significant insight into the workings of the communist system in *The Lives of Others* but is hardly mentioned in critical analyses of the film is the husky, lowly employee of the Stasi with whom Captain Wiesler, the boss in this situation, shares the watching shifts, the recording devices and earphones. Cheerfully clueless about other matters, he just does his job, even enjoys it (particularly when he becomes witness to the lovers' most intimate moments), mumbles apologies when he is criticized for being late, and is pleased when he is praised. He perceives only one ledge of authority above himself: Wiesler, his boss. We, the audience, know that Wiesler is caught under the pressure of his own boss, Colonel Grubitz, who in turn is caught under an even higher power, the minister of culture. The whole hierarchical pattern of authority and responsibility, false or corrupt, is revealed in this dark, dirty, unheated attic.

In the Czech film the representatives of Nazi power who appeared, typical of Hřebejk's comic genius, in semi-ridiculous moments during the action, find their end. One German medical officer who had boasted of having sterilized a thousand of the "Roma trash" has committed suicide. Again, the ingrained irony of the film leaves us in an opaque moral space: in case we might feel some sort of regret for the demise of the young man out of sympathy extended humanely even to an enemy, we are made quickly to realize the real reason for our possible regret—as the only medical doctor at hand, he was desperately needed for the delivery of Josef's baby. The other representative of Nazi power, an aging officer (who had been drinking merrily with Josef when the latter pretended to collaborate) who lost his son in the war and whose grandson (a mere child soldier at the end of the conflict) had just been shot as a deserter is being pushed through the streets by the Czech militia and now stands helplessly against a wall enduring the slaps of a child in his mother's arms. Again, this possibly justified albeit grotesquely funny gesture of revenge is likely to evoke an odd feeling in the audience because the wrathful mother can be recognized as the wife of the citizen who, years earlier, upon discovering David, the escaped Jewish neighbor, tried but failed to get the attention of the German police to arrest him. The grimly ironic implication of this scene becomes clear when we realize that this neighbor now, when the regime has changed, has rapidly morphed into the leader of the local armed militia, and his wife, having appeared several times at key moments, peering, greedy for news, from behind the safety of her curtained window, now stands there as a figure of revenge, admonishing her children to express her newly found contempt and anger at the defeated enemy.

The end of the film dissolves all this. Its final sequence shows Josef happily pushing a pram with his new baby son across the ruins of his town, as those who perished (the Jewish family and the German boy soldier) appear to him in the distance like a friendly vision. It is a wondrous final scene—a healing fairy-tale ending to a story about the horrors and dangers of the absurd murky reality a small town at the center of Europe experienced during the war and enemy occupation.

Self-Censorship and the Perpetuation of Evil

It bears repeating that at the core of both films is the notion that the absurd senselessness of the system and its ubiquitous lies are internalized by the population and become habitual and hence "natural." Self-censorship, the most noxious of censorships, has become a prevalent human quality. It causes an individual's disintegration into several selves that, as it were, keep watch over each other. The Czech communist regime invented a politically useful euphemism for such a situation. The period after the country was once again—this time from the other side—occupied by tanks in August 1968 was officially termed "normalization." In the films the normal or normalized attitude of the characters is revealed repeatedly as the tense attitude of self-censorship. When Josef in *Divided We Fall* gets a lesson from his manipulative friend Horst on how to train himself to achieve a facial expression that does not betray what he thinks, we witness an amusing but grim lesson in self-censorship. When Georg Dreyman assures the Stasi officer who has been in charge of the house search that left his apartment in shambles that everything is left "in bester Ordnung," in perfect order, he obviously practices self-censorship. It remains for us to ponder: how does constant self-censorship affect persons who practice it? Drawn into the sphere of the totalitarian system, they "may surrender their human identity in favor of the identity of the system . . . they may learn to be comfortable with their involvement, to identify with it as though it were something natural and inevitable and ultimately . . . come to treat any non-involvement as an abnormality, as arrogance."[9] Although this would obviously be stretching a point, it might be of some interest to extend the thought by asking in what way the self-censorship under a coercive regime differs from the form used in a democracy today? Could we think here of today's phenomenon of "political correctness," a socially or personally imposed form of language that specializes in certain avoidances and substitutions? Is it disputable or at least unfair to suggest an opaque comparison with the language practiced constantly under totalitarianism that was never named?

The theme of evil is present in the films discussed here but it is less obvious. In *Divided We Fall* it temporarily emerges as we see the innocent victims (the Jewish family going, still hopeful, to their deaths). But what may concern us more in this context is how the workings of evil are implied in the constant anxiety and sudden bouts of icy fear and agonized uncertainty displayed yet concealed by the characters.

Apart from the slimy minister wielding his power from the top of the communist system's hierarchy, the obvious representative of evil, the "devil," in *The Lives of Others* initially seems to be Wiesler, the Stasi captain. Here lies the main dramatic, political, and ethical interest of the film. The same question seems to wedge its way into any argument concerning this film, as it also did in these pages. As we know, Wiesler changes diametrically and indeed becomes a sort of savior, risking not only his job but also his life. Can Donnersmarck's film be criticized (as it has been) for projecting a black-and-white message? The Czech film discussed here seems to avoid possible starry-eyed conclusions, lifting us from the dark background into a fairy-tale dimension and leaving us there with a shrug and a smile. But it could be argued such a black-and-white understanding of *The Lives of Others* oversimplifies matters. In the last minutes of the film we see Wiesler, a gray and hardly noticeable figure, pushing a newspaper cart along the street. Dreyman, now knowing about his act of courage, passes by in a taxi. The audience, probably yearning for a satisfying resolution in the form of some compensation for the gallant "hero," has to watch the taxi go by. The resolution, realistically leaving Wiesler under the new regime in a lowly menial job, allows him to enter, in his imagination at least, the "lives of the others" when he discovers the book that recognizes in him "a good human being." Will Wiesler recognize himself in its pages? This seems no longer important. The film ends with his clutching the book and answering (to a salesperson who offers to gift wrap it): "This is for me." This irresistible double entendre closes the film.

Approaching the topic from an entirely different point of view, we might think of Brecht (who plays a significant part in the "conversion" in *The Lives of Others*). In his play *Life of Galileo* the protagonist also strikes a compromise, clearly out of fear, against his own convictions. His fear of torture leads him to recant his discovery and form a pact with the powers of the church. Brecht has an idealistic pupil call out: "Unhappy the land that has no heroes!" Galileo, who has just proved that he is not a hero, answers by inverting the phrase: "Unhappy the land that needs heroes!" There are no heroes in the films under discussion. Or does Wiesler come close to being one? How would Brecht have commented on him or on the author who gave him life in his film script?

The main figures in each film are faced with having to make certain fateful decisions, while only vaguely or not at all aware of their moral weight. In neither of the films does the relevant character express his or her decision (for better or for worse) in words. This shows the refusal of the filmmakers to dwell on the complexity of the situations with even a shadow of moralizing. As a person who lived as "dissident" under a coercive political system as well as a playwright dealing with such issues on stage, Václav Havel could be considered as speaking for these filmmakers who show us the workings of two "absurd" political systems. "The absurd playwright does not have the key to anything," writes Havel. "He sees his role in giving form to something we all suffer from, and in reminding us, in suggestive ways, of the mystery before which we all stand equally helpless."[10]

My discussion of these challenging films leaves another and larger question open: what do these films tell us, who live in another time, in another country, aware of and faced with different problems? The films give us a message many of us might feel we don't need any longer because it refers to the past. But although the allure of totalitarian regimes has faded, ideological temptations are still very much with us. We ought never to forget the boundless human capacity for self-deception. The films remind us that the amazing but also dangerous ability of human beings to "make the best of things," usually cited (and often justifiably) as an admirable quality, can lead us into an illusionary world that mimes success and happiness but can also spell dependence from which there is no escape, confusion about who we are, and above all loss of a sense of value. About the possibility to change our view of the world, the films show us, if we care to notice, that we can overcome fear (Josef), engrained habits of assumption and thought (Wiesler), and recognition of our own weakness (Horst and Christa-Maria). The Czech writer Pavel Kohout brilliantly captures the problem here in a scrap of a conversation from his rollicking novel *I Am Snowing,* in which the characters are swaying between Nazism and communism. The ebullient, lovable heroine with a checkered past—personally as well as politically—asks a run-of-the-mill schoolteacher, "Did you teach your children that . . . how did it go? You can live decently off a lie but only with truth can you have a decent life? Am I saying it right?"[11]

Turning with a smile—possibly a wistful one—to Mrożek's lion, with whom I opened these remarks, we may find that the lion was well aware of societies suffering under absurd and brutal regimes. Continuing this thought, we might think of Gayus, the lion keeper, who could have entered the world of our films, having learned the ways of behavior—balancing acts—such as an absurd regime requires. If the films ignite sparks of understanding and perhaps recognition in the minds of today's audience, their appeal will be a lasting one.

Notes

1. Sławomir Mrożek, *The Elephant,* trans. Konrad Syrop (New York: Grove, 1962), 43–45.

2. "Divided we fall" follows "United we stand" in John Dickinson's revolutionary "The Liberty Song." The literal translation of the Czech title is "We have to help each other." This phrase is repeated by different characters multiple times during the film. It is used as a folksy expression and could be ironic depending on the occasion.

3. Manès Sperber, *Sieben Fragen zur Gewalt* (Munich: DTV, 1978), 29 (the translation is my own).

4. C. S. Lewis, *The Screwtape Letters,* rev. ed. (New York: Collier Books, 1982), 43.

5. Aldous Huxley, *Point Counter Point* (London: Chatto and Windus, 1947), 389–90.

6. Timothy Garton Ash, "The Stasi on Our Minds," *New York Review of Books,* May 31, 2007, 6.

7. Wolf Biermann, *Ein deutsch-deutscher Liedermacher* (A Political Songwriter between East and West), trans. Leslie A. Wilson, North American tour 1992, Goethe Institut.

8. Ivan Klíma, *The Spirit of Prague and Other Essays,* trans. Paul Wilson (London: Granta Books, 1994), 119.

9. Václav Havel, *Open Letters: Selected Writings, 1965–1990* (New York: Vintage Books, 1992), 143.

10. Ibid., 133.

11. Pavel Kohout, *I Am Snowing: The Confessions of a Woman of Prague,* trans. Neil Bermel (New York: Harcourt Brace, 1994), 233.

Part 4

THE LIVES OF OTHERS AND THE HISTORY OF THE GDR

Sebastian Koch (as Georg Dreyman).

8

FICTION OR LIVED HISTORY?

On the Question of the Credibility of *The Lives of Others*

Manfred Wilke

Translated by Dirk R. Johnson

The attempt to show the mechanisms of communist dictatorship from the perspective of a Stasi officer went against the standard victim-perpetrator debates held in Germany after 1990 on the question of membership in the Ministry for State Security (Ministerium für Staatssicherheit, or MfS). East German society's self-liberation from the Socialist Unity Party of Germany (Sozialistische Einheitspartei Deutschlands, or SED) and its most important instrument of repression in the peaceful revolution of 1989 went hand in hand with moral condemnation of that organization. It became a matter of justice and of German democracy's political morality to rehabilitate the victims of the Stasi regime after German reunification.

It was already provocative as such to turn a captain of state security into a positive hero. But then this was only amplified by showing Captain Wiesler's transformation while he spies on a writer. Wiesler refuses to serve. The film reminds us that even state security functions only through the work of individuals, and these individuals can change. The discussions surrounding the film began with its credibility and with the historical burden of the facts in the script. As the film was shown in theaters, the automatic response was: was there ever any form of divergent behavior or opposition within this ministry? Doesn't the script make use of a fiction that puts the Stasi and its activities into a better light?

The scriptwriter and director of the film are one and the same. Florian

Henckel von Donnersmarck knew that he would be criticized. He had already discussed the first draft of the script with me. One of the questions concerned state security "evaders." My response was that there weren't many of them, but that there were members of the MfS who opposed the leadership, who got out of the country, or who spied for the West German secret service. For example, the first two ministers of state security—Wilhelm Zaisser in 1953 and his successor Ernst Wollweber in 1958, two old communist revolutionaries—dared to oppose the SED general secretary, Walter Ulbricht. Both lost their positions and Ulbricht installed Erich Mielke as minster of the MfS; he had served as state secretary since the founding of the ministry in 1950. Mielke remained in that post until 1989. During his tenure, Major Gerd Trebeljahr and Captain Werner Teske, two dropouts from the organization, were condemned and executed in 1979 and in 1981, respectively. In 1979, Werner Stiller crossed over to West Germany and blew the cover of a group of MfS spies. He had previously led a network of agents among scientists in West Germany and had served as a double agent for the West German secret service.

As the minister of state security, Erich Mielke was merciless toward "traitors"; within the organization, he made that abundantly clear, threatening: "We are not immune from having a scoundrel among us once in a while. If I were to know that right now, he would be dead by tomorrow. A quick verdict! I can have such an outlook since I am a humanist." He declared this to his generals in 1981—and he added: "All that nonsense about whether or not to execute is garbage, Comrades. Execute—even without a verdict if necessary."[1]

No such fate threatens Wiesler at the beginning of the film. He is portrayed as a conscientious MfS officer who is asked to clear up a case of "desertion of the republic" in the Stasi Detention Center in Berlin—Hohenschönhausen. A sleep-deprived inmate is being forced to reveal the name of a man who had helped someone else "desert the republic." "Illegal border-crossing" was, according to the criminal code of the GDR (paragraph 213), a "crime against the state order" and could lead to two years in prison. Just preparing for and attempting to "flee the republic" were considered criminal offenses. In his investigation, Wiesler tries to determine if this was a case of "enticement to desertion of the GDR" or of trafficking in humans (paragraph 132).[2]

This paragraph also served to prevent escape from the GDR. After the internal German border was secured in 1952 and the Berlin Wall was built in 1961, there were those in the West willing to help people escape. The GDR regarded their illegal activities as criminal and they were prosecuted. Anyone who actively helped a person to get "abroad" could be sentenced to up to eight years in prison, according to the criminal code of the GDR.

Separation of powers went against the principle of dictatorial power in the SED. The MfS was not only responsible for spying on its citizens for subversive political behavior but also for investigating political crimes, including "desertion of the republic." In his history of the MfS, Karl-Wilhelm Fricke came to the following verdict about the role of state security in the political proceedings of the GDR: "In reality, state security from the very beginning decisively influences the course of investigation and its subsequent proceedings."[3] The MfS also suggested to the prosecution the extent of the penalty.

The director of the film did not want to make a pure Stasi movie but rather to show the role and significance of the secret police for the SED dictatorship. At the same time he wanted to produce a thriller that would meet Hollywood expectations. The film makes the problem of the hierarchical connection between party and secret police a more personal one, and the character of Hempf (in his role as a member of the SED central committee) embodies the state party. In the name of the party Hempf orders the Stasi officer Grubitz to spy on the writer Georg Dreyman. This sets in motion Operation Dreyman, which then becomes the basis for the film's narrative.

For the MfS, the term "operative procedure" (*operativer Vorgang*, or "OV") meant the highest level of conspiratorial or concealed surveillance of suspicious individuals. What the MfS stressed—here in the administrative jargon of state security in 1976—was the preventive nature of the OV: "The goal-oriented development of operative procedures is a preventive measure to stop the effective emergence of hostile-negative energies, to prevent the introduction of possible damages, dangers, or other possible harmful consequences of hostile-negative activities and thereby to contribute in an important way to the continuous execution of the policies of the party and the state."[4] With this, the ministry officially determined the operative importance of OVs.

As a scholarly consultant to the film, I was responsible for the historical accuracy of facts in the script. But if I was the historical expert, Ulrich Mühe became for the director the specialist regarding the film's atmosphere. Mühe deservedly won an Oscar for his precise and emotionally distant portrayal of Wiesler. At this point I would like to introduce my personal memory of the actor. By 1989, Mühe was already a highly regarded actor at the Deutsches

Theater in East Berlin. By the early 1990s, he had gone through his Stasi records. According to his own account, he had washed his hands of the GDR. He acted on stage in Hamburg and Vienna in the 1990s, putting the state and his oppressive experiences behind him. By the time he assumed the role of Captain Wiesler, he played it without hatred or anger; he claimed he only needed to remember.

Donnersmarck chose the character of the MfS captain to project a single communist's crisis of faith during the final phase of the GDR. That represents the underlying theme of *The Lives of Others*. In the first instance, the film treats the deeply Christian questions of transformation and redemption as exemplified in Wiesler's refusal to serve. Donnersmarck's original idea for the film was inspired by a report by the Russian writer Maxim Gorky, who had chronicled Lenin's admiration for Beethoven's "Appassionata." Someone who experiences true art can no longer serve as a slave to dictatorship. Art is capable of piercing the armor of ideological worldviews and of reactivating individual conscience. To illustrate such a conflict of conscience, the director uses the words of Lenin quoted by Gorky. Lenin explains why he can't listen to Beethoven's music too often, drawing from it the opposite conclusions: "[This music] attacks the nerves. One is tempted to utter sweet stupidities and to stroke the heads of people, who live in such a disgusting hell and are able to produce something so beautiful. But nowadays, one shouldn't stroke people's heads; one's hand will be bitten off. One must smash in their heads, smash them in without pity, although we are, according to our own ideals, against all forms of violence against other human beings. Hm, hm, it is a devilishly difficult task!"[5]

At the beginning of the film, Wiesler is a devoted communist and, as such, a true believer, if we are to assume that communism was a secular religion. At the same time he is turned off by the cynical careerism of some comrades, reflected in the film in the person of his supervisor, Grubitz. When Wiesler, who lives alone, complains to Grubitz about the pressures of protecting socialism—"Don't you sometimes wish that communism would have already arrived?" he asks—Grubitz prescribes the services of an MfS prostitute as a cure for his depression—hardly true solace for a faithful communist. The noble goal should be to abolish all inequality between people, to abolish the state, and to bring about earthly paradise through violent socialist revolution. Wiesler yearns for this form of earthly happiness. It is an understandable wish, considering the dreary everyday reality of life in the "real existing" socialism of the GDR, where nothing then seemed to indicate that happiness was just around the corner, even though the Communist Party had pledged to achieve that goal politically.

Ever since the communist takeover of Russia in 1917, this visionary end goal of history was imperiled by socialism's imperialist enemies—at least according to the self-legitimizing fiction of the dictatorship. Already on December 20, 1917, Lenin had founded in response the All-Russian Commission to Combat Counterrevolution and Sabotage, or Cheka.[6] MfS members therefore proudly called themselves the Chekists of the GDR. Wiesler was obliged to make the following pledge: "As member of the Ministry for State Security, I will fight alongside the protective and security organs of the Soviet Union and its allied socialist countries against the enemies of socialism, even at risk to my life, and will fulfill all my duties to protect the state."

The Chekists needed the motivating forces of both faith and hatred to succeed mentally in their struggle against enemies both internal and external. While Wiesler still held onto the emotional qualities of a committed communist, the careerists' faith had turned into cynicism; only hatred remained. The interrogation scenes at the beginning of the film show the function of such hatred. It allowed the MfS to deal with suspects it interrogated as individuals only from a criminological point of view. Even if the person were not yet convicted, an arrest alone proved that he or she was an enemy or hostile-negative "element." The political mission of the MfS was to intervene actively and threateningly into the "lives of others" in order to change those lives at a fundamental level if they did not conform to party expectations. The party's expectations for "its people," both inside and outside the party, were laid out in programs, plans, directives, and clear parameters, such as those in the criminal code. At the root of their actions stood a dualistic Marxist-Leninist worldview motivated by class struggle that communists promoted in the GDR and in the world. The world political opposition between West and East was secured by the existence of two separate states in a divided Germany. This dichotomized worldview, structured conceptually, was binding, and it allowed the SED and its Chekists to give political categories to human behavior both within and without the GDR. This reduction of humans to categories affected artists and writers in particular. Minister of Culture Hempf unabashedly refers to Stalin when he says that writers are "engineers of the soul" who need to be controlled and utilized by the state. The conceptual elimination of personal traits permitted the MfS to categorize the "others" they had to spy on and combat, and it allowed them to convert those "others" into objects of hatred. Combined with the hatred of one's enemies, which was required by Chekists in their work, there was a faith in communism and the happiness of future generations. MfS captain Wiesler lives and works with such self-awareness until he assumes control of Operation Dreyman.

The MfS considers the writer Dreyman to be loyal to the party. But apparently Culture Minister Hempf, who has risen through the career ranks of the ministry, mistrusts him and orders an "operative procedure" against him. Wiesler is called on to organize this surveillance, instructed to hand over all his findings directly and only to Grubitz. After the suicide of a blacklisted theater director, Dreyman decides to publish the GDR's suicide statistics, confidential since 1977, in the West German newsmagazine *Der Spiegel*. He enters into negotiations with a *Spiegel* correspondent in his apartment, thinking that it could not be bugged. The correspondent agrees to publish the story and assures him anonymity.

At this point the question returns: is this fiction or lived history? To be able to answer that, I will first need to describe the process a GDR writer had to go through to be allowed to publish in the West. Such potential publications had to go through the copyright office, which was controlled by the state. In the case of an article on suicide, it would have been impossible to get that permission. Statistics such as these were confidential and to publish them would have violated a series of paragraphs in the GDR criminal code. The film hints at such paragraphs without explicitly mentioning them. For example,

Paragraph 97 (Espionage)
If a person collects for a foreign power confidential information or material detrimental to the interests of the German Democratic Republic, its institutions or its representatives, or for a secret service or for foreign organizations and their helpers; if he reveals such material or such information to them, transfers it over to them or in any other way makes it accessible to them; he will be convicted with no less than five years in prison.

Paragraph 99 (Treasonous Transfer of Information)
If a person transfers nonconfidential information detrimental to the interests of the German Democratic Republic over to places or individuals mentioned in Paragraph 97; if he collects or makes it accessible to them; he will be convicted with a prison sentence of between two and twelve years.

Paragraph 219 (Illegal Contacts)
If a person contacts organizations, institutions, or individuals whose goal is to pursue activities directed against the state order of the German Democratic Republic, or makes contact aware of such goals or activities, he will be convicted for up to five years.

Dissidence, opposition, and resistance within the Soviet Empire were common topics for the Hamburg newsmagazine *Der Spiegel*. It published texts written by Soviet dissidents and Polish and Czech civil rights leaders as well as literature forbidden in the GDR. Included among the writers forbidden in the GDR were Robert Havemann and Jürgen Fuchs, whose "memory protocols" of the time he spent under investigative arrest in Hohenschönhausen appeared in *Spiegel* in 1976–1977. The director used those protocols as a source for the interrogation scenes at the beginning of the film.

In January 1978, the newsmagazine published the manifesto of the Union of Democratic Communists in Germany from within the GDR. The publisher cited "mid- and high-level SED functionaries," who had requested anonymity for obvious reasons, as its sources. After 1989 it was disclosed that the man primarily responsible for the manifesto was Professor Doctor Hermann von Berg, a historian at the Humboldt University–Berlin. During the 1960s, Berg had worked for the press office of the GDR Ministers' Council. He was in charge of West German journalists, and GDR Minister President Stoph had sent him as a delegate to West Germany to help prepare the ground for the new policy of *Ostpolitik*. At the same time he reported as an informant (*inoffizieller Mitarbeiter*, or IM) to the main office for reconnaissance in the MfS. Hubertus Knabe revealed this information when he published the MfS file. A few years later, the historian was fed up with conditions in the GDR, and he entrusted his manuscript to East German *Spiegel* correspondent Ulrich Schwarz to be published. The so-called *Spiegel* Manifesto—which unleashed for a short time a hefty public debate involving both the *Pravda* in Moscow and the *Neues Deutschland,* central party organ of the SED—begins with a position statement toward the Soviet Union: "The political bureaucratic orthodoxy in Moscow has, in an objective sense, become reactionary. . . . It pursues a great-power politics that ignores the international workers' movement or its so-called brother nations." Stalinism and National Socialism are both conceived as "twins" due to their terrorist qualities. The manifesto describes conditions in the GDR through statements couched as suggestive questions. One such question: "Why is the GDR the world leader in divorces, suicides, and alcohol abuse?" The main target was the "clique at the top," which "did more damage to the idea of socialism in Germany and Europe than all so-called enemy propaganda." The criticism culminates in this statement: "No ruling class in Germany has sponged off the people and protected itself against the people as much as the two dozen families who treat our country like their own private commissary. . . . Take a close look at them: has any one of these self-appointed leaders come up with a single idea or written a book or an article? In any area of special-ization or even in the field of politics? . . . These political bureaucrats are painfully vain. Just count their official titles: We, Erich & Co., by the Mercy of Brezhnev, King of Prussia, etc."[7] The "clique at the top" responded to the manifesto's publication by closing the *Spiegel* office in East Berlin. The MfS arrested Hermann von Berg, stripped him of his professorship, and had him deported to West Germany.

The *Spiegel* Manifesto inspired the director in his portrayal of Drey-man's actions in the film. The manifesto's characterization of the top ruling families in the GDR informs Wiesler's change of heart. Wiesler soon finds out that the real reason that the "comrade culture minister" ordered him to spy on the writer was personally motivated. The love affair between the actress Christa-Maria Sieland and the writer annoys the minister. Hempf then uses his position as minister of culture to force an affair with Frau Sieland—the film presents their affair as "illicit sexual relations with a subordinate." In order to get his romantic rival out of the way, Hempf orders Grubitz to initiate an OV against the writer. The state has become a self-service shop for personal aggrandizement. The zealous MfS lackey Grubitz makes it clear to Wiesler that they both "have a lot to gain from this story . . . or to lose."

It is the moral corruption of the SED's "clique at the top," as criticized in the *Spiegel* Manifesto (a clique to which Hempf belongs), that turns Operation Dreyman into a goad for moral self-examination on the part of the communist Wiesler. Was it really a struggle against imperialist "diver-sion," or was the MfS being misused in order to manipulate a minister's love affair to his advantage? Hatred of the enemies of socialism is of little service to one confronted by such moral quandaries. Who is the enemy of socialism in this situation? The harassed actress; the writer, who until then had refused to take a stand in the internal debates in the GDR; or the minister, the party representative who had ordered him to find incriminat-ing evidence against the writer so as to pressure the actress to break off her relationship? Wiesler begins to encounter personal doubts in a situation where the friend-enemy schema no longer applies. It is at this point that the director introduces music as the catalyst in Wiesler's decision making. The "Sonata for a Good Man" frees him from his Chekist esprit de corps and initiates his transformation.

For the first time he questions his obligation to serve. A boy, shown playing, asks him if it is true that he works for the Stasi. Wiesler responds with his own question, asking the boy if he even knew "what that meant, the Stasi?" The boy responds: "They are bad men, who lock other people up . . . so my father says." Instinctively Wiesler wants to know the name of the boy's father but stops himself in midsentence. Members of the MfS were there to ensure "socialist legality" and his duty would have required him to uncover the father's name. To make such a statement was considered a crime, and a paragraph in the criminal code of the GDR dealt with it:

Paragraph 220 (Public Disparagement)
A person who disparages the state order or the organizations of the state, its institutions or its social organizations or its activities or measures in public will be convicted with up to three years in prison.

The boy absolves him of his actions: "But you are not an evil man."[8]

Wiesler is still completely loyal when Hempf initially hopes the Stasi will find something incriminating in Dreyman's apartment, but things become more serious after Wiesler's inner break: Dreyman decides to take a stand, agitating against conditions in the GDR with his *Spiegel* article on GDR suicide rates. Now Captain Wiesler cements the break. He keeps his supervisor in the dark about this criminal offense and falsifies information in the investigative protocols. Further, he tries to protect the actress from the minister's encroachments and tries to prevent Hempf from banning her from public performance. He uses his position as an MfS officer to protect her from persecution. He is forced to interrogate the newly arrested Christa-Maria Sieland in Hohenschönhausen to uncover the hiding place in Dreyman's apartment where the "evidence," the typewriter Dreyman used to type his *Spiegel* article, is concealed. Wiesler already knows the location through his surveillance. He now sees his chance. He commits the actress to work as an MfS informant (IM) so that he can release her after her confession. But his attempt at rescue ends in tragedy.

Before his supervisor Grubitz can get his commandos to search Dreyman's apartment, Wiesler has already removed the typewriter. The end of Operation Dreyman also ends Wiesler's career in the MfS.

By this time Mikhail S. Gorbachev had become the general secretary of the Soviet Communist Party. The *Neues Deutschland,* which heralds this news, lies on the passenger seat next to Grubitz as he puts an end to Wiesler's career. Here the film makes a symbolic reference to the beginning of the SED dictatorship's demise.

The writer discovers for the first time the identity of his "guardian angel" after he opens the MfS file on his case; this file contains Wiesler's falsified reports. With this, the film makes a subtle case that victims of repression and historians should have access to MfS files after the reunification of Germany in 1991. It was a form of belated self-liberation when victims could find out the identity of those who had served in the GDR security state, where by 1989 approximately 13,000 of the 91,000 employees were directing an army of 170,000 unofficial informants to realize the SED's fantasy of total surveillance of the country.

The film takes place during the GDR's final days. Again the question returns: is it fiction or is it lived history? Did Wiesler's change of heart and his resistance have any significance for the fate of the GDR? Officers in the MfS were members of the SED. As "guardians of socialism," they possessed a singular esprit de corps; they considered themselves elite. But even within their ranks there were growing doubts about conditions in the GDR after Gorbachev acceded to power in 1985. They experienced this in their work, but above all in the paralysis of the SED leadership, which had seemed to close its eyes to reality. Wiesler changes when he understands that the SED functionaries no longer believe in communism either. They are concerned with their privileges, their sybaritic lifestyle, and their personal power. He does not have energy to resist; he can only refuse to serve.

This internal renunciation was quite prevalent within the SED by 1989. In the course of the peaceful revolution there was a series of resistant actions taken by SED functionaries to thwart party dictates that ended up promoting peaceful revolution. On October 9, 1989, when the SED leadership in Leipzig tried to put a violent end to the Monday demonstrations through the use of increased police force, three regional secretaries of the SED, together with the director Kurt Masur, resisted the measure and signed an appeal against the use of violence. One day earlier the lord mayor of Dresden, Wolfgang Berghofer, received a group of demonstrators to discuss the situation in the city. His colleague in East Berlin acted in similar fashion; he involved the opposition in the city's investigations into police actions against demonstrators on October 7–8, 1989. Thanks to such measures, the SED power monopoly began to crumble on the spot in cities and communities throughout the GDR. Finally, one should mention the opening of borders in Berlin on the night of November 9–10, 1989. The borders were secured by an officer of the border police, who was responsible for their military protection, and by the passport control unit of the MfS, which supervised the flow of traffic. On that night, Major Manfred Sens of the border police and Lieutenant Colonel Harald Jäger of the MfS shared command over the border crossing on Bornholm Street. At 23:30, both men decided to stop their controls, allowing people free access from East to West. The Wall was open.

With the character of Wiesler, the film focuses on one man's broken biography from the days of the GDR, and it convincingly shows the mechanisms of repression in the SED-controlled state. *The Lives of Others* reveals how a single communist during the final days starts to understand that he is not chasing after enemies to realize a dream of humanity but is instead spying on people who wish only to fashion their own lives. He has been manipulated to act in the interest of a cynical clique at the top of party and state.

Donnersmarck frequently sought out advice in making this film. He accepted that advice, but the script is his own labor. His questions served the purpose of self-enlightenment; they were not meant to confirm a predetermined verdict. His goal was to produce a film that would have a fictitious story but would incorporate accurate historical details. The material for his narrative was based on the final phase of the second German dictatorship in the last century. Through his efforts, he was able to create an authentic film that leaves an indelible impression.

Notes

This essay was published in German as "Fiktion oder erlebt Geschichte? Zur Frage der Glaubwürdigkeit des Films *Das Leben der Anderen*," in *German Studies Review* 2008, Vol. 31, No. 3. Reprinted by permission.

1. This infamous quotation from Mielke can be found in Jens Gieseke, *Die hauptamtlichen Mitarbeiter der Staatssicherheit* (Berlin: Links, 2000), 385. Mike Dennis renders it slightly differently in *The Stasi: Myth and Reality* (Harlow: Longman, 2003), 39.

2. This reference and those that follow to the criminal code of the GDR can be found, in English, in *Penal Code of the GDR of January 12, 1968*, vol. 2 of *Law and Legislation in the German Democratic Republic* (Berlin: Association of German Democratic Lawyers, 1968).

3. See Karl Wilhelm Fricke, *Die DDR-Staatssicherheit: Entwicklung, Strukturen, Aktions-felder* (Cologne: Verlag Wissenschaft und Politik, 1982).

4. See Dennis, *The Stasi,* 114.

5. See Georg Lukács, *Lenin: A Study on the Unity of His Thought* (Cambridge, MA: MIT Press, 1971), 94.

6. Translator's note: This was the initial name for the Soviet state security organization that later took on various other names: GPU, OGPU, and KGB.

7. "Das Manifest des Bundes Demokratischer Kommunisten Deutschlands," in Dominik Geppert, *Störmanöver: Das "Manifest der Opposition" und die Schließung des Ost-Berliner "Spiegel"-Büros im Januar 1978* (Berlin: Christoph Links Verlag, 1996), 164, 172, 177, 174–75.

8. Though appearing in the published screenplay, this line is not spoken in the actual film.

9

The Ghosts Are Leaving the Shadows

Wolf Biermann

Translated by Lucy Powell

There are increasing numbers of West people in Germany who dilettant-ishly play the role of the noble procrastinator. In an argument about the involvement of East people in the crimes of the GDR regime, they prefer to opt out for the worldly-wise option of holding their tongues. This sort of eloquent silence always sets a twisted Hamlet soliloquy ringing in my ears:

> To be or not to be . . . No . . . to get involved or better not . . . that is the question. Whether 'tis nobler in the mind to keep stubbornly quiet about the Stasi troubles of the Ossis, or to dive headlong into a sea of slanging matches . . . No! I'm a Wessi, who has never had to suffer that sort of repression and who has never lived under the weight of a dictatorship. So I won't take an inflated moral stand; I prefer to confess modestly to being one of the little people, with fears and weaknesses. Whether I would have been courageous in the GDR or cowardly, whether I would have gone along with everything or at least cautiously refused, or whether I might even have dared oppose the regime—I cannot say. And this is why I'd rather not judge these things, not to mention judging the people who—who knows—only swam with the tide or, in good faith that they were doing the right thing, collaborated with the secret police or, simply in ignorance or fear, and with great sadness in their hearts, inflicted misery on others. I'll keep out of all this. I thank providence that I

was never forced to denounce, inform on, or torture anybody, and I'm very thankful that I never had to find out. Luckily it's all over, it's all in the past.

You come across this bogus declaration of bankruptcy more and more. But this sort of shabby modesty is nothing but a cowardly flight to what Immanuel Kant called "self-imposed immaturity." Anyone who says, "Who knows if I would have become a pig?" is only issuing themselves a precautionary whitewashing coupon for swinishness. No matter how you might have behaved back in the days of fear and danger, all that matters in the here and now is that you don't deny or downplay the wretchedness of others.

Two months ago, I was sitting in the formerly East German Kollwitz Platz in Berlin's Prenzlauer Berg district with five friends. Marianne Birthler gave us a sneak DVD preview of a film from a young unknown director about the GDR: *The Lives of Others.* All of us watching the film had opposed the regime; some of us were even its scarred jailbirds. When I read the name of the director, it occurred to me that this Florian Henckel von Donnersmarck had sent me the draft script for his film about the GDR secret police (the Stasi) two years or so ago. At the time I had flicked through it irritably. I wanted nothing to do with a project like this. I was convinced that this novice, this naïve upper-class kid who had been graced with being born so late in the West would never ever be capable of tackling this sort of GDR material, either politically or artistically.

When we'd finished watching the film, I was astounded, confused, pleasantly disappointed, and cautiously enthusiastic. A heated argument ensued. Two of my friends thought the film was full of inaccurate details. A minister of culture could never have had so much influence on the Stasi apparat as the film showed. After all, the MfS, or Ministry for State Security, was strictly and staunchly what it was set up to be and what it wanted to be: "the shield and sword of the party"—no more, no less. A lieutenant colonel in Erich Mielke's company would never ever have taken marching orders from some comrade minister! The decisions were always made by the party leadership; the state was only the executive organ. And there was absolutely no way that the Stasi would have been drawn into exercising its powers at the behest of a cultural functionary just because this flaccid individual had got the elderly hots for some GDR starlet who lived with her ambitious and successful GDR playwright.

And another inaccuracy: the film portrayed the young writer as someone who conformed to the system. But only truly oppositional writers were "operatively handled," informed on, tapped, and followed to that extent. And and and! And young officers of the MfS would never ever have goofed about in plain clothes in their academy lecture hall! These and other details are just plain wrong. And! And! And anyway the film put a soft pedal on the totalitarian reality.

I was among those in our friendly circle of experts who considered these fuzzinesses beside the point. The basic story in *The Lives of Others* is insane and true and beautiful—by which I mean really very sad. The political tone is authentic; I was moved by the plot. But why? Perhaps I was just won over sentimentally because of the seductive mass of details, which look like they were lifted from my own past between the total ban on my work in 1965 and denaturalization in 1976. So uncertainty and suspicion linger on: if such Saul-Paul conversions of Stasi officers really did take place, where were similar shining examples after the fall of the Wall? No one explained themselves publicly or privately to me or my "degenerate" friends, still less apologized for a crime, which only onlookers in the East and West ring seats of the historical boxing ring could waive off blithely . . .

When I watch this film through the eyes of my dead friend the writer Jürgen Fuchs, of course it rings home that in the Hohenschönhausen remand prison things were a lot more brutal than they are in this film. The mild-tempered Jürgen Fuchs would have had a fit had he been sitting there with us. He would presumably have said: "Now the myrmidons of the dictatorship are being humanized! GDR life grew more brutal, more gray, and more terrible by the day. Are Stasi criminals like Mielke and Markus Wolf being softened in the wash like poor old Adolf in the last days in the Führerbunker under the Reich's chancellery?"

I cannot know whether the wonderful conversion of the Stasi chief is a historical lie or an artistic understatement. We are all addicted to evidence of people's ability to change for the good.

I know that decades ago Aleksandr Solzhenitsyn was out to achieve the greatest effect, but it was not in one of his thick books where all the horrifying mass murders and systematic horrors in *The Gulag Archipelago* are truthfully described and listed with encyclopedic meticulousness. No, it was in his very first novella, *A Day in the Life of Ivan Denisovich*, that he tried to achieve the strongest effect in the world. Here Solzhenitsyn does nothing more than describe one of the more pleasant days of an ordinary prisoner in an ordinary labor camp in the Stalin era, with no attractive torturing: a refined piece of underexaggeration. And it was precisely this age-old device that succeeded in breaking down people's inhibitions in East and West about facing unbearable truths. And Solzhenitsyn even managed to reach people in the USSR who knew the blow-by-blow details firsthand because there too, after the Twentieth Party Congress following Khrushchev's secret speech about the crimes of the Stalin era, this little book went into print—sadly, only for a brief period. However, the effect was long lasting and in a back-to-front way it took effect in the GDR, back to front because it was printed only in West Germany.

Back to our film, *The Lives of Others.* This is the story: a professional people "corroder," a bull-headed "fighter on the invisible front," gets corroded himself. The MfS captain Gerd Wiesler is a tough cookie but he softens up. He eavesdrops via phone bugs on lovers and then after hours he sneaks back to the "actually existing socialist"–tiled coffin of his modern flat and creeps into his empty bed. Another time in his sterile room, he answers the call of nature with a fifteen-minute rent girl from the MfS sex service. This man is at least as lonely as his victims in solitary confinement and incomparably worse off than the actress and her writer, whom he and his subordinates have to listen in on and shadow round the clock.

In the attic above the bugged flat he transcribes word for word the discussions and the silences of the intellectuals he is "operatively handling." And he is increasingly seduced by their liveliness. By the end of the story he is ruined for this wretched job as a "people corroder." With a beautiful twist he goes kaput while professionally making others kaput, and this is the fairy-tale variation of the "deformation professionelle."

I have similar stories to tell involving two women when I lived at Chauseestraße 131. I lay in the clutches of two brave fighting ladies who were working in Mielke's service and who had the special mission of defeating the "songwriter" and people's enemy with erotic weapons, and who then de-conspired and deserted Mielke's erotic brigade.

This film was able to convey things to me that I could never have imagined "being real."

In the ten thousand pages of my Stasi files, I found around 215 aliases of a number of unofficial employees, vulgo: *Spitzel,* or informers. Of course I know many of their faces. The documents are also strewn with the real family names of umpteen official employees, all officers: in other words, higher-ranking pen pushers, like comrades Reuter and Lohr, in other words, characters like those in the film. The artwork lends these faceless scoundrels the facial expressions of the actors, which I can now read. Lohr and Reuter worked for many years as part of the Central Operative Operation "Poets" on systematically "corroding" me—as the chemical terminus technicus of Stasi jargon phrases it. Two of the twenty or so measures against dissidents stand there, typed in a long list by two Stasi index fingers on the office typewriter: "Destruction of all love relationships and friendships." Another: "Faulty medical treatment."

I have never attempted to get personally acquainted with any of these high-ranking criminals since the collapse of the GDR. These ominous apparitions are almost all still alive and they are drawing pensions as civil servants of the reunified Bundesrepublik Deutschland. And it's clear that hardly any of these perpetrators have ever forgiven their victims. And what's more, these senior lackeys of the GDR who got off the hook so comfortably have certainly never sought out a discussion with the people they systematically pursued for decades on end.

Certainly, they were somewhat altered as film characters, but for the first time I saw these phantoms as human beings, right down to their inner contradictions. The ghosts are stepping out of the shadows. Sometimes a work of art can have more documentary clout than actual documents, whose truth is doubted both by the perpetrators—of course—and, more painfully, by readers of the documents who bore easily.

Captain Wiesler's superior, Lieutenant Colonel Anton Grubitz, is played by the actor Ulrich Tukur. This strong character actor lends the ideologically encrusted silhouettes in the cave of my mind human features at last, behind which the remains of a face even emerge. And so the cardboard cutout villains in my life are finally given the experience of real flesh and blood, and I can even make out in each ravaged human countenance the flashing of all the colors in the black-and-white rainbow.

Ulrich Tukur rose to fame when twenty or so years back in Peter Zadek's production of Joshua Sobol's *Ghetto* at the Hamburger Schauspielhaus, he gave a brilliantly brutal performance as a young SS man—in other words, the more interesting villain. I saw the controversial play back then—all skeptical, eyes squinted together. In a television feature, Tukur mentioned that he perhaps enjoyed playing difficult, cynical, and cruel characters because in his own life he'd never had anything to do with that sort of suffering, conflict, or adversity. His private life had so far been without any real catastrophe or profound desperation or disappointments.

Yeah, right! I thought, Tukur, you philosophical clown, you don't need the experience of being imprisoned in a ghetto. A brilliant actor like you doesn't need an SS father and doesn't need to have been a real Stasi man.

An artist so loved by the muse doesn't first have to wade through vile netherworlds and bloodbaths.

I can't get over it that such a West-born directing greenhorn like Donnersmarck and a handful of established actors are able to deliver such an unbelievably realistic genre study of the GDR with what is probably a purely invented story. He didn't go through any of it! And yet a young man like this can have his say! This West boy is obviously quite adequately equipped to judge and even condemn. Not only can he have his say, he has something to say. And he doesn't need any whitewashing coupons.

Every life, even the so-called easy, well-protected ones, sharpen the way you look at things. Even a conflict-lite CV provides the most protected child from a good home with the capacity to know misery and what is crooked and what is straight. In the darkest reaches of our hearts, we all know what heartache and bliss mean, treachery and cowardice, uprightness and bravery.

Which is why this director succeeded, without the painful lessons of a GDR socialization, in conveying what it felt like to be subjected to a Kafkaesque dictatorship. Florian Henckel von Donnersmarck shows us what a crazy and complicated mix of good and evil is contained within the human breast, and in what dreadful disarray. The most disconcerting things about pigs are their human traits. But despite all the complicated complications in human affairs, what Father God said in the Bible to all his earthly children still holds: "Let your yes be yes and your no be no."

In the past, my ass! We obviously carry this deep in our soul-genes: nothing is really completely over. And nothing is all in the past.

A lot of people in both the East and West are sick to the teeth of the discussions about the Stasi and the GDR dictatorship, and between you and me: I'm just the same. After my Stasi ballads from 1966, my lampoons of the corrupt old men in the Politburo, and my polemical essays after the fall of the GDR, I don't need any more. But I don't trust myself on this issue. This debut film makes me suspect that the truly deep-reaching confrontation with Germany's second dictatorship is only just beginning.

And perhaps those who never experienced all the misery should take over now.

Note

The English translation of this essay originally appeared at signandsight.com, March 29, 2006, and is reprinted with permission.

10

AGAINST FORGETTING

A Conversation with Joachim Gauck

Paul Hockenos

Joachim Gauck, born in 1940 in the Baltic Sea port city of Rostock, was a Protestant pastor in the German Democratic Republic (GDR). He was a staunch proponent of democracy and human rights, though not a member of an oppositional group. When the Berlin Wall fell, he was one of the cofounders of the New Forum alliance and was elected on its ticket in January 1990 to the first (and last) democratic parliament in East Germany. Mr. Gauck was also chairman of Gegen Vergessen—Für Demokratie (Against Forgetting— For Democracy), an NGO that fights left- and right-wing extremism and promotes coming to terms with the legacy of the two totalitarian regimes in German history. He remains a prominent voice in Germany on these issues, appearing regularly in the media and in public.

This interview (conducted for this volume) took place on September 29, 2011, in Mr. Gauck's offices in downtown Berlin. Paul Hockenos conducted the interview and subsequently translated it into English.

Paul Hockenos: When did you first see *The Lives of Others* and what was your initial reaction?

Joachim Gauck: I saw the film before it opened to the public since I was asked to write a review for the German magazine *Stern*. I was greatly impressed from the get-go, not least because the film had an incredible cast, from the lead roles all the way to the smaller supporting roles. Donners-marck succeeded brilliantly in inspiring this cast, which included some of

Germany's most famous actors and actresses. But above all I was moved by the atmosphere of fear that it conveyed. The film was a haunting expedition into a bygone world. I titled the review "Ja, so war es!" (Yes, It Was This Way!).[1] The film revisits a time when people's everyday lives were blighted by fear and conformity. I call this the "fear-conformity syndrome." The film portrays the audacious, arrogant attacks of the state against "the others," in this case artists. Everyone who sees the film understands why the past for so many isn't really past. The injuries or even just the impressions that we carry around are evident even today, long after the demise of the dictatorship. So intensive was the pressure to conform, so omnipresent was the fear.

PH: But not everybody was as impressed as you were, particularly many of those who had lived in the East. In fact, the film provoked a good deal of fierce criticism.

JG: I knew from the beginning that there'd be resistance and from three very different corners: from the former dissidents, from part of the old establishment, and from the broad ranks of the conformists (*die Angepassten*). The former anticommunist dissidents inevitably retorted, "Here comes a Wessi trying to tell *us* an East story." They pointed out that there's a lot that's not strictly factual, as if the film were a documentary. So they latched onto inaccuracies in certain scenes, like the construction of the surveillance system in the attic of an apartment building. This was indeed a bit bizarre. It never happened that way. But the scene provided a great, evocative image, and after all it's a feature film. Yet many took scenes like that one as proof somehow that the director and the scriptwriter hadn't engaged adequately with the material, which simply wasn't the case. They had prepared very thoroughly, in fact for several years.

This reaction from the ex-dissident circle is a protest against what they understand as an expropriation of their experiences. They were victims and now they're concerned they're no longer in possession of their own narrative. They feel like they're just ingredients in a larger-than-life story that others are telling regardless of the facts.

Because a feature film is not a historical documentary, it can be freer with the historical facts. It can portray the Stasi protagonist as better than this type really was, as long as it doesn't sugarcoat the whole story and end up an outright falsification. But the opposite is the case with this film: it unmasks; it doesn't sweeten. Take the figure of the culture minister who must have the beautiful actress. He gets her. Where allegiance comes up short, fear and the prospect of losing her career make her act.

Then there's the former establishment. They don't like any kind of documentation, any retelling, or any scholarly research into the brute facts of the dictatorship. They're not even sure that it was a dictatorship.

The final group, always the largest in any dictatorship, is those who lived quite well by conforming. This included the cultural elite. They say, "Oh, it wasn't like that at all. If it had been, then we would have noticed it and we'd have resisted it in a very different way." A well-known Berlin actor said, "How should I explain this to my children? It simply wasn't this way!"

In terms of remembering dictatorships, it is incredibly important to recognize the milieu from which certain memories emerge. Almost always in the immediate aftermath of dictatorships there is a nostalgic wistfulness about the days of the dictatorship. This happened right after World War II: there was a classic expression then in Germany, "Not everything was bad under the Führer." Hitler divided human beings into those whose lives were worthy and those whose were not and brought so much destruction and so much suffering and terror, yet still people didn't think about these brutal facts but rather said, "Well, we didn't notice anything and everybody had work. There was the war and this with the Jews, but not everything was bad." This "not everything was bad" motif obstructs an inner reckoning—it prevents shame, guilt, mourning, all of these things.

In West Germany there was a vigorous debate and discussion about memory and the Nazi years. The "guilt question" was integral to the 1960s student movement in the Federal Republic. Alexander and Margarete Mitscherlich's 1967 book, *Die Unfähigkeitzutrauern* (The Inability to Mourn) had a huge impact, even though I think this book should have been read a bit more carefully.[2] Some of its theses are certainly open to critique, but it prompted many Germans to think more deeply about the end of the dictatorship. The mass movements and an array of publications like the Mitscherlich book enabled West Germany, as civil society grew stronger, to bring elements of guilt, recognition of guilt, the ability to mourn and express shame, into the public consciousness.

And this was so strong that by the 1970s it was no longer a healthy self-consciousness. The West Germans became too self-conscious. In the 1950s they repressed it, proud of their economic miracle, then came the student movement and a new narrative began about the German who could never be trusted. Many Germans didn't even want to be "Germans" at all but rather saw themselves as "Hamburger" and "European" or "Bavarian" and "European." That's what you heard then. But this has changed somewhat since reunification and we're on the road to a healthy normalization. That's very welcome.

PH: Does the film accurately portray everyday life in the GDR?

JG: Yes, generally, although again there are some who think otherwise. Take those people who weren't part of the communist leadership but were functionaries of one kind or another, who may never have had any contact with the Stasi. They think this portrayal of everyday life in the film is exaggerated. In fact, they simply didn't notice it. Such a stratum is not uncommon in tyrannical regimes. In despotic Arab regimes, in China, in the Nazi era, there are people who had relatively apolitical jobs and managed to live their lives and get by without problems.

This film is so remarkable because it takes the perspective of the oppressed to explain this period in history. As a pastor, I come from circles in which the relationship to the regime ranged from standoffish to outright oppositional. In these circles the presence of the state security was palpable at all times. I experienced how in our youth groups sixteen- and seventeen-year-olds were recruited to act as informants. They came right to me and told me about it. I was so furious that even minors were being recruited that I marched into the city hall and asked the person responsible for church issues whether this was in the spirit of their party, to recruit teenagers as informants? Anyone who belonged to these kinds of religious circles or even anyone who had an opinion of their own knew very well how intensively the Stasi worked.

Of course, there were those who didn't know exactly, those who had made their peace with the regime and had internalized it so thoroughly that their conformity was simply a given aspect of the way things were. This existence isn't akin to the life of a citizen but rather to the life of an obedient subject. In premodern societies it was quite normal to be a subject. Likewise, many people in the GDR didn't even recognize their own powerlessness. Under kings and queens, if you're upstanding and loyal, then nothing can happen to you.

But there is one scene that illustrates perfectly how fear can be used as an instrument of power even among this category of people. It is the scene in which the neighbor of the playwright Georg Dreyman, an older woman, happens to witness the Stasi searching Dreyman's apartment. She's told by the Stasi officer that she "hasn't seen anything" and that the state security knows very well that her daughter studies medicine. The woman then knows exactly what is at stake. She won't say anything to anybody about it. This latter period of the GDR dictatorship was different than the Stalinist period, when dissenters were abducted, tortured, and murdered. In this later period the regime had on kid gloves. Its instruments were softer and clearly on display: we can lift you up; we can bring you down. The old woman reacts at once because she knows this without thinking. This scene is priceless because it stands for a vast array of intimidations and similar measures relied upon by the regime.

Those people who claim that they were never intimidated by these kinds of measures—well, it's only because they've forgotten. For example, even putting the Stasi aside for a minute, there was a phenomenon called *Kadergespräche*, or "cadre talks." Say you're a teacher at a school and you're supposed to be promoted, or a professor who wants to become head of the department. Inevitably comes the question: "Are you a member of our party?" And at that moment one feels enormous pressure to conform. Some intellectuals are so flexible that they act as if they are genuinely convinced socialists when in fact they're just bending to the pressure. It is a humiliating experience and people don't want to remember humiliating experiences—neither the perpetrators nor the victims. That's why they often black out their own powerlessness as they experienced it. They remember it as if they were normal professionals in their fields like, say, professors anywhere else, and then maybe add as an afterthought, "Oh, well, yes, one had to be a member of the party." But this person doesn't talk about the moment when he had to join the party.

I have a brother who is a sailor, a ship's engineer. He eventually gained the qualification required to be a ship's chief engineer. His superior congratulated him and asked, "So are you already in the party?" Those who didn't want to join would often say, "Oh, I'm really not mature enough yet for these kinds of important issues." This response gave the impression that there could be hope he'd join at some point in the future, just not at the moment. It might work. Or the response might be, "Yes, well, if you're not mature enough for the party then you're not mature enough to be in charge on a ship." So you remain as second or third in command. My brother didn't join the party and then a couple of years later they wouldn't even let him on board a ship at all. This happened a million times over, and whoever says he doesn't know it is either lying or repressing it. For example, every single school had a principal who was in the SED [Socialist Unity Party, the communist party], every one, even in such a little country like ours.

PH: And is the work of the Stasi portrayed accurately in the film?

JG: Yes, very much so. The film starts with a very interesting scene: a taped interrogation is played in front of a class of cadets at the Stasi's officer-training facilities, where they're taught the techniques of the state security. This includes perfidious and scurrilous methods that violate people's most intimate space, in this case the capturing and preserving of their personal body odor. This scene is in the film because Donnersmarck saw how astounded visitors to the archives were when they saw these little yellow strips of cloth bottled up in sealed jars and stored away there. It is a small example of how arrogant a regime can be in a dictatorship: people's most intimate spaces aren't off limits; civil liberties count for nothing.

The communist model could be established only with the help of a strong repressive apparatus, including a strong secret police. Contrary to democracies, in communist states the intelligence service and the secret police are one, like the Gestapo was in the Third Reich. In the Federal Republic, an example of a *Rechtstaat* [a state based on the rule of law], the Federal Office to Protect the Constitution does not have policing responsibilities. When the basic liberties of the individual are not protected, when there are neither administrative courts (*Verwaltungsgerichte*) nor constitutional courts, and where power is absolute, then there is nothing to stop the state from breaching the private sphere.

The film shows this at a number of levels: the covert searching of apartments, the coercion of informants, the bugging of the bedroom, the blackmailing of people in difficult situations. Take the case of the leading lady, who has a drug addiction. The Stasi knows this and uses it: "We can take care of this for you. Yes, it's criminal but if you're with us we'll help you out." It is extremely realistic. This happened all the time. This means of recruiting IMs [*inoffizieller Mitarbeiter,* nonstaff informants] wasn't the rule, but neither was it uncommon. It wasn't the rule because it could also trigger a defensive reaction. The rule was to talk and talk and talk until eventually the person in question caved in.

The German writer and playwright Carl Zuckmayer wrote a play called *The Devil's General* in 1946,[3] which became a popular film in the 1950s. It's not a historical work, but Zuckmayer reaches out to begin a discourse about Nazism with Germans after the war. *The Lives of Others* does this in much the same way, but with communism. Of course, many of our former human rights activists complained that it was a fairy-tale Saul and Paul story, the transformation of a perpetrator to a helper. They rightly point out that this type doesn't appear anywhere in the archive's files. But the story is fiction and the author poses the question to those who had power twenty years ago: *could* you have acted this way? So it invites them to ask themselves what was possible within the parameters of their individual situations. This is the film's greatest accomplishment. The Stasi officer's actions were not outside the realm of the possible.

Moreover, there were examples of people within the system who wanted out. For example, the last death sentence in the GDR was carried out in 1981 against a Stasi officer convicted of treason for making plans to escape the country. So there were people in the Stasi who were prepared to question. But such a transformation as in *The Lives of Others* didn't happen. The film underscores that we always have a choice, even in dictatorships. We don't have every choice, but we can act in many different ways. The film portrays this well. The theater director changes his mind; the Stasi officer changes his mind; Dreyman changes his mind. There are people who want to help the truth come to life. And one has more allies than one thinks when one looks around closely. The film poses the stark question: is civil courage something for you too?

PH: Did the film provoke an important debate in Germany?

JG: Looking back on it today, I'd say this wasn't the case. The important debates, at least among those involved in the issues, were already well under way. The real accomplishment of the film was the portrayal of a serious political issue in the form of a popular cultural product. As a feature film in movie theaters everywhere in Germany in 2006 and 2007, it disseminated a certain judgment about the dictatorship that had already been established through scholarship, books, conferences, and media debates in the 1990s. So the film enabled our rejection of the dictatorship to be reflected by a much broader public, one that usually isn't interested in political discourses.

In Germany we have experience with narrative elements of film or other cultural products that pick up a topic anew. Take, for example, the 1970s American TV series *Holocaust*, which tells the story of the Holocaust like in a soap opera through a single family, the Weisses. Serious historians like

Claude Lanzmann and Raul Hilberg probably rolled their eyes and said, "Oh, God! How banal!" But the series was on television at a time when everyone could watch it. It thus had enormous reverberations and impact. My parents, who lived in the northern city of Rostock, cried when they saw it. As a young person I had asked them whether they had noticed the persecution of Jews in Rostock. They said, "No, not at all." They couldn't tell me anything. But after they had seen the TV series, thirty years after the events, suddenly I heard names of Jewish classmates of my father, names of Jewish lawyers from my hometown. I witnessed my parents moved in a way I had never seen before.

Germany's experience with this film is so fascinating because it was after the waves of political education and well after the student movement discourses. But then came the series—a generation after the war—and with it another wave of introspection, not with new analysis or facts but with an emotional element and comprehensible in a different way because ordinary people's personal histories were tied up with a political theme. That's why I'm always skeptical when political discourses—even those delegitimizing a dictatorship—are confined to scholars and pedagogues. That's one of the greatest assets of this and other such films: through tragedy or even sometimes through comedy, people can distance themselves from the subject matter and recognize something for the first time.

PH: One of the essays in this book addresses the issue of moral corruption. Does the film correctly portray the difficulty of living a moral life in a dictatorship like the GDR?

JG: A feature film naturally has to spice things up and condense the passage of time. But we are, for example, confronted with the question of how one goes about publishing a critical text in a dictatorship. What do I have to do as a playwright or theater director in order to continue to work as such? We see this in the character of Jerska, a blacklisted director and typical resident of the Berlin district of Prenzlauer Berg, who says, "No, I'm simply not going along with this charade any longer." He's an artist and has crossed the Rubicon: he won't make compromises anymore. There were these people—and his character takes his own life in the film. Others simply picked up and left the country. Our greatest poets left the GDR, figures like Sara Kirsch, Peter Huchel, Reiner Kunze, Günter Kunert, and many, many others. They left; others disappeared into suicide. This kind of brutality isn't always immediately visible in the late phases of a dictatorship. But you see this very clearly in the film, as if through a magnifying glass.

This very realistically reflects a time when the regime is no longer Stalinist but is nevertheless ready and willing at all times to break people. And if people don't go along with it, then their life space is restricted or their futures snuffed out. And that's why in such societies there are different grades of conformism, from unconvinced minimal loyalty to ultra-conformity. The ultra-conformist is not only a member of the state party but also a secret police informant who spies on his peers. That's the highest form of betrayal: a snitch who's not even a professional snitch, but rather does it for a higher good. An excellent example of this type is one of Germany's current editors in chief, Arnold Schölzel, who runs a dubious communist newspaper called *Junge Welt.* He clearly betrayed many of his colleagues in the GDR period, yet he won't admit even today that it was wrong. His loyalty at the time was elsewhere, he says. This is one of the tricks of dictatorships: they manage to win the loyalty of such people by transforming the values of the past into the highest values of the party that rules the country.

PH: Some critics charge that *The Lives of Others* is a typical West German take on the GDR. Is it?

JG: It is sometimes the case that a picture becomes clearer when viewed from a distance. We're still writing books about the Roman Empire and ancient Greece. We weren't there and nevertheless we make judgments and win new insights. Of course, eyewitnesses will always be important. But the first-person participant may not be in the best position to abstract from the event, sometimes because he is still so shocked and traumatized by it. Thus they are also easily offended when they feel that the source of their trauma is being trivialized. "This wasn't like that!" they say. "This officer could never have existed! Only a Bavarian count could concoct such a figure! Life was much worse than that!" They simply don't grasp the artistic endeavor behind the attempt to explain how brutal it really was by transforming it into a work of fiction. A cooler, distanced perspective is often very, very important.

PH: The first wave of films about life in the GDR were comedies. I think of *Sun Alley, Good Bye Lenin!* and *Heroes Like Us.* And then with *The Lives of Others* came the tragedies. Why? Does it reflect a shift in the process of remembering the GDR?

JG: Perhaps it's actually good that the tragedies didn't come out first. There were plenty of TV documentaries and other products that were duly hardnosed on topics like forced adoptions, prison conditions, political justice, etc. As for these comedies, well, they weren't always comedies. *Sun Alley* isn't really a comedy. There are fantasy and humorous elements in it, but a tough message comes through. Take the boy who because of a record album becomes a victim of border troops. That's terrible. Or in *Good Bye Lenin!* where the mother constructs this cozy socialist world upon a lie, namely, that the father abandoned the children. In fact, he wrote one letter after another but they landed behind a kitchen cabinet. That's not funny at all. I know people who cried watching *Good Bye Lenin!* What's interesting about this approach is that it didn't try to shock people. You can also get distance from something by laughing at it. With humor you can unpack something that you hadn't dared to touch before. So you can't say this approach is undemocratic. It's another artistic form to get to the heart of the matter at hand. And this is often not recognized by our political activists. Of course, there are also nostalgic products, too, the likes of which you can find on television these days. But these films don't fall into that category. They're serious films and deserve to be taken seriously.

PH: Are you satisfied with the way that Germany has addressed the GDR legacy?

JG: Essentially, yes, though we also created a serious problem for ourselves. The agents of the regime party, namely, the state security, were treated more rigorously than the regime's actors themselves. We managed to remove Stasi informers, even some who were relatively unimportant, from public service while important leading party officials—from the district, municipal, and central committee levels—remained uncontested in top positions. Thus we didn't have a decommunization analogous to denazification in postwar Germany.

The postcommunist forces claimed there was a witch hunt, which is nonsense. The renewal of the public service in eastern Germany wasn't driven by ideological criteria. The ultra-conformists who actively worked against their fellow countrymen were deemed "less trustworthy" and this was an impediment for them to serve in the public sector. An autonomous, federal authority was established to administer these files and then share them with eligible persons according to legal norms. We also shared relevant files with the public institutions when it concerned civil servants. It thus was sometimes the case that the rights of the former rulers and their former subordinates were compromised. Admittedly, this kind of lustration is an intervention into personal rights. But compared to the rights of victims, who had no external confirmation they were oppressed, it was of secondary consequence. And that's why German lawmakers opened the secret police files to our authority.

What we didn't do—and what we should have done—is put the leading strata of the SED on a par with the senior officers of the Stasi. The failure to do so caused an imbalance. It was a mistake made by the democratic forces that were in the parliament in 1989. It was a lack of will. We thought a general declaration that the SED was a criminal organization didn't reflect reality. The SED wasn't just the leadership but rather 2.3 million members, most of whom entered the party to ensure themselves and their families economic and political security. It wasn't because they wanted to repress other people. And that's why it seemed unfair to undertake a full-scale de-communization. The Czechs did this. But to us it looked disproportionate. We could, however, have pushed through a limited form of de-communization that vetted the operational representatives of the regime as we did their peers in the Stasi. Here we failed.

PH: How is the legacy of totalitarianism still reflected in Germany's eastern states?

JG: Not only in Germany, but everywhere in the world where people are powerless over an extended period of time, political relations are formed the likes of which we know from premodern times. This subject mentality has an impact on society. Sometimes different vocabulary is used: the Nazis employed the term "allegiance" (*Gefolgschaft*) and the communists wanted "conviction." They wanted us convinced that we grasped the goal of history and the party as the avant-garde, as the cutting edge of progress, and so on. . . . This is a semantic trick to disguise the real power relations, namely, an excess of power for the few and the powerlessness of the many. This power is not invested by God's grace as in the times of absolutism but rather the *Weltgeist* [world spirit] evokes this specific form of rule. We are the last phase of history's progress. The cleverest and most important of us are in this party and the leadership represents this progress. And who wants to be against progress? So you have to approve this authority for eternity.

This is the Leninist mantra—once communists have power, they should never give it up.

This disrespect for the will of the majority is an explicit rejection of the European and North American democratic project. All of those elements integral to the evolution of this project—the rule of law, separation of powers, civil liberties, human rights—were disparaged or minimalized in order to consolidate the power of the regime. Naturally, a lot of people can't see through this because they are apolitical, especially many artists and actors. For the most part, actors are the type who when given good contracts will say they didn't notice anything. In the Nazi period it was the same way. And it exists in every dictatorship. If you go to Chile there are a lot of people who'll say that everything wasn't bad under Pinochet. They don't discuss how the military dictatorship secured its absolute power or what crimes it committed. They experienced a certain security in their milieu and for this they are thankful.

These kinds of divided discourses are typical. The real legacy of dictatorships is not the "captive mind" that the Polish poet and Nobel Prize recipient Czesław Miłosz describes—although there is this, too—but the accommodation of powerlessness. Powerlessness becomes the norm. The internalizing of the oppressor is a phenomenon we know from rape victims. Kids say, "That can't be wrong since it was Father" or an uncle. "They were kind." The soul protects itself by a loving internalization of the perpetrator. We see this in societies in which powerlessness is denied. Supposed or actual material security is posited as a fundamental value, but behind this vanishes the basic rights and freedoms of citizens.

This accommodation of powerlessness leaves a kind of blight across all postcommunist societies. All transitional societies are marked by a deep division: some wake up, grasp the new situation, and relish being a citizen. The others say it's impossible, it's all a pack of lies, it was always like that but now has a new name. The fearfulness engendered by the dictatorship then looks for new objects of fear. These feelings of inferiority can thus be perpetuated. The psyche duplicates what it learned under the previous regime in the new political process. This legacy of the dictatorship weighs heavily on transitional societies: fewer people exercise their own initiative or creativity, and they shirk self-responsibility. These are elements essential to civil society.

But when you've already learned in school how to adapt and conform—no school newspaper, no class speaker; when you don't have a proper trade union in workplaces; when you have no vote; when universities have no research freedom; and there is no media freedom—then this principle of subjugation is normal. And the principle of resisting the system is abnormal. The eastern German or Soviet populations lived this for forty-five or fifty-six or seventy years—they ceased to be *citizens in any meaningful sense.* There can be a minority who learns more quickly. You see this more strongly in countries like Poland where there is a deeply rooted love for freedom and a tendency to see the whole process more positively than in eastern Germany or the former Czechoslovakia. Apart from the economic and environmental disasters caused by communism, the most tragic legacy is this perpetuated, internalized powerlessness.

PH: There's a debate in Germany about closing the Stasi Archives and winding down the processing of the GDR past. When will Germany finally be finished with coming to terms with the GDR past?

JG: Look how grotesquely inaccurate the many predictions were that Germany's coming to terms with the National Socialist past was finally at an end after the Wall fell, that the Germans would eventually forget about it. On the fiftieth and sixtieth anniversaries of the war's end and the defeat of the Nazi dictatorship there was a tremendous flood of scholarly publications and a rich debate over issues such as the war, war guilt, Nazi crimes, and the Holocaust. That's why it's very hard to predict when a debate over the past will be over.

But it could become marginalized and diluted for a very banal reason. Four-fifths of today's Germans are western Germans. And of the eastern Germans only roughly half see any point in processing the GDR past. Moreover, eastern Germany isn't a closed niche. There is no special eastern German discourse, but rather discourses like the delegitimation of dictatorship happen with western German scholarship and on a European level, not in a little snow dome just for eastern Germans. Will western Germans continue to examine this second failed German democracy project with the intensity it deserves?

Moreover, there is a great danger it will be overshadowed by the dominance of the Holocaust discourse. I'm a German and will always see Nazi rule and the Holocaust as a black hole in history. But when the western Germans claim that it was only Nazi rule that devastated Europe, then they're making a serious historical mistake. In Poland, Ukraine, the Baltics, and elsewhere live people who dreamed of freedom, dignity, and human rights.

Some of them experienced not only powerlessness but death. It is a grave illusion to think that remembrance of the Holocaust is enough to secure democracy. There are many very different ways that our democratic values can be annulled. Western Europe lacks a feeling for the seriousness of this narrative, something that we former inhabitants of the GDR share with the Central and Eastern Europeans.

There are European intellectuals who say that anticommunism is somehow uncool, and that it doesn't belong in democratic political culture. But you can only think this if you're far enough away from the suffering that Soviet communism inflicted. In fact, the West has to learn that there are two kinds of anti-communism. One stems from conservative arrogance, such as that in the United States and West Germany. This variety is useless. The other variety stems from suffering, the deprivation of rights, and powerlessness. And if you're not able to feel this, then you lack something as a human being. And, sadly, western Germany and western Europe still have to learn this. The seriousness of the threat of communism to our democracy project has to be respected.

Notes

1. See Joachim Gauck, "Ja, so war es!" *Stern,* March 25, 2006.

2. Available in English as *The Inability to Mourn: Principles of Collective Behavior* (New York: Grove, 1975).

3. Available in English in the volume *The Devil's General and Germany: Jekyll and Hyde,* ed. Volkmar Sander (New York: Continuum, 2005).

11

EAST GERMAN TOTALITARIANISM

A Warning from History

Peter Grieder

The Lives of Others is not a documentary but a movie. The purpose of a movie is to entertain rather than to inform. So why debate its historical accuracy? Because its screenwriter and director, Florian Henckel von Donnersmarck, claims that the film is fundamentally authentic.[1] His "close historical consultant," the renowned historian Manfred Wilke, vigorously defends its historical credibility in this volume and elsewhere.[2] Furthermore, the Oscar-winning blockbuster succeeded in renewing the debate about life in the former German Democratic Republic (GDR), also known as East Germany, to which historians are particularly well qualified to contribute. Many ordinary people imbibe their history from motion pictures and cultural artifacts rather than academic publications, making an investigation of historical reliability wholly legitimate. The first section of this essay will focus on how truthfully *The Lives of Others* engages with the theme of East German totalitarianism.[3] In so doing, it will explore certain aspects of where the movie reflects historical reality and where it does not.[4] The second section will advance an interpretation of the film as a salutary warning to democratic societies in the early twenty-first century.

The Lives of Others and East German Totalitarianism

Totalitarianism may be summarized as "the concerted but disguised attempt by a state to exercise total control over, coerce, integrate, manipulate, mobilize, and seduce its population in the name of an ideology, regardless of the extent to which this was actually achieved in practice."[5] As Friedrich and Brzezinski explain, one of the basic features of a totalitarian dictatorship is "the terror of the secret police systematically exploiting modern science, and more especially scientific psychology."[6] It is this secret police control, in the form of the GDR's Ministry for State Security (MfS), or Stasi, that is examined in *The Lives of Others.*

Despite winning seven Lolas of the German Film Prize in 2006, the film received a somewhat mixed reception in Germany.[7] On the one hand, "the cultural and political establishment"[8] hailed it as a powerful antidote to the wave of *Ostalgie* (nostalgia for the East) that had been sweeping eastern Germany since the 1990s. This was a result of a clever marketing strategy by Donnersmarck, which somewhat unfairly compared *The Lives of Others* to earlier, "less serious" movies about the GDR, the most famous being *Good Bye Lenin!* and *Sonnenallee.*[9] Writing in the weekly magazine *Der Spiegel,* Reinhard Mohr described it as "the first German feature film to tackle seriously throughout, without Trabant-nostalgia, Spreewald-cucumber romanticism, and other folkloric tomfoolery, the kernel of the German Democratic Republic that collapsed in 1989—the systematic intimidation, oppression, and repression of its citizens in the name of 'state security.'"[10] On the other hand, *The Lives of Others* was criticized by some historians and "professional film people" for having an "ostalgic" theme itself in that it depicts a Stasi captain, Gerd Wiesler, protecting the celebrated playwright Georg Dreyman and his actress girlfriend, Christa-Maria Sieland, whom he is supposed to be observing.

There is no evidence such a thing ever happened in the GDR. Of course, this does not mean that it did not or could not have happened. If, like Wiesler, the officer had successfully covered his tracks, the incriminating evidence would either have been destroyed or never recorded in the first place. In any event, the Stasi files are so voluminous that one cannot completely exclude the possibility of such a documented case coming to light in future. Be that as it may, Dr. Hubertus Knabe, director of the memorial at the former Stasi prison at Hohenschönhausen in Berlin, was so incensed by what he saw as Donnersmarck's artistic license that he denied him permission to film there. According to Knabe, a strict division of labor and internal MfS surveillance would have prevented a Stasi captain from exercising so much control over a single operation.[11] These factors would certainly have disrupted Wiesler's task but not rendered it impossible. Anna Funder, author of the acclaimed *Stasiland,*[12] supports Knabe's objections: "to understand why a Wiesler could not have existed is to understand the 'total' nature of totalitarianism."[13] Moreover, she insists, Stasi officers were "true believers" hardened by "institutional coercion." They would never have wanted to save those they were spying on.[14]

Yet Knabe and Funder miss a more fundamental point. A perfect totalitarian system has never existed and never will. While East Germany came closest to realizing the dystopia of George Orwell's *1984*, it still ranks as the least inefficient of the Soviet bloc regimes. The "human factor" can never be discounted, even in a police state as obsessive as the GDR. Hence the main supposition of *The Lives of Others*, while unlikely, is not implausible. There were Stasi employees and informers, the latter known as *inoffizieller Mitarbeiter* (IMs), or "unofficial colleagues," who engaged in dissent. Wilke cites the cases of two officers, Major Gerd Trebeljahr and Captain Werner Teske, who were executed in 1979 and 1981, respectively.[15] At least ten MfS personnel paid with their lives for attempting to change sides.[16] Garton Ash knew of "full-time Stasi operatives who became disillusioned, especially during the 1980s."[17] As the GDR sank deep into crisis during its final decade, the possibility of such disillusionment grew, despite or even because of the ministry's increasingly repressive modus operandi after 1987.[18] With their dense networks of informers, Stasi officers were well aware of the shortcomings of what had become known as "really existing socialism"—a term used to distinguish it from the coming communist utopia. Wiesler himself gives an indication of this when he asks his superior, Lieutenant Colonel Anton Grubitz, who heads the culture department at the MfS: 'Don't you sometimes wish that Communism was already here?'"[19] By 1989 some Stasi employees favored reform.[20] Not all were hopelessly indoctrinated drones. To believe that they were is to subscribe to a view of totalitarianism as an ideal type rather than as a really existing historical phenomenon. If the Soviet leader, Mikhail Gorbachev, could make the transition from hard-line communist to supreme reformer within a few short years, then the much smaller transformation being portrayed in *The Lives of Others* is certainly realistic. Unless historians see Stasi officials as fallible human beings rather than mindless automatons, they will not be able to empathize with them. In empathy lies the key to historical understanding.

When Timothy Garton Ash interviewed the former Stasi major Klaus Risse in the 1990s, he came away with the distinct impression that he was a "good man." By this he meant "a man with a real goodness of heart and a conscience that is not switched off at the office door."[21] Risse's father had died "on active service" during the Second World War. The family had lost everything it owned in the bombing raids. His mother, an agricultural laborer, kept them alive. Then the East German state began to provide support. Klaus was a bright pupil, and the government awarded him the highest scholarship to attend a boarding school. Aged eighteen, he had to decide on a career. He hoped "to study fishery at university." But the Stasi said, "Do something for the state which has done so much for you." So he became an employee of the MfS.[22] Thus it came to be that this fatherless, destitute child of the Second World War was pressured into working for one of the most sinister secret police organizations of the twentieth century. Those state benefits he had received as a vulnerable youngster provided the means for his recruitment. The victim had become a victim again, this time by entering the ranks of the main perpetrators.[23] How Wiesler came to work for the Stasi is not elucidated in *The Lives of Others*. But it is worth noting that Risse might not have been so exceptional. Elsewhere, Garton Ash writes: "In many hours of talking to former Stasi officers, I never met a single one whom I felt to be, simply and plainly, an evil man."[24] One is reminded of this at the end of the film. After the fall of the GDR, Dreyman discovers from his Stasi file that Wiesler had been protecting him. By way of gratitude, he dedicates his novel *Sonata for a Good Man* to the former Stasi captain, identified by his MfS moniker HGW XX/7.

According to Mary Fulbrook, the doyenne of GDR studies in the United Kingdom, totalitarianism theory entails adopting "an essentially dichotomous approach in separating cleanly between repressive, totalitarian 'state' and innocent, oppressed 'society.'"[25] What she does not acknowledge, though, is that totalitarian polities rule *through* rather than *over* society. Totalitarianism is the invasion and occupation of society by the state—a state that has itself been hijacked by and subjugated to a political party,[26] in the GDR's case, the Socialist Unity Party of Germany (SED). Such dictatorships embraced the "totality" of society, fusing it with party-state structures. Collaboration and participation were essential prerequisites for a system that, by definition, drew the entire population into its remit. As the anticommunist dissident and future president of Czechoslovakia, Václav Havel, perceptively observed in 1978, the crucial "line of conflict" did not run between rulers and ruled but rather "*de facto* through each person, for everyone in his or her way" was "both a victim and a supporter of the system."[27] He drew attention to the way that every person was, to a greater or lesser degree, implicated in the regime: "Individuals . . . must *live within a lie*. They need not accept the lie. It is enough for them to have accepted their life with it and in it. For by this very fact, individuals confirm the system, fulfil the system, make the system, *are* the system."[28] Of course, none of this makes the Stasi any less culpable for the evils of East German totalitarianism.

The Lives of Others departs from cold war stereotypes in that it explores the complexity of state-society relations under the watchful eyes of the totalitarian MfS. The film cannot be written off as a tale of "heroes, victims and villains,"[29] a type of history writing that Fulbrook rightly warned against in the 1990s.[30] Stasi captain Wiesler is a perpetrator, a dissenter, and to some extent a victim, in that he suffers demotion for protecting Dreyman and Sieland. Dreyman is simultaneously a supporter of socialism, a critic of the system, and a victim of its excesses. Sieland is also a loyal socialist, a victim of the regime, and a perpetrator, in that she agrees to work (albeit under duress) as an informer for the Stasi. To depict the film as a tale of "a few good men" and one "bad" woman is therefore simplistic.[31] Sieland is victimized by the patriarchal MfS in the form of one of its former officers, the predatory culture minister, Bruno Hempf, who wants to have a sexual relationship with her, and Wiesler's careerist superior, Grubitz. Both are irredeemably malevolent characters. While "the two leading male figures are given the chance to mature through the failing woman," claims that the film itself is misogynist because of the "weak, seduced and guilty" female heroine can be taken too far.[32] Sieland is not the only person in the movie to be broken by the system.

The question then arises as to whether the film "steers uncomfortably close" to "a moral relativism that ends up blurring the distinction between perpetrator and victim," as Garton Ash has claimed.[33] Its portrayal of a "good" Stasi captain has been criticized in some quarters for downplaying the evil of the Stasi and distracting attention from the real heroes of the GDR, the dissidents.[34] Yet these objections are somewhat overstated. Wiesler's ruthless record as MfS captain is made very clear at the start of the film, when he interrogates a prisoner, identified only by his number, 227. Something of what the founding mother of totalitarianism theory, Hannah Arendt, memorably termed "the banality of evil"[35] is evident here.[36] By "banality of evil," Arendt meant the almost mechanical perpetration of immoral acts by ordinary individuals who were in no way psychologically disturbed. As Owen Evans argues, Wiesler's chilling treatment of Prisoner 227 and use of a recording of the interrogation to instruct students at the MfS university in Potsdam converts "the obvious suffering of an individual into material for supposed academic analysis."[37] When one of the students asks whether depriving the prisoner of so much sleep did not amount to inhumane treatment, Wiesler silently places a black mark next to his name. Shortly after observing Dreyman for the first time at the theater, Wiesler suggests putting him under surveillance, describing the playwright as "exactly the arrogant type I always warn my students about."[38] The suffering and courage of all the Stasi's victims are treated with great pathos throughout the film. It is important to remember that there are two heroes at the center of this story: the first is Wiesler, the second is Dreyman.

According to Garton Ash, the "conversion" of Wiesler "seems implausibly rapid and not fully convincing."[39] Yet this interpretation can be questioned. First, as Mary Beth Stein perceptively points out, "Wiesler undergoes an evolution, not a conversion. He does not defect but remains a (smaller) cog in the machinery of surveillance until the opening of the Wall."[40] This renders the plot much more believable, as the idea of a Stasi captain becoming a fully fledged dissident in the context of the film might have stretched the imagination too far. Second, Wiesler was a true believer in the Stasi's ideological mission to protect the SED. This was typical of an MfS officer, immediately making him credible as a historical character. It is precisely *because* he was a principled communist that he was genuinely appalled by the abuse of ministerial surveillance powers to victimize a politically reliable artist and his partner. Lunching in the Stasi canteen with Grubitz, Wiesler insists on sitting with the rank and file rather than at the officer table. When Grubitz queries this, Wiesler remarks: "Socialism must begin somewhere, after all." When Grubitz then tells Wiesler that the purpose of Operation Lazlo is to help Hempf to sideline his rival, Dreyman, so that he can have a sexual relationship with Sieland, Wiesler asks him: "Is that why we joined up? Do you still know our oath 'shield and sword of the party'?"[41] Other Stasi officials would also have balked at such a rare form of corruption, convinced as they were of their own professionalism and the purity of Marxist-Leninist ideology. Third, the emotionally impoverished existence of Wiesler made him particularly vulnerable to the seductions of the forbidden world he was observing. He had no life at all outside spying and lived merely to monitor the lives of others. The fourth and probably decisive factor is Wiesler's growing love for Sieland, which gains in poignancy throughout the film because of its understated nature. Love can be a truly transformative force, all the more so against the background of searing loneliness. When love transforms, it often does so quickly. One is reminded of A. J. P. Taylor's observation, "Revolution is for society what a passionate love is for the individual; those who experience it are marked for ever, separated from their own past and from the rest of mankind."[42] Finally, there is the humanizing impact of art, here in the form of a piano piece called "Sonata for a Good Man" given to Dreyman by his friend the blacklisted theater director Albert Jerska (which Wiesler overhears while eavesdropping) and a Bertolt Brecht poem called "Memory of Marie A." (an allusion to the heroine of the plot, Christa-Maria Sieland), which he removes from the artists' flat. Although great art has been used to aestheticize totalitarianism, its ability to harvest love and redemption is a central theme of the movie. Garton Ash's criticism that it would have taken "more than the odd sonata and Brecht poem" to melt a Stasi man's heart neglects the first four factors.[43]

The film accurately portrays some of the methods employed by the East German police state. Wiesler spends much of his time in the attic of Dreyman's apartment block, wearing a pair of headphones and eavesdropping on the lives of the playwright and his actress girlfriend. According to Evans, "All of the equipment featured in the film was actually used by the MfS for such operations."[44] Then there were the searches of Dreyman's flat and the preservation of smell samples from suspects so that they could be tracked by sniffer dogs.[45] The film is set in 1984, the year of George Orwell's famous novel by that name, when violence and physical torture were no longer favored methods of the MfS. Instead, there was "what Hubertus Knabe has called a system of 'quiet repression' (*lautlose Unterdrückung*)"[46] that reflected the ministry's exploitation of "scientific psychology" in the manner outlined by Friedrich and Brzezinski above. In the carefully honed totalitarian jargon of the Stasi, this was known as *Zersetzung* (decomposition).[47] The main victim of this in the film is Jerska, whose life has been rendered worthless by the MfS. This is particularly evident at Dreyman's birthday party when Paul Hauser, a journalist friend of Dreyman's, accuses one of the other guests of working for the Stasi and thereby helping to destroy Jerska. A favorite Stasi tactic was to spread false rumors of this nature in order to sow mistrust and "decompose" the groups they were monitoring. Zersetzung also made it easier for the regime to hide its human rights abuses in an era of détente and *Ostpolitik*,[48] when securing financial credits and international recognition from the West were top priorities.[49]

Some of the Stasi's psychological techniques are on display during Wiesler's breaking of Prisoner 227 at the start of the film. First there is sleep deprivation combined with endless interrogation. Then there are threats to incarcerate his wife and send his children to a state orphanage, eerily reminiscent of Nazi *Sippenhaft,* a policy that held all family members responsible for the crimes of one. Later in the film, Grubitz is shown enthusing over a PhD thesis he supervised with the cumbersome title "Prison Conditions for Political-Ideological Subversives of the Art Scene according to Character Profiles." Displaying the classic totalitarian mania for crude categorization, the dissertation claimed there were only five types of artist. Grubitz labels Dreyman type 4—a "hysterical anthropocentric"—who required nothing more than ten months' solitary confinement without trial to cure him of his condition.[50]

The Stasi worked with carrots as well as sticks. When Wiesler enters Dreyman's apartment to install bugging equipment, he is seen by Mrs. Meineke, the neighbor living in the flat opposite. "One word about this to anyone," Wiesler threatens the poor woman, "and tomorrow your Masha will lose her place to study medicine. Understood?"[51] Immediately afterward, he orders his colleague to buy her a gift to reward her cooperation. The Stasi was very adept at playing on people's weaknesses. In Sieland's case, this is an addiction to drugs, for which she is arrested on a tip-off from Hempf. In fear of losing her cherished career as an actress, Sieland agrees to become an IM ("Marta") and denounces Dreyman, who has anonymously published an illegal article in the West German magazine *Der Spiegel.* Wiesler, who wants to uncover the whereabouts of the subversive typescript so that he can remove it and thereby save both Dreyman and Sieland, goes through the motions of totalitarian blackmail: "Think of what the state has done for you your whole life long. Now you can do something for the state. And it will thank you."[52] As Sieland leaves the Stasi prison, Grubitz tells her: "Do not forget. You are now an IM. That means duties such as complete conspiracy and confidentiality. But also privileges." He then slips her some narcotics.[53]

What *The Lives of Others* does so brilliantly is capture the possibilities of secret police control in a totalitarian state. In the process, it helps to illuminate a key aspect of "late totalitarianism" in the GDR. As the film shows, the "tentacles" of "the Stasi octopus" were long enough to penetrate the most intimate private sphere.[54] After the regime collapsed, a number of real-life cases came to light documenting how members of the same family had been turned against each other. The most famous is that of the opposition activist Vera Wollenberger, who learned from her Stasi file that her own husband, Knud, code-named IM Donald, had been informing on her for years. Then there was the author Hans Joachim Schädlich, who discovered that he had been spied on by his elder brother.[55] The potentially devastating consequences of secret police surveillance are vividly highlighted in the film.

This totalitarian control was imposed by the Stasi not just on society but on the Stasi itself. So-called UMs were deployed to spy on the MfS.[56] Again, we see that the ministry was intertwined with the East German population, not separate from it. The instance in the movie of a Stasi second lieutenant, Axel Stigler, demoted for repeating a joke about SED general secretary Erich Honecker, is completely believable. Political humor in the GDR was no laughing matter as far as the authorities were concerned. Witticisms at the expense of the regime could result in being blacklisted. In 1984, an East German television presenter was debarred from his profession for making political gags in public.[57] Although they could do little to stop them,[58] wisecracks about socialism were beyond a joke for the SED leaders.

Both Wiesler and Stigler end up working in a cellar of Department M, the MfS division responsible for monitoring the country's postal service. There they steam open letters until the fall of the Berlin Wall. The letter-steaming machine used in the film is authentic. Over the forty-year existence of the GDR, the Stasi "opened up to 400 million items of mail using steam, chemicals, irons and ultrasonic baths," according to an exhibition in East Berlin entitled An Open Secret: Postal and Telephone Surveillance in the German Democratic Republic.[59] Apparently, "women with 'sensitive fingers' were trained to handle sealed envelopes; if they sensed a photograph, the mail was opened with a primitive dry-ice machine to prevent damage to the print."[60] Despite a legal clause protecting "the inviolability of postal communications," Stasi officers were stationed at every post office in the land.[61] Their surveillance was extremely thorough, with every piece of domestic and foreign mail being inspected "at least to the extent of someone casting an expert eye over the outside of the envelope, the name of the sender and the addressee."[62] Anything that looked remotely suspicious was opened and, if necessary, confiscated. In East Germany's second city of Leipzig during the 1980s, 120 MfS employees opened between 1,500 and 2,000 letters each day.[63] The 154 operatives assigned to Department M of Region Halle scrutinized 15,779,715 items of postage in the first three months of 1989 alone, submitting 85,478 memos to various MfS departments concerning their contents.[64] To quote John O. Koehler, "All letters and parcels sent to or received from a non-communist country were opened surreptitiously. The operation was established to catch spies and enemies of the regime; but over the years, it evolved into organized mail robbery. Money sent by

West Germans to their relatives in the East for the purchase of goods available only in hard currency shops was systematically removed."[65] Allan Hall reports that "operatives were instructed to remove stamps from intercepted mail for forwarding to the German Book Export and Import Company, a Stasi firm that sold the stamps to Western collectors for hard currency."[66] In *Snowleg*, a poignant and well-researched historical novel on the East German secret police, the author, Nicholas Shakespeare, describes a visit to the Stasi museum in Leipzig. On display are "an assortment of fake rubber stamps from Brussels, Tokyo, Buenos Aires, to make it look as if letters had in fact reached their destination and the Leipzig Post Office was simply returning them to sender, 'Name Unknown.'"[67]

The Lives of Others highlights the wooden totalitarian jargon of the SED state and its Stasi protectors.[68] Officially, there was neither censorship nor blacklisting in a republic that purported to be "democratic." Pseudo-democracy is a defining characteristic of totalitarian regimes.[69] When Dreyman makes an appeal on behalf of his blacklisted friend Jerska, he is chastised by the culture minister: "Blacklisting? Such a thing does not exist in our country. You should choose your words more carefully."[70] The Orwellian double-speak of the SED leadership was completely divorced from the reality of life in the GDR.[71]

That said, the ideological work of the secret police could perhaps have been explored more deeply in the film.[72] The Stasi was above all an "ideology police."[73] East Germany was more of an "ideological state" than its Warsaw Pact allies. Bulgaria, Czechoslovakia, Hungary, Poland, and Romania existed as countries before the cold war started, whereas the GDR was born of that conflict and died with it. This made it the archetypal cold war polity.[74] In November 1989, the famous East German writer Stefan Heym wrote that "the raison d'être of the German Democratic Republic is socialism."[75] This was the only Soviet bloc satellite to refer to itself as the Workers' and Peasants' State[76] or Workers' and Peasants' Power. Since it was an ideologically saturated realm, the Stasi's role as "shield and sword" of the Communist Party could have been pointed up more strongly. One scene where Wiesler spies on neighbors he suspects of "speculative hoarding of goods" (*spekulative Warenhortung*) was cut from the final version.[77] If the question of ideological conformity and nonconformity had been investigated in greater depth, it might also have been possible to depict how some writers successfully pushed back the boundaries of official cultural discourse, as studies by Karen Leeder and Helen Bridge have shown.[78]

Instead, the plot is built around the sexual lust of the culture minister and SED Central Committee member Hempf. His abuse of unaccountable power was undoubtedly easier in a totalitarian polity where the government controlled so much of people's lives. It also enables the film to probe the connection between welfare and oppression in the GDR[79] (the Stasi stops a dentist from providing Sieland with semi-illicit drugs because of the latter's refusal to have a sexual liaison with Hempf). In a liberal democracy, such corruption might have been exposed by a free press, fond as it is of prying into politicians' private lives. Moreover, a minister for culture in the West would never have enjoyed such overwhelming power over an actress's career in the first place. In communist countries, artists were supposed to be servants of the state and "engineers of the human soul" (a quotation attributed to Stalin and recapitulated by Hempf);[80] in the West they are free to criticize the state, whether it subsidizes them or not. The totalitarian reach of the Workers' and Peasants' Power is encapsulated in Sieland's exclamation to Dreyman: "Don't I need this entire system? . . . But you get into bed with them, too. Why do you do it? Because they can destroy you as well, despite your talent and your faith in it. Because they determine what we play, who is allowed to act, and who can direct."[81] Significantly, the Stasi denies Dreyman's close friend Hauser permission to travel to the West to address a cultural conference.[82] As Hempf himself puts it: "The party in fact needs artists but the artists need the party far more."[83]

The Lives of Others focuses on the cultural intelligentsia. Paradoxically, given the latter's ideological proclivity toward socialism, it was heavily penetrated by the MfS.[84] This makes Dreyman and Sieland, who are both idealistic socialists, credible characters. East German intellectuals enjoyed a privileged existence compared to their fellow countrymen so long as they toed the party line. Many artists and writers had contacts in the West, making them both useful and suspect to a regime that craved international recognition. Stasi surveillance of this milieu was stepped up after the expatriation of the dissident communist balladeer Wolf Biermann on November 16, 1976, ending Honecker's "no taboos" policy in the realm of art and culture. Only ten days later, the scientist and philosopher Professor Robert Havemann, a close friend of Biermann's and the country's most distinguished communist dissident, was placed under house arrest.[85] Artists and writers who signed open letters of protest against Biermann's treatment were subjected to an array of state reprisals. Many, like Jerska in *The Lives of Others*, were blacklisted. Others were ejected from the state-controlled Writers' Union, incarcerated, or expelled from the GDR.[86] During the 1980s, East Berlin's alternative "Prenzlauer Berg scene" was significantly steered by the Stasi, using the performance artist and "perfect spy" Sascha Anderson.[87] When the MfS was abolished in 1989–1990, Department XX/7, which oversaw important areas of cultural life in the GDR, employed about forty full-time staff and the highest number of IMs, totaling 350 to 400.[88] According to Mike Dennis, "In 1989, 49 out of 123 members of the executive of the Writers' Union had been or still were Stasi collaborators, and 12 out of the 19 members of the Presidium were former or current IMs."[89] Even Hermann Kant, president of this official body, was unmasked as a Stasi informant (IM Martin).[90] Christa Wolf, one of the GDR's most celebrated authors, wrote a book about her experiences under MfS surveillance[91] but was later revealed to have served briefly as an IM herself under the alias Margarete.[92]

Another question the film raises is the high suicide rate in East Germany. The GDR was certainly a world-beater in this respect, something the country's leaders were desperate to conceal. *The Lives of Others* contains one certain suicide, that of the blacklisted theater director Jerska, and another suspected one, that of Sieland. When Jerska hangs himself after a seven-year ban on practicing his profession, Dreyman writes his anonymous *Spiegel* article in which he addresses the taboo subject of suicide in the "workers' and peasants' paradise." The article is composed on a typewriter smuggled into the GDR from West Berlin in order to prevent the Stasi from tracing its typeface. Its argument is that the high suicide statistics are a consequence of political repression under state socialism. Yet according to a seminal study by Udo Grashoff,[93] this was not generally the case. Decisive reasons, according to him, were the area's traditions and Protestant heritage. Thuringia and Saxony had displayed high suicide rates since the mid-nineteenth century. For cultural and religious reasons, Protestant regions tend to record more cases of suicide than Catholic ones. Certainly the SED dictatorship failed to improve the situation. As *The Lives of Others* makes clear, when the figures rose in 1977, the party forbade their dissemination.[94]

In causing Jerska's suicide and harassing Sieland, the Stasi inadvertently turns Dreyman into the very "hostile-negative force" (to use the ministry's jargon) it was supposed to "render harmless." This is emblematic of the ultimately self-defeating nature of GDR totalitarianism. The SED's punishment of critical but generally sympathetic cultural figures undermined its own support base, a point conceded to me by the Politburo's former ideological spokesman, Kurt Hager, when I interviewed him in the early 1990s.[95]

Biermann's expatriation permanently blighted relations between the party and key members of the cultural intelligentsia. As Martin McCauley notes, "Until 1976 there had been a net inflow of writers and artists into the GDR but after that date it became an exodus."[96] Prior to that year, Biermann had not even been popular among his compatriots; afterward he was feted as "a political martyr."[97] According to Garton Ash, the Stasi kept a total of forty thousand pages on the singer.[98]

The MfS undermined domestic support for East Germany because most of the population regarded it "as a hostile element."[99] This is illustrated in *The Lives of Others* when a little boy asks Wiesler in the lift of his apartment block: "Are you really with the Stasi?" "Do you even know what that is, the Stasi?" comes the reply. The child gives an answer that could have had serious consequences for his family: "They are bad men, who imprison others, says Daddy." Wiesler deliberately refrains from asking the boy to give him his father's name, something he was required to do as a Stasi captain.[100] According to Armin Mitter and Stefan Wolle, the "bloated, inefficient and expensive Stasi apparatus harmed the GDR more than all the opposition groups put together."[101] Obsessive-compulsive state control was therefore one of the main reasons for the GDR's ultimate failure, although not collapse, which could only occur once the Kremlin had withdrawn its backing.[102] This is made clear in the film as Gorbachev becomes Soviet leader just as Wiesler is being demoted in March 1985. Within five and a half years, Gorbachev's liberalizing reforms in the USSR had led to the downfall of the "first 'Workers' and Peasants' State' on German soil."[103]

One of the fundamental debates about *The Lives of Others* among Germans is whether it accurately depicts everyday life in the GDR. According to Cheryl Dueck, "Viewers were attracted to the look of the film, that is, the recognizable aesthetic of the décor, clothing, and social groups within the German Democratic Republic, as well as the familiarity of the East Berlin cityscape."[104] At a symposium in Washington, DC's, German Historical Institute on April 30, 2007, "several panellists thought that the film had done well in capturing the atmosphere of the place and time." They particularly commended its rendering of "the repressive political climate in the GDR, one of suspicion and mistrust that permeated nearly all levels of society."[105] However, by his own admission, Donnersmarck deliberately accentuated the drab colors of East Germany, thereby heightening the oppressive atmosphere. As a commentary in the newspaper *Die Zeit* observed: "Donnersmarck does not want realism, but a metaphorical hyperrealism."[106]

It is no criticism of *The Lives of Others* to say that another film is needed that captures the impact of the Stasi on the wider population in the Workers' and Peasants' State.[107] This would enable a deeper examination of Arendt's "banality of evil" concept. As Garton Ash has pointed out, "Nowhere was evil more banal than in the net-curtained, plastic-wood cabins and caravans of the German Democratic Republic."[108] When Wiesler threatens Dreyman's neighbor Mrs. Meineke, it is one of the few scenes in the film to engage with the world of ordinary East Germans, even if it does speak volumes. A single movie cannot be expected to portray all aspects of state surveillance without losing focus.

According to Stein, since only 1 to 2 percent of GDR inhabitants were involved in spying on another 1 to 2 percent of their compatriots, the absence from the film of ordinary people "who neither supported nor resisted the regime" exaggerates the repressiveness of the GDR.[109] This is to underestimate somewhat the impact of the MfS, which touched the lives of everyone to a greater or lesser degree, whether they were under direct surveillance or not. As Gary Bruce puts it, "One can no more place a boundary around the Stasi than one can encircle a scent in a room."[110] The fear of the secret police was pervasive, and many East Germans behaved as if the Stasi was omnipresent, even though it was not.[111] David Childs noted this fear when visiting the GDR in 1978; Timothy Garton Ash kept coming up against it while living there during the early 1980s.[112] In 1990, 72.6 percent of East Germans believed that there was "complete surveillance" in the GDR, although five years later the figure had declined to 42 percent.[113]

At the start of *The Lives of Others,* the viewer is told that the Stasi consisted of 100,000 staff and 200,000 informers.[114] Garton Ash maintains that in 1988 the MfS had more than 90,000 full-time personnel and over 170,000 IMs.[115] In 1989, the number of informers was between 174,000 and 176,000.[116] All this to control a population of approximately 16.4 million.[117] Dennis has determined that "in any given year throughout the 1980s, about one in 50 of the country's 13.5 million adults were working for the Stasi on the home front, either as an officer or as an informer."[118] According to Koehler, if one includes people who supplied information on a part-time basis, the ratio is one informer per 6.5 citizens.[119] Since many MfS records did not survive the 1989 revolution, the precise number of IMs may never be known, although 500,000 has been given as a credible estimate.[120] As Dennis points out, there was one full-time MfS employee per 180 citizens in the GDR, which made it "the largest secret police and secret security apparatus in the Soviet empire and probably in world history."[121] It is often forgotten that Stasi surveillance was augmented by other organizations. These included the official trade union (FDGB), the communist youth movement (FDJ), SED factory cells (GO), the People's Police and their collaborators, neighborhood associations, "educators," the printed media, and the Agitation Commission of the SED.[122] Margot Honecker, wife of the party's general secretary and the GDR's minister for people's education between 1963 and 1989, "ordered every teacher to report all incidences of deviation by pupils from the communist line."[123]

Paradoxically, given the extent of state monitoring, most East Germans, according to Fulbrook, could still "experience their everyday life as 'perfectly normal.'"[124] Jeannette Madarász concurs, stating that between 1971 and 1987 "life in the GDR was ordinary for the majority of the population."[125] Bruce takes a different view: "It would not be an exaggeration to state that every East German citizen has a 'Stasi story,' either personally or that of a close acquaintance. Some of the brushes with the secret police were mild, some were harrowing, but all of them reveal a life that was anything but 'ordinary.'"[126] Of course, notions of what is "normal" and "ordinary" are relative, and memories can be misleading. Even if people genuinely believed that their lives were normal in the context of 1984, this was sometimes a misconception. Many East Germans were ignorant of exactly what the Stasi was doing until after the regime collapsed. In *The Lives of Others,* Dreyman finds out that he had been under surveillance only in November 1991, some two years after the fall of the Berlin Wall. He is even more incredulous when he is told that this surveillance was of the "comprehensive" variety.[127] Others, consciously or unconsciously, blotted out the repressive aspects of the system by concentrating on their work, pursuing hobbies, or building families. However, Fulbrook is undoubtedly correct when she writes that although "many East Germans lived with a sense of oppression and fear . . . the climate of fear was the outer parameter of existence" in this police state; "it did not have to be a feature of everyday life."[128] In any case, most citizens were too busy with other things to worry incessantly about the Stasi. Thus the debate between those who stress the normality of daily existence in the GDR and those who emphasize its repressive nature is unnecessarily polarized. The film cannot convey this widespread perception of normality because the plot is built around a small group of dissident artists.

Funder rightly points out that the fate of Wiesler after 1990—he is shown delivering junk mail to people's homes—was not typical of erstwhile MfS officials, who generally did far better out of German reunification than their victims.[129] Neither are reconciliations between Stasi spies and their quarries very common, although they are surely possible. While in various respects *The Lives of Others* is stylized history, the film cannot be dismissed simply as a "fairy tale."[130] After all, it does shed light on certain totalitarian practices in the GDR. Garton Ash gives a characteristically cogent assessment of its historical authenticity: "It uses the syntax and conventions of Hollywood to convey to the widest possible audience some part of the truth about life under the Stasi, and the larger truths that experience revealed about human nature. It mixes historical fact (several of the Stasi locations are real and most of the terminology and tradecraft is accurate) with the ingredients of a fast-paced thriller and love story."[131] The GDR has been dead for more than two decades now but many of its former inhabitants are still alive. Small wonder, then, that the movie sparked off such a "vigorous debate"[132] in Germany. Nevertheless, as Dueck observes, "most critics and audience discussions end on a positive note."[133] In dramatizing history for the purposes of catharsis and redemption, the film can help heal the wounds of the "second German dictatorship."[134]

A Warning from History

The Spanish-born philosopher, essayist, poet, and novelist George Santayana once warned: "Those who cannot remember the past are condemned to repeat it."[135] While *The Lives of Others* should serve to educate post–cold war generations about the dangers of dictatorship and overweening state control, for the general public outside Germany rarefied discussions about the film's historical accuracy with regard to everyday life in the GDR are beside the point. Here we have to guard against a variant of what might be called *Ostphobie* (phobia toward the East) that pours scorn on the Workers' and Peasants' Power, with the clear implication that such malign state intrusion could never occur in a Western democracy. "The past is a foreign country," we tell ourselves comfortingly. "They do things differently there."[136]

Yet at the time of writing, the British government is consulting on a draft Communications Data Bill[137] which, if passed into law, would monitor all the electronic correspondence, social networking activity, and Web site visits of everyone resident in the UK. Furthermore, this monitoring would take place in real time. Although the content of telephone and e-mail messages is apparently to remain hidden (at least for the time being), there are some doubts about whether this is even technologically feasible. Be that as it may, it is possible to construct a very detailed profile of somebody by analyzing his or her browsing history and who he or she communicates with over the telephone and Internet. To quote Sir Tim Berners-Lee, inventor of the Worldwide Web: "The amount of control you have over somebody if you can monitor internet activity is amazing. You get to know every detail, you get to know, in a way, more intimate details about their life than any person that they talk to because often people will confide in the internet as they find their way through medical websites . . . or as an adolescent finds their way through a website about homosexuality, wondering what they are and whether they should talk to people about it."[138] Berners-Lee has even gone so far as to describe the government's plans as a "destruction of human rights."[139] According to N02ID, a pressure group set up to "stop the database state": "Traffic data tells a different story to reading mail. And a much more detailed one: who you contact, how, where from, for how long, what you read and watch, what games you play, what you search for; all your online and telephone habits and most of the technical details of your equipment and software."[140]

The policy was first mooted by Gordon Brown's Labour administration in 2008, which proposed storing all the information on a single database owned by the government.[141] Its Orwellian connotations were not lost on the general public and the idea had to be abandoned in April 2009.[142] Three years later, the proposal is to give the intelligence services the right to access existing databases without a warrant, which effectively amounts to the same thing. Communication service providers (CSPs) would be required to store "records of billions more communications."[143] Such a monstrous extension of state monitoring could never have been contemplated by the Stasi, which operated in an offline world. Although the MfS went in for general as well as targeted surveillance,[144] it never quite achieved the maxim of "blanket surveillance" (*flächendeckende Überwachung*). The 6 million paper files the ministry left behind (2 million of which were on West Germans)[145] ran to 185 kilometers,[146] not including all those others it managed to destroy. Yet this vast data mountain now seems somewhat less remarkable given the surfeit of information being collected on the "free" citizens of the West.[147]

Since the terrorist atrocity of 9/11, Western democracies have become surveillance societies far more sophisticated than that of the GDR. This has been made possible by revolutionary technological advances since the end of the cold war. Another factor is the move toward a culture in which most people have become accustomed to being observed in some form or other. Indeed, they are hardly conscious of it. One need only mention the ubiquitous closed-circuit television cameras in Great Britain, which is now the most watched nation on Earth.[148] In 2006, there were as many as 4.2 million CCTV cameras in the UK—approximately "one for every 14 people."[149] As early as August 2004, Britain's information commissioner, Richard Thomas, warned that the country risked "sleepwalking into a surveillance society." According to the *Times,* he said "that there is a growing danger of East German Stasi-style snooping if the State gathers too much information about individual citizens."[150] Two years later, Thomas declared: "Today I fear that we are in fact waking up to a surveillance society that is already all around us."[151] On the same day, one of the writers of an academic report compiled by the Surveillance Studies Network averred that the United Kingdom was "the most surveilled country" among Western industrialized nations.[152] In 2007 the respected human rights organization Privacy International classified Great Britain and the United States as "endemic surveillance societies," in the same league as Russia and the People's Republic of China.[153] The organization also found that Britain was "the worst Western democracy at protecting individual privacy."[154] It would not be an exaggeration to claim that the UK is metamorphosing from a liberal into an illiberal democracy. Nonetheless, most British citizens, like many ordinary East Germans before them, believe that they live "perfectly normal lives." This is because notions of normality have evolved and surveillance is deemed to be benevolent, its encroachments occurring only incrementally or invisibly.

What has all this got to do with *The Lives of Others,* you might ask? A great deal. *The Lives of Others* is not a film primarily about ideological surveillance but about the abuse of surveillance powers by the government. Now, of course, while all totalitarian states are surveillance societies, not all surveillance societies are totalitarian states. But even in putatively democratic polities where the purposes of monitoring are generally benign, such extensive powers are bound to be misused, particularly as those doing the snooping have to work in secrecy. To quote Tim Berners-Lee again: "The idea that we should routinely record information about people is obviously very dangerous. It means that there will be information around which could be stolen, which can be acquired through corrupt officials or corrupt operators, and [could be] used, for example, to blackmail people in the government or people in the military. We open ourselves out, if we store this information, to it being abused."[155] Confidential personal data collected under the last Labour government in Britain was repeatedly lost or leaked, regardless of the safeguards.

Neither will panoptic surveillance be very effective at deterring criminals, who can encrypt their data or find alternative means of communication. Those primarily affected will be the overwhelming majority of people who never commit any crimes. The proposed legislation will simply add mountains of irrelevant information to existing stockpiles, making it even more difficult to find all-important "needles" in a vastly enlarged "haystack."[156] According to James Ball, "More than a trillion emails a year are sent from the UK."[157] Stasi officials drowned in masses of minutiae, becoming victims of their own attempts at omniscience. The ears of the MfS were long, but the space between them was often rather limited.[158] Even with the wonders of modern computer technology, Western intelligence services run the risk of being unable to see the wood for the trees. In the end, it is human beings, not computers, who will have to sift and evaluate all this new material.

East German officials used to quip that "trust is fine but surveillance is better" (*Vertrauen ist gut, Kontrolle ist besser*).[159] Originally attributed to Lenin, the quote is also said to have been used by the GDR's minister for state security, Erich Mielke.[160] Whatever its provenance, the motto could just as well have been adopted by the governments of Tony Blair, Gordon Brown, and David Cameron. "Trust" is supposed to come entirely from the innocent citizens being put under surveillance, who are sometimes accused of paranoia if they object to being watched. Yet the government refuses to trust its own population, turning everybody into potential suspects. If creating a "suspect society" is not paranoid, then what is? One is reminded of Brecht's observation after the popular uprising of June 17, 1953, in East Germany: "The people had forfeited the confidence of the government and could win it back only by redoubled efforts. Would it not be easier in that case for the government to dissolve the people and elect another?"[161] In Britain, we are fundamentally altering the relationship between state and society in favor of the state, when in a free society it should be exactly the other way round. The state should be accountable to the people, not the people to the state. "Nothing to hide, nothing to fear" goes the mantra. Theoretically, in a perfect world, those with nothing to hide *would* have nothing to fear. But we do not live in a perfect world and hopefully never will because perfect worlds exist only in the minds of totalitarians. Putting people who have nothing to hide under surveillance is not just an unnecessary violation of their privacy but also a gigantic waste of resources. An all-encompassing surveillance apparatus is being constructed that, if it falls into the wrong hands, could resuscitate the totalitarian monster of the twentieth century.

Nobody should be complacent enough to think that liberal democracy could never again slip into existential crisis. If and when it does, there is a surveillance system already in place for the unscrupulous regimes that might follow. Their misuse of the "database state" would make the Stasi seem tame by comparison. Italy was a democracy in 1922. By 1925 it was a fascist dictatorship. Germany was a liberal democracy in 1932 and a totalitarian state by 1933. People should ask how the Nazis managed to round up so many communists within a few short weeks of coming to power. Part of the answer lies in their use of police records collated by the Weimar Republic.[162]

Of course, the risk of a totalitarian resurgence in the West is extremely remote at present. The real and extant danger is that of "sleepwalking" into a comprehensive surveillance state by a series of small steps. There is no totalitarian design here. Mielke's dystopian objective "to know everything and to report on everything worth knowing"[163] is not being pursued by the current British government. That said, we should not take our civil liberties for granted. Information is power. Whatever the intentions behind it, blanket surveillance is wholly inappropriate in a democratic society. The road to hell is paved with good intentions and the most powerful law in history is the law of unintended consequences. Big Brother is already watching the people of the United Kingdom, even if it is not the Big Brother of George Orwell's *1984* or 1984 in East Germany. *The Lives of Others* should serve as a timely warning from history.

Notes

1. "Audio Commentary on Feature and Deleted Scenes by Writer and Director Florian Henckel von Donnersmarck," *The Lives of Others* DVD (Lionsgate, 2007); Jens Gieseke, "*Stasi* Goes to Hollywood: Donnersmarck's *The Lives of Others* und die Grenzen der Authentizität," *German Studies Review* 31, no. 3 (2008): 581.

2. Manfred Wilke, "Wiesler's Umkehr," in *Das Leben der Anderen: Filmbuch von Florian Henckel von Donnersmarck* (Frankfurt: Suhrkamp, 2006), 205–17; Manfred Wilke, "Fiktion oder erlebte Geschichte? Zur Frage der Glaubwürdigkeit des Films *Das Leben der Anderen*," *German Studies Review* 31, no. 3 (2008): 589.

3. The term "totalitarian state" to describe the GDR is used by Donnersmarck himself. See "Audio Commentary on Feature and Deleted Scenes."

4. See also Owen Evans, "Redeeming the Demon? The Legacy of the Stasi in *Das Leben der Anderen*," *Memory Studies* 3, no. 2 (2010): 164–77; Timothy Garton Ash, "The Stasi on Our Minds," in *Facts Are Subversive: Political Writing from a Decade without a Name* (London: Atlantic Books, 2009), 328–41; Daniela Berghahn, "Remembering the Stasi in a Fairy-tale of Redemption: Florian Henckel von Donnersmarck's *Das Leben der Anderen*,"

Oxford German Studies 38, no. 3 (2009): 321–33; Gieseke, "*Stasi* Goes to Hollywood"; Thomas Lindenberger, "Stasiploitation—Why Not? The Scriptwriter's Historical Creativity in *The Lives of Others*," *German Studies Review* 31, no. 3 (2008): 557–66; Mary Beth Stein, "*Stasi* with a Human Face? Ambiguity in *Das Leben der Anderen*," *German Studies Review* 31, no. 3 (2008): 567–79; Anna Funder, "Tyranny of Terror," *Guardian*, May 5, 2007, http://www. theguardian.com/books/2007/may/05/featuresreviews.guardianreview12 (accessed April 23, 2012); Neal Ascherson, "Beware, the Walls Have Ears," *Observer*, March 11, 2007, http://film. guardian.co.uk/print/0,,329741495-3181,00.html (accessed April 23, 2012).

5. Peter Grieder, "In Defence of Totalitarianism Theory as a Tool of Historical Scholarship," *Totalitarian Movements and Political Religions* 8, no. 3 (2007): 565.

6. Carl J. Friedrich and Zbigniew K. Brzezinski, *Totalitarian Dictatorship and Autocracy* (Cambridge, MA: Harvard University Press, 1956), 10.

7. Evans, "Redeeming the Demon?" 164.

8. Lindenberger, "Stasiploitation—Why Not?" 558.

9. Ibid., 559.

10. Reinhard Mohr, "*Das Leben der Anderen*: Stasi ohne Spreewaldgurke," *Der Spiegel*, March 15, 2006, http://www.spiegel.de/kultur/kino/0,1518,druck-406092,00.html (accessed April 23, 2012).

11. Funder, "Tyranny of Terror"; also see Stevan Pfaff, "*The Lives of Others*: East Germany Revisited?" *German Historical Institute Bulletin* 41 (Fall 2007): 111.

12. Anna Funder, *Stasiland* (London: Granta Books, 2003).

13. Funder, "Tyranny of Terror."

14. Ibid.

15. Wilke, "Wiesler's Umkehr," 205. On informers who switched sides, see Lindenberger, "Stasiploitation—Why Not?" 560; and Garton Ash, "The Stasi on Our Minds," 335.

16. "Das war die DDR. Teil 4: 'Schild und Schwert,'" in *Eine Dokumentation über die Geschichte und den Zeitgeist der Deutschen Demokratischen Republik* (video, 1993).

17. Garton Ash, "The Stasi on Our Minds," 335.

18. Mary Fulbrook, *Anatomy of a Dictatorship: Inside the GDR, 1949–1989* (Oxford: Oxford University Press, 1995), 236.

19. "Drehbuch," in *Das Leben der Anderen: Filmbuch von Florian Henckel von Donnersmarck*, 35. These lines appear in the original screenplay but have been cut from the DVD version.

20. Edward N. Peterson, *The Secret Police and the Revolution: The Fall of the German Democratic Republic* (Westport, CT: Praeger, 2001), 268.

21. Timothy Garton Ash, *The File: A Personal History* (London: Flamingo, 1997), 177.

22. Ibid., 172–73; quotes on 173.

23. Grieder, "In Defence of Totalitarianism Theory," 579. See also Grieder, *The German Democratic Republic* (Basingstoke: Palgrave Macmillan, 2012), 5–6.

24. Garton Ash, "The Stasi on Our Minds," 335.

25. Mary Fulbrook, "The Limits of Totalitarianism: God, State and Society in the GDR," *Transactions of the Royal Historical Society* 7 (1997): 49.

26. Grieder, "In Defence of Totalitarianism Theory," 569.

27. Václav Havel, *Václav Havel; or, Living in Truth: Twenty-two Essays Published on the*

Occasion of the Award of the Erasmus Prize to Václav Havel, ed. Jan Vladislav (London: Faber and Faber, 1989), 53.

28. Ibid., 45. This paragraph has been drawn from Grieder, *The German Democratic Republic,* 10–11. See also Grieder, "In Defence of Totalitarianism Theory," 570.

29. Jennifer Creech, "A Few Good Men: Gender, Ideology, and Narrative Politics in *The Lives of Others* and *Good Bye, Lenin" Women in German Yearbook* 25 (2009): 101, 103–4, 117.

30. Mary Fulbrook, "Heroes, Victims and Villains," in *Rewriting the German Past: History and Identity in the New Germany,* ed. Reinhard Alter and Peter Monteath (Amherst, MA: Prometheus Books, 1997).

31. Creech, "A Few Good Men."

32. Lindenberger, "Stasiploitation—Why Not?" 562.

33. Garton Ash, "The Stasi on Our Minds," 336.

34. Anna Funder, "Eyes without a Face," *Sight and Sound* 17, no. 5 (2007): 16–20, cited in Evans, "Redeeming the Demon?" 168.

35. Hannah Arendt, *Eichmann in Jerusalem: A Report on the Banality of Evil* (New York: Penguin, 1963).

36. Evans, "Redeeming the Demon?" 166.

37. Ibid.

38. *The Lives of Others* DVD.

39. Garton Ash, "The Stasi on Our Minds," 335.

40. Stein, "*Stasi* with a Human Face?" 571.

41. "Drehbuch," 59–60.

42. A. J. P. Taylor, *Europe: Grandeur and Decline* (Harmondsworth: Penguin, 1985), 40.

43. Garton Ash, "The Stasi on Our Minds," 335.

44. Evans, "Redeeming the Demon?" 167.

45. Garton Ash, *The File,* 16.

46. Mike Dennis, *The Stasi: Myth and Reality* (Harlow: Longman, 2003), 112.

47. Ibid.

48. West Germany's policy of rapprochement toward the Soviet bloc in general and the GDR in particular, introduced during the late 1960s.

49. Grieder, *The German Democratic Republic,* 70.

50. *The Lives of Others* DVD.

51. "Drehbuch," 43.

52. *The Lives of Others* DVD.

53. Ibid.

54. John O. Koehler, *Stasi: The Untold Story of the East German Secret Police* (Boulder, CO: Westview, 1999), 9.

55. Garton Ash, *The File,* 18.

56. Fulbrook, *Anatomy of a Dictatorship,* 49.

57. "Das war die DDR. Teil 4: 'Wir sind das Volk,'" in *Eine Dokumentation über die Geschichte und den Zeitgeist der DDR.*

58. See *Die besten Witze aus der DDR* (Vienna: Tosa Verlag, 2003). For an excellent study of humor under communism, including the GDR, see Ben Lewis, *Hammer and Tickle: A History of Communism Told through Communist Jokes* (London: Weidenfeld and Nicolson, 2008).

59. Allan Hall, "A Sneak Preview of How Stasi Made GDR a Nation of Spies," *Times,* March 25, 2002, 17, *Times Digital Archive* (accessed April 25, 2012).

60. Ibid.

61. Koehler, *Stasi,* 143.

62. John C. Schmeidel, *Stasi: Shield and Sword of the Party* (London: Routledge, 2008), 21.

63. David Childs, *The Fall of the GDR: Germany's Road to Unity* (Harlow: Longman, 2001), 38.

64. Gary Bruce, *The Firm: The Inside Story of the Stasi* (Oxford: Oxford University Press, 2010), 6.

65. Koehler, *Stasi,* 143–44.

66. Hall, "A Sneak Preview."

67. Nicholas Shakespeare, *Snowleg* (London: Vintage, 2005), 253.

68. See Wolfgang Bergsdorf, "Politischer Sprachgebrauch und totalitäre Herrschaft," in *Die totalitäre Herrschaft der SED: Wirklichkeit und Nachwirkungen,* ed. Wolfgang-Uwe Friedrich, 23–36 (Munich: C. H.Beck, 1998).

69. Eckhard Jesse, "War die DDR totalitär?" *Aus Politik und Zeitgeschichte,*October 7, 1994, 15.

70. "Drehbuch," 34.

71. Stein, "*Stasi* with a Human Face?" 573–74.

72. Ibid., 569–70.

73. Siegfried Mampel, *Das Ministerium für Staatssicherheit der ehemaligen DDR als Ideologiepolizei: Zur Bedeutung einer Heilslehre als Mittel zum Griff auf das Bewußtsein für das Totalitarismusmodell* (Berlin: Duncker and Humblot, 1996).

74. See also Peter Grieder, "When Your Neighbour Changes His Wallpaper: The 'Gorbachev Factor' and the Collapse of the German Democratic Republic," in *The 1989 Revolutions in Central and Eastern Europe: From Communism to Pluralism,* ed. Kevin McDermott and Matthew Stibbe (Manchester: Manchester University Press, 2013), 76–77; Grieder, *The German Democratic Republic,* 129.

75. Quoted in Wolfgang-Uwe Friedrich, "Bürokratischer Totalitarismus—Zur Typologie des SED-Regimes," in Friedrich, *Die totalitäre Herrschaft der SED,* 17.

76. John Connelly, *Captive University: The Sovietization of East German, Czech, and Polish Higher Education, 1945–1956* (Chapel Hill: University of North Carolina Press, 2000), 284.

77. See "Extended and Deleted Scenes," *The Lives of Others* DVD.

78. Karen Leeder, *Breaking Boundaries: A New Generation of Poets in the GDR* (Oxford: Clarendon, 1996); Helen Bridge, *Women's Writing and Historiography in the GDR* (Oxford: Oxford University Press, 2002). See also Grieder, *The German Democratic Republic,* 118.

79. For a conceptualization of East Germany as a totalitarian welfare state, see Grieder, *The German Democratic Republic,* particularly 2–6.

80. "Drehbuch," 31, 32.

81. Ibid., 82. See also Stein, "*Stasi* with a Human Face?" 572.

82. "Drehbuch," 74, 80.

83. Ibid., 33. See also Stein, "*Stasi* with a Human Face?" 572.

84. Mike Dennis, *The Rise and Fall of the German Democratic Republic, 1945–1990* (Harlow: Longman, 2000), 145–46.

85. Hermann Weber, *DDR: Grundriß der Geschichte, 1945–1990* (Hannover: Fackelträger, 1991), 324.

86. Martin McCauley, *The German Democratic Republic since 1945* (London: Macmillan, 1983), 186. See also Grieder, *The German Democratic Republic*, 75.

87. Schmeidel, *Stasi*, 90–91.

88. Stein, *"Stasi* with a Human Face?" 572.

89. Dennis, *The Stasi*, 117.

90. Stein, *"Stasi* with a Human Face?" 573.

91. Christa Wolf, *Was bleibt: Erzählung* (Frankfurt: Luchterhand, 1992).

92. Dennis, *The Stasi*, 118.

93. Udo Grashoff, *"In einem Anfall von Depression . . . " Selbsttötungen in der DDR* (Berlin: Christoph Links Verlag, 2006).

94. Ibid., 470. See also Grieder, *The German Democratic Republic*, 117.

95. Author's interviews with Kurt Hager, December 1, 1992, and April 6, 1994.

96. McCauley, *The German Democratic Republic*, 186.

97. Jeannette Madarász, *Conflict and Compromise in East Germany, 1971–1989: A Precarious Stability* (Basingstoke: Palgrave Macmillan, 2003), 120. See also Grieder, *The German Democratic Republic*, 75–76.

98. Garton Ash, *The File*, 19.

99. David Childs and Richard Popplewell, *The Stasi: The East German Intelligence and Security Service* (Basingstoke: Macmillan, 1996), 177.

100. "Drehbuch," 78.

101. Armin Mitter and Stefan Wolle, *Untergang auf Raten: Unbekannte Kapitel der DDR-Geschichte* (Munich: C. Bertelsmann Verlag, 1993), 538.

102. See Grieder, *The German Democratic Republic*, chaps. 5, 6.

103. See Grieder, "When Your Neighbour Changes His Wallpaper."

104. Cheryl Dueck, "The Humanization of the Stasi in *Das Leben der Anderen*," *German Studies Review* 31, no. 3 (2008): 599.

105. Pfaff, *"The Lives of Others*," 111.

106. Cited in Dueck, "The Humanization of the Stasi," 601.

107. See Lindenberger, "Stasiploitation—Why Not?" 565.

108. Garton Ash, "The Stasi on Our Minds," 335.

109. Stein, *"Stasi* with a Human Face?" 569.

110. Bruce, *The Firm*, 12.

111. John Burgess, *The East German Church and the End of Communism* (New York: Oxford University Press, 1997), 106.

112. Childs, *The Fall of the GDR*, xii; Garton Ash, "The Stasi on Our Minds," 329.

113. Bruce, *The Firm*, 9.

114. *The Lives of Others* DVD.

115. Garton Ash, *The File*, 74.

116. See Schmeidel, *Stasi*, 26; and Dennis, *The Stasi*, 6.

117. Dennis, *The Stasi*, 4.

118. Ibid., xi.

119. Koehler, *Stasi*, 9.

120. Ibid., 8.

121. Dennis, *The Stasi,* 79.

122. Bruce, *The Firm,* 184. See also Grieder, *The German Democratic Republic,* 114.

123. Kate Connolly, "No Remorse: Margot Honecker Defends East German Dictatorship; Wife of Erich Honecker Breaks 20-Year Silence to Lament Demise of GDR," *Guardian,* April 3, 2012, 15.

124. Mary Fulbrook, *The People's State: East German Society from Hitler to Honecker* (London: Yale University Press, 2005), 8.

125. Madarász, *Conflict and Compromise,* 195.

126. Bruce, *The Firm,* 145.

127. "Drehbuch," 150.

128. Fulbrook, *Anatomy,* 55.

129. Funder, "Tyranny of Terror."

130. Berghahn, "Remembering the Stasi in a Fairy-tale of Redemption."

131. Garton Ash, "The Stasi on Our Minds," 333.

132. Dueck, "The Humanization of the Stasi," 600.

133. Ibid.

134. See ibid., 607.

135. George Santayana, *The Life of Reason; or, the Phases of Human Progress: Introduction and Reason in Common Sense* (New York: Charles Scribner's Sons, 1920), 284.

136. This famous quotation is the opening sentence in: Leslie Poles Hartley, *The Go-between* (London: Hamilton, 1953), 9.

137. See "A New Era for Privacy—No Snoopers' Charter: Policy Officer Sophie Farthing Looks at the New Draft Communications Data Bill—How Low Will the Government Stoop and How Far Will It Snoop?" *Quarterly Newsletter of Liberty* (Summer 2012): 6–7. This bill, dubbed the "Snoopers' Charter" by its critics, was shelved in April 2013 following protests from privacy campaigners and the opposition of the Liberal Democrats within the Conservative-led coalition. However, in June 2013 former Central Intelligence Agency (CIA) employee and U.S. National Security Agency (NSA) contractor Edward Snowden revealed that secret mass surveillance of e-mails, telephone calls, and Internet traffic was already happening through the PRISM and Tempora programs of the NSA and British Government Communications Headquarters (GCHQ), respectively. Some argue that the NSA's capture and storage of ordinary citizens' metadata violates the Fourth Amendment to the U.S. Constitution, which states: "The right of the people to be secure in their persons, houses, papers, and effects, against unreasonable searches and seizures, shall not be violated, and no Warrants shall issue, but upon probable cause, supported by Oath or affirmation, and particularly describing the place to be searched, and the persons or things to be seized."

138. Ian Katz, "Tim Berners-Lee Urges Government to Stop the Snooping Bill. Exclusive: Extension of Surveillance Powers 'A Destruction of Human Rights,'" *Guardian,* April 17, 2012, http://www.guardian.co.uk/technology/2012/apr/17/tim-berners-lee-monitoring-internet/print (accessed April 25, 2012).

139. Ibid.

140. "The State Isn't Going to Read All Your Email—It's Worse than That," *NO2ID Newsletter,* 2nd ser., no. 5, April 25, 2012.

141. "Giant Database Plan 'Orwellian,'" *BBC News,* October 15, 2008, http://news.bbc. co.uk/1/hi/uk_politics/7671046.stm (accessed May 3, 2012).

142. "UK Government Drops 'Orwellian' Database Plans," *Neowin,* April 27, 2009, www. neowin.net/news/uk-government-drops-orwellian-database-plans (accessed May 3, 2012).

143. "A New Era for Privacy," 6.

144. Bruce, *The Firm,* 91–93.

145. "Das war die DDR. Teil 4: 'Schild und Schwert.'"

146. Dennis, *The Stasi,* 7.

147. See Timothy Garton Ash, "Our State Collects More Data than the Stasi Ever Did: We Need to Fight Back," *Guardian,* January 31, 2008, http://www.guardian.co.uk/ commentisfree/2008/jan/31/immigrationpolicy.politics/print (accessed April 23, 2012).

148. Ibid.

149. "Britain Is 'Surveillance Society,'" *BBC News,* November 2, 2006, http://news.bbc.co.uk/1/hi/uk/6108496.stm (accessed April 26, 2012).

150. Richard Ford, "Beware Rise of Big Brother State, Warns Data Watchdog," *Times,* August 16, 2004, 1, *Times Digital Archive* (accessed April 26, 2012).

151. "Waking Up to a Surveillance Society," press release from the information commissioner's office, November 2, 2006, http://www.ico.gov.uk/upload/documents/ pressreleases/2006/waking_up_to_a_surveillance_society.pdf (accessed April 26, 2012).

152. "Britain Is 'Surveillance Society.'"

153. Anthony B. Newkirk, "The Rise of the Fusion-Intelligence Complex: A Critique of Political Surveillance after 9/11," *Surveillance and Society* 8, no. 1 (2010): 1, http://www.surveillance-and-society.org/ojs/index.php/journal/article/viewFile/fusion/ fusion (accessed April 26, 2012).

154. "Britain Is 'Surveillance Society.'"

155. Katz, "Tim Berners-Lee Urges Government to Stop the Snooping Bill."

156. James Ball, "Triumph of Surveillance: Vows to Protect Online Privacy Are Exposed as Hollow by a Plan to Vastly Extend Online Monitoring," *Guardian,* April 3, 2012, 28.

157. Ibid.

158. Grieder, *The German Democratic Republic,* 91.

159. Childs, *The Fall of the GDR,* 36.

160. Stein, "*Stasi* with a Human Face?" 572.

161. See "The Solution," in *Bertolt Brecht Poems, 1913–1956,* ed. John Willet and Ralph Manheim, with the cooperation of Erich Fried (London: Eyre Methuen, 1981), 440.

162. Richard J. Evans, *The Coming of the Third Reich* (London: Penguin, 2004), 331.

163. Dennis, *The Stasi,* xii.

Part 5

THE STASI IN THE GDR

Ulrich Mühe (as Gerd Weisler).

12

THE STASI

An Overview

Jens Gieseke

Translated by Mary Carlene Forszt and David Laurence Burnett

Editors' note: The following is an abridged version of an essay on the Stasi that first appeared in the indispensable volume A Handbook of the Communist Security Apparatus in East Central Europe, 1944–1989, *edited by Krzysztof Persak and Łukasz Kamiński, published by the Institute of National Remembrance in Warsaw in 2005. Gieseke's contribution, like the others in that volume, is truly comprehensive and extraordinarily detailed. For reasons of space, the present version has been reduced in size. We have also included an abbreviated version of Gieseke's extensive bibliography so readers can direct themselves to this literature. Gieseke's in-text citations refer to works listed there.*

1. Organization and Structures of the Security Apparatus

The inner security apparatus in the German Democratic Republic (GDR) was divided into two ministries: the Ministry of the Interior (MdI), with the German People's Police (Deutsche Volkspolizei—DVP) as the regular, "public" police force, and the Ministry for State Security (MfS) as the political secret police and intelligence service. For a brief period, from July 1953 to November 1955, State Security was formally subordinate to the Ministry of the Interior in the form of a permanent secretary's office, though in reality it was always independent. This contribution deals systematically only with the Ministry for State Security as the core institution of the communist security apparatus. The People's Police is dealt with only where it was directly involved in politically motivated repression.

By its origin and design, the Staatssicherheit (or, more colloquially, Stasi) was a secret police organization that watched over and fought against opponents of the party dictatorship—or those it held to be such. It could arrest people and keep them prisoner in its own interrogation and detention facilities until they could be brought to trial. Additionally, it strove to bring the whole of society under its control. At the same time, the GDR's State Security Service was one of the world's most successful intelligence services for espionage and counterespionage. Over the decades the apparatus grew into a large-scale bureaucracy with numerous additional tasks: it provided bodyguards to protect leading East German functionaries and operated the Politburo settlement in Wandlitz (near Berlin); it placed passport inspectors at border crossings and monitored the flow of traffic between East and West Germany; it monitored and was involved in weapons and technology trade; and finally, it ran a sports club, FC Dynamo Berlin, which won the national football championship on numerous occasions.

In the cold war context, it saw itself as part of the global system conflict between socialism and "imperialism" that was being waged on German soil between two separate states. Due to this situation, inner political and social conflicts were viewed in principle as being controlled by West German or other "imperialistic" secret services and "enemy" organizations. Accordingly, internal "counterintelligence" and external "reconnaissance" closely cooperated, thereby blurring the boundaries between intelligence service activities and domestic repression.

It goes without saying that the paradigm for the MfS was the Soviet secret police, founded by the Bolsheviks in 1917 and developed under Stalin into institutions (State Political Administration [GPU], All-Russian State Political Administration [OGPU], People's Commissioner for Internal Affairs [NKVD], People's Commissioner for State Security [NKGB]) of mass terror within society and the party. Like all members of the socialist "brother organs," MfS employees liked to describe themselves as "Chekists" in the spirit of the legendary Extraordinary Commission for Combating Counterrevolution and Sabotage of 1917.

2. The Methods of Security Apparatus Operational Work (Surveillance Techniques and Technologies)

The main methods of the State Security Service during the early years consisted of arbitrary arrests and extorting confessions using unceasing nightly interrogations and other torture methods. These aimed to prove that the person under arrest was involved in espionage activities for Western intelligence services and underground organizations such as the Task Force against Inhumanity, the Association of German Youth, or the Eastern offices of the Western political parties and trade unions. Nor did the Stalinist mindset adopted during industrialization accept production stoppages as a result of worn-out or overloaded machines, wanting to expose them instead as hostile acts of sabotage.

In the course of de-Stalinization in 1956–1957, the standard practice of continuous interrogation and other types of torture was eventually called into question. From spring until autumn of 1956, the number of arrests made by the MfS substantially decreased. Only after the closing of the sector border in Berlin did the MfS resume drastic measures, arresting East German citizens who protested against the construction of the Wall as well as other personae non gratae previously spared in order to avoid unrest (and thus a further increase in the number of flights to the West). Direct compulsion therefore remained at the core of MfS practice, backed by the equally effective use of the unspoken threat. However, other methods of intelligence service surveillance took on greater importance. Following the consolidation of political power after the building of the Berlin Wall in August 1961 and the new de-Stalinizing impulses of the Twenty-second Congress of the Communist Party of the Soviet Union (CPSU) in October 1961, the MfS's frame of reference shifted somewhat. The Socialist Unity Party of Germany (SED) leadership under Ulbricht was looking to expand its remit.

On the one hand, the changes affected secret police practices: investigators and prison warders less frequently committed open brutalities against prisoners; prison conditions, while still degrading, were eased somewhat. The repertoire of criminological and intelligence-gathering techniques was expanded; the permanently increasing number of full-time employees and the quantitative and qualitative improvement of the informant network made it possible to extend secret police operations into the main battle lines of opposition activities. On the other hand, preventive reconnaissance of potential trouble spots became a field of operations as important as direct persecution.

From 1964 onward, the MfS established a network of "security representatives" headed by the inspection division of the Council of Ministers. In
the head offices of the economic bureaucracy (ministries, public offices) of
the centrally regulated organizations of the state-owned factories as well as
in the 459 most important combines, enterprises, and institutions, the security representative positions were filled with officers on special assignment
(OibE). After 1968 the top economic OibE was the head of the Inspection
Department in the Council of Ministers, Harry Möbis.

The efforts of the GDR leadership to establish an international reputation
and the "hostile" influences that entered East Germany through Western
contacts, which were growing by leaps and bounds, curtailed the leeway of
the MfS to use openly forceful measures. Nevertheless, the State Security
did not take these changes as an opportunity to limit its activities—on the
contrary, it increased the degree of concealed surveillance and modified its
methods. With the help of the considerably expanded network of unofficial
informers, not only was every "hostile" activity to be exposed in its incipient
stages, it was to be combated by conspiratorial means (means that would
not be recognizable to the person targeted by the Stasi).

Arrests could arouse the interest of Western journalists accredited in the
GDR. Therefore, everything had to be done first to "switch off" human rights
activists and people wanting to defect. Among other things, along with the
"operational psychology" methods increasingly integrated into MfS work in
the 1970s, covert "demoralization measures" were taken up to cause or stir
up conflicts between group members, to weaken or thwart their connection
to church institutions, and to limit or squelch the opposition's commitment.

It was decisive that the State Security was not recognizable as the real
wire puller in these operations. Such measures were supposed to be used
when "due to political and political-operational reasons in the interest of
realizing a greater social benefit, the respective operational procedure was
not to be concluded with criminal prosecution" (directive 1/76)—for example, if direct repression would have caused too much outcry and thereby
endangered German-German negotiations.

Even in the 1970s and 1980s the State Security Service did not limit
itself to such methods but also arrested citizens when this seemed necessary and it had gathered sufficient "evidence." Then Main Department IX
came into action, the so-called examination organ of the MfS. This department also took proceedings out of the hands of the People's Police if they
were "politically-operationally" relevant for other reasons, for example, if

full-time employees or unofficial informers were involved too. The interrogators and watchmen only rarely used physical force, but they used the whole gamut of "white torture" (emotional pressure) to induce the interrogated person to make statements or confess to crimes. In the course of preferring charges and court proceedings, the examination organ of the MfS had a significance that far exceeded its formal position. In effect, the State Security Service directed the scene in political trials right up to the verdict; in prominent cases it asked state and party leader Honecker for a "suggestion" about the sentence.

The MfS reserved for itself the right to seal up sections of inquiry files that contained "unofficially" gained information. The public prosecutor's offices and courts responsible for political trials were under the cadre policy control of the MfS. They were infiltrated by unofficial informers and, in important positions, by officers on special assignment. They maintained intensive personal contacts with the leaders of the MfS inquiries. Not least of all, in some cases the State Security Service worked together with the defense lawyers.

During preliminary proceedings the prisoners were detained in the interrogation/detention centers of line XIV. There they were exposed to various types of torment: the cells could be bugged; in addition, the MfS employed fellow prisoners as "cell informers." They were supposed to spy on prisoners in exchange for privileges. While sentenced political prisoners normally served their sentences in other East German detention centers, the State Security in special cases (such as those involving MfS employees who had deserted) kept prisoners in their interrogation/detention centers, where some of them were imprisoned as so-called numbered prisoners.

Apart from the methods of arrest and direct persecution, the MfS had the entire secret service and criminological system at its disposal. This included the collaborative work of unofficial informers (see below) as well as diverse methods of technical surveillance.

Division M and its territorial offshoots monitored post and package shipments. They had their own rooms in the main post offices of the GDR, in which MfS employees (in this case mostly women) checked the post by both random and targeted sampling. Postal monitoring played a pivotal role as early as the 1950s due to the high volume of letter and parcel post crossing over the German-German border. By the 1980s, MfS postal inspectors could handle around ninety thousand letters and sixty thousand packages a day. During holiday seasons such as Christmas and Easter the figures were considerably higher. The MfS even invented its own machines, enabling it to automatically open and reseal large quantities of letters.

Department 26 was responsible for audio and visual surveillance measures of every kind, including telephone surveillance and observation of rooms using "bugs" and cameras. This branch of the MfS grew alongside the expansion of the private telephone network in the GDR. Department 26 at MfS headquarters alone grew from 65 employees in 1955 to 436 in 1989. Added to this were corresponding units in the regional administrations and district offices. In 1989 the district offices each had sixteen to one hundred and the regional administrations two hundred to five hundred bugged lines available for simultaneous use. In East Berlin alone, twenty thousand telephones could be tapped at the same time.

Shadowing and, if necessary, arresting individuals fell under Main Department VIII's area of responsibility. In 1989 nearly forty-five hundred staff members were employed in this line at the central and regional administrations. A "dovetailing" service unit that was aimed more at external tasks was Main Department III. It was supposed to monitor radio traffic in the GDR and also, at the same time and with considerable effort, the line-of-sight radio links between West Berlin and the Federal Republic as well as conversations via radio telephone in the Bonn area. It is said that between thirty thousand and forty thousand telephone connections were tapped in the West. Technical equipment and related items were provided by the Operational-Technical Sector (OTS) and the Department for Weapons and Chemical Services (BCD). The MfS even secretly took body scent samples of supposed dissidents and marked objects with radioactive substances. Finally, the paths of "official" influence and information via the SED party machinery, the People's Police, the government administrations and economic apparatuses, the cadre sections, army district defense commands, and mass organizations were equally important. This all added up to a policy of "total surveillance"—with bugs and cameras, telephone, radio and postal surveillance, searches of flats and workplaces, and shadowing of suspects.

3. The Main Focuses of Security Apparatus Activities: Stalinism, 1950–1956

In the early years—until February 1956—the Stasi established itself as an instrument of "bureaucratic terror" in SED social politics and in the German-German conflict of systems. Top priority was given to the struggle against enemy organizations working out of the West: the Eastern offices of the Social Democrats, Christian Democrats, and the Liberal Democratic Party as well as the German Federation of Trade Unions, the Investigating Committee of Free Lawyers (a shelter for judges, public prosecutors, and administrative officials purged from their positions), and the militant Task Force against Inhumanity. Added to this were offices such as the American radio broadcaster in Berlin, RIAS, and—of course—the secret services, including the West German Gehlen Organization (precursor of the Federal Intelligence Service). Also considered as "hostile organizations" were concerns and enterprises based in the Federal Republic whose assets had been expropriated in the GDR.

It goes without saying that all of these offices had sources in the GDR. Yet the SED and State Security did not content themselves with finding merely these. The fateful logic of Stalinism meant that, in principle, anyone and everyone holding a deviating opinion or position or those who, even through no action of their own doing, became an object of scrutiny were declared to be secret agents, saboteurs, and bandits in the service of these "enemy headquarters." In actual fact, the SED was waging a cold civil war on the home front and beyond the demarcation line with the aim of carrying through its course of political and social transformation.

The Stasi arrested, for instance, politicians of the "bourgeois" parties that had been forced into line, such as Foreign Minister Georg Dertinger (Christian Democrat) in December 1952, accused of being a spy, and the minister for trade and supply Karl Hamann (Liberal Democrat) on charges of being a saboteur. Numerous Social Democrats who refused to accept the course of the Unity Party or were to be removed from their posts for other reasons also became victims. Many young people were also arrested: for example, for distributing leaflets protesting the political course. All of these persons arrested were given long prison sentences. Nearly twenty-eight hundred Jehovah's Witnesses were likewise arrested between 1950 and 1955 for allegedly being American agents. With the remilitarization of the GDR in 1952 (creation of the Barracked People's Police) the Protestant youth group Junge Gemeinde—which with its open atmosphere of pacifism offered a sanctuary for many young people still traumatized from the Second World War—likewise came under pressure.

The inner terror reached its pinnacle in the wake of the Second Party Conference of the SED in July 1952. It was here that Walter Ulbricht proclaimed the "Construction of Socialism" in the GDR, thereby ushering in a new stage of the transformation process. The party conference resolved: "One should bear in mind that the intensification of the class struggle is inevitable and that the working people must break the resistance of hostile forces."

Many farmers, craftsmen, and merchants were brought to court for alleged "economic crimes." At the same time the GDR adopted from the Soviet Union the draconian disciplining of workers. The "Law for the Protection of National Property" prescribed tremendous penalties for minor offenses: workers were sentenced to a minimum of one year imprisonment for stealing a coal briquette or a pound and a half of sauerkraut. In more serious cases of theft one ran the risk of being sentenced to the "twenty-five years" notorious in Soviet law—spent there in a "work-reform camp" and in the East German case in a penitentiary.

Moreover, during the Stalinist purges in the early 1950s the MfS carried out, together with the Central Party Control Commission, investigations against purported "elements hostile to the party" as well as alleged Trotskyites and Titoists. Among the most prominent victims were the deputy chairman of the West German Communist Party (KPD), Kurt Müller, and the East German railways director, Wilhelm Kreikemeyer, whose death while in MfS custody remains unclarified even today. Even the leading functionary Paul Merker, a Politburo member since 1927, was expelled from the SED in 1950 and arrested by the MfS in 1952. Because of his contacts to the alleged American spy Noel Field, he was at first slated to become the main defendant in a show trial. In 1955 he was sentenced to eight years in prison. The court acquitted him in July 1956 as a result of the subsequent political thaw.

During the uprising on June 17, 1953,[1] the MfS had to prove its usefulness in the face of inner disturbances. The guard units protected party and government buildings, including the House of Ministries in Berlin, while the employees of other service units formed task forces to arrest the "ringleaders" or tried to protect MfS buildings. Since Wilhelm Zaisser (first minister for state security, 1950–1953) had forbidden shooting at demonstrators and the MfS employees had not been suitably trained, only the Soviet troops saved the secret police from disaster. Demonstrators stormed the district offices in Bitterfeld, Görlitz, Jena, Niesky, and Merseburg and shot an employee in front of one Magdeburg prison. In Rathenow an irate mob lynched a man well known in the town as a former K-5 (Branch 5 of the Criminal Investigation Department) member.

The Stasi reacted to the June crisis by building up its own information system and taking greater precautions for a potential civil war. It began setting up independent information groups that were supposed to combine their collected reports into "mood reports." Due to the small size of the groups and the lack of qualified personnel, however, their usefulness remained limited.

With defeat on June 17, 1953, being averted only by the Soviet army, the SED leadership prepared more intensively for the eventuality of military conflict or domestic unrest in the GDR. In 1954, with this aim in view, the leadership formed a Security Commission as well as district and local operational staffs in which the State Security was also represented. MfS guard units in the former provincial capitals (except for the Berlin Guard Regiment) were combined with some of the stand-by police units, which had previously been under the authority of the Ministry of the Interior, to form the "domestic troops." Together with the border and transport police, they were subordinated to Deputy Minister Gartmann in 1955. Because Ernst Wollweber (minister for state security, 1953–1957) regarded these large newly formed units as a foreign body in the MfS, they were put under the authority of the Ministry of the Interior in the spring of 1957. This meant that the Berlin Guard Regiment was the only military unit left in the MfS. In November 1956, with the Hungarian Revolution and the June crisis in mind, the Politburo approved a multistage plan to suppress civil unrest using armed East German troops as well as Soviet troops if necessary. According to the "first stage," the People's Police, armed MfS units, and the paramilitary task forces of the working classes (*Kampfgruppen*) would suppress disturbances using "simple police means" such as water cannons and by sealing off areas. NVA (National People's Army) units would only be called into action in exceptional situations.

Foreign espionage, now part of the ministry, began to increase in importance as of 1955, when a slight détente emerged in East-West relations. The East European secret services "compensated" accordingly with a course correction. Secret activity aimed at the West was to be substantially expanded, with regard both to espionage and to subversive actions in the opposing camp. The MfS district administrations formed their own espionage departments and the Western assignments of the counterintelligence lines were expanded. In line III (national economy), for example, working groups were set up for activities against Western manufacturing concerns. Among other things, they were supposed to engage in industrial and military espionage. The work against "internal enemies" was to take second place to this new main area of emphasis.

De-Stalinization and Recovery, 1956–1971

With the revelations of the Twentieth Party Congress of the CPSU in February 1956 Ulbricht endeavoured to limit the repercussions. Numerous political prisoners were released (see below) and uncertainty spread as to the future tasks of State Security. Secret police in general became the target of a wave of criticism. The "specter" lasted little more than half a year, however. The inner disturbances in Poland and Hungary, combined with the revolt of party intellectuals and students in the GDR, gave Ulbricht cause for a renewed change in policy: he shifted the main emphasis from direct actions against Western intelligence services and underground organizations to the internal opposition forces in the GDR, which had been influenced, "softened up," and "subverted" by "imperialist" ideology. Erich Mielke (minister for state security, 1957–1989) willingly took on this change in policy, having demonstratively rejected the criticism of Stalin at the Twentieth Congress of the CPSU. Nor did he later make any secret of his admiration for the "great Soviet leader."

In 1957–1958, following the new party line of the Thirty-fifth Plenum of the Central Committee, Mielke further developed the MfS definition of the enemy under the concept of "political-ideological subversion" (*politisch-ideologische Diversion*—PID). He traced all forms of domestic opposition in socialist countries back to the influence of "imperialistic enemy headquarters," whether there were direct, provable intelligence incursions or only intellectual influence. The Stasi trained its sights particularly on positions both within the SED and outside the party supporting democratic socialism critical of Stalinism. These were castigated as "social democratism [*sic*], opportunism, revisionism." The "PID doctrine" was the State Security's justification for its constantly growing presence in all areas of life in the following decades.

Between the Fifth Party Conference of the SED in 1958 and the construction of the Berlin Wall in 1961, the main task of the MfS lay in the fight against illegal border crossing. Those who inspired and organized such actions were to be arrested. In addition, in 1959–1960 a large number of employees were engaged in the recruitment of fighting brigades pushing forward the collectivization campaign in agriculture. Farmers were put under pressure through interrogations and threatened by drumhead courts with punishment for real or fictitious offenses if they were not prepared to join the collective farms. The fight against allegedly omnipresent "political-ideological subversion" provided Mielke with a legitimate reason to build up State Security into a "government office authorized to exercise control over the rest of the apparatus of state," as senior SED functionary Hermann Matern complained in 1962.

At this point the future role of the Stasi in the walled republic had by no means been decided by the party leadership: the important KGB role model was having to reorient itself during the thaw under Khrushchev; Ulbricht was propagating the "socialist human community" and had initiated reforms; the army and police had to accept budget cuts. But just as Honecker succeeded in mobilizing the "conservative" interests of the party against any spirit of reform, so Mielke succeeded after 1963–1964 with his ideas for the development of State Security. In the 1960s the MfS systematically enlarged both its internal analysis and its secret official reporting to the SED leadership. The MfS took the economic reforms of the "New Economic System" after 1963 as an opportunity for amplified activities in the national economy. Already it had jealously guarded the surveillance of the ambitious and politically sensitive buildup of an aviation programme in the GDR, riddled with purportedly "unreliable" engineers, as its own pilot project. Nevertheless, the scheme was abandoned by the Politburo in 1962—even the MfS had been unable to prevent its failure. Exposing hostile activities in the economy was, according to Mielke, the main task of the MfS in contributing to an increase in productivity.

In the spirit of prevention, the Stasi not only strove to be broadly present in every area of society but also expanded into personnel-intensive police tasks that only indirectly concerned secret police activity. These included passport controls at the border crossings of the GDR in 1962 and the supervision of holiday traffic crossing the intra-German border in 1963–1964. The working groups formed for these purposes were united in 1970 in Main Department VI. This additional area of responsibility arose from the experience gained during 1963–1966, when a limited border pass agreement had been in effect, enabling inhabitants of West Berlin to cross over to the Eastern part of the city for the first time since 1961. The MfS had set itself the task of surveilling the onslaught of approximately 1.2 million visitors during the Christmas season of 1963. To this end it had obliged all employees to work on special task forces. Additionally, the border intelligence unit of the border police (already under the leadership of a covert MfS officer on special assignment since 1959) was placed under MfS authority, while a division of labor was determined with the military espionage unit of the

National People's Army. The State Security Service thereby consolidated its position vis-à-vis the other armed forces.

"Personal protection" was an area of influence that took on a special meaning and atmosphere when it involved state and party functionaries: the MfS provided not only bodyguards but also the complete staff of the Wandlitz Politburo settlement, right down to the sales personnel in the special supermarket supplied with Western products. The total care and provision of functionaries and their families living there was dispensed from the hand of the MfS.

The Stasi discovered a broad field of activity in the propaganda war against the Federal Republic in the 1960s. It used the collection of Nazi materials it had been building up since the 1940s to denounce actual or supposed Nazi perpetrators who held office in Bonn: for example, in politics, business, and law enforcement. The Eichmann trial in Jerusalem 1961 as well as the Nazi trials in the Federal Republic provided the occasion to tap a continuous-observation pool of former concentration camp staff tracked down in the GDR, providing stool pigeons but also, if required, the accused. Party and MfS staged trials in absentia against politicians in Bonn and released incriminating documents (forged if necessary) in the West. On the other hand, they kept investigative reports to themselves about the whereabouts of Nazi perpetrators, such as Erich Gust, the alleged murderer of KPD leader Ernst Thälmann, in order to be able to accuse the West German judicial authorities of inaction and lack of zeal.

Finally, the Stasi prepared itself more intensively for possible actions involving civil unrest or national defense. All employees received military training. The sabotage unit of the MfS (which had existed since 1953) received reinforcements from the NVA's special forces for "partisan operations." These had also trained West German Communists as underground fighters and had built up a logistic network in the Federal Republic. In 1964 Mielke ordered special training for individual military specialists (radio operators, divers, parachutists, and explosives specialists). In addition, from 1959 on the first indications can be found for plans to intern "hostile-negative" forces in the case of unrest. The mobilization directive 1/67 thus contained a detailed system for the creation of isolation camps. Moreover, the MfS guard regiment was developed substantially, in 1967 receiving the honorary name Feliks E. Dzierzynski after the founder of the Extraordinary Commission for the Battle against Counterrevolution and Sabotage (Cheka), and by 1970 numbering approximately seventy-nine hundred.

In a nutshell, the State Security Service during the 1960s developed into a post-Stalinist, large-scale bureaucracy, a "general enterprise for security, securing power and oppression" (Henke et al. 1995–). The "Prague Spring" in 1968 and its violent end at the hands of Warsaw Pact troops proved to be a test case for the efficiency of the apparatus. This (historically final) attempt at reforming communism along humane, democratic lines corresponded in almost textbook fashion to the MfS's perception of the enemy and its "political-ideological subversion." The Stasi took part with its own forces in turning the course of events in Czechoslovakia; after the successful suppression it helped the Czechoslovakian secret police to purge its apparatus of reformers and reconsolidate it. In the GDR itself there was a wave of over twenty-one hundred protests and more than five hundred investigative proceedings, mainly for "propaganda hostile to the state," against East German citizens who had publicly shown their solidarity with the cause of the Prague Spring. But the MfS could sum up: "There was no serious discord or unrest nor were there any occurrences, involving larger population groups, which could have expanded into political actions against the GDR and the measures taken by the five Warsaw Pact states" (quoted in Tantzscher 1994, 35). In this respect the State Security Service had absolutely fulfilled its repressive function. Preventive surveillance, however, had been shown to have gaps: not even a quarter of all registered protest cases had been solved, and in those in which the MfS was successful, it turned out that they mostly involved individuals who had not previously attracted negative attention.

The Honecker Era, 1971–1989

The foreign policy of the GDR in the 1970s, which concentrated on international recognition and thus required a partial opening to the West, confronted the Ministry for State Security with an "extraordinarily crucial test." The aim of the state and party leadership, to break through the foreign-policy isolation of the GDR and to draw legitimacy from the creation of this international reputation, demanded concessions with regard to the social opening of the GDR. The domestic consequences of this development were to be offset by the State Security. The SED reacted to the German-German Basic Treaty of December 21, 1972, with extensive security measures in order to keep the contacts of East German citizens to West Germans, which greatly increased after this time, under control.

The international debate about the observation of human and civil rights and above all the signing of the Final Act of the Conference on Security and Cooperation in Europe (CSCE) in Helsinki in 1975 also became challenges. This guarantee of freedom of expression and freedom of domicile, officially recognized by the GDR, was used by many East Germans as an occasion to demand changes in domestic policy. In addition to the quantitatively rather small but politically significant civil rights initiatives, citizens wanting to leave the country became a central target of MfS persecution. The "driving back of unlawful migration requests" became one of its most important tasks.

In the view of the party and MfS leadership, the consequences of tolerating "political-ideological subversion" could be witnessed in one of the GDR's neighbors and allies. As in Czechoslovakia in 1968, the MfS attempted in 1980–1981 to influence the conflict in Poland, which had been triggered by the founding of the independent trade union Solidarity and culminated in the imposition of martial law. In 1980 an MfS operational group had been set up in Warsaw, with branches in four additional Polish cities, and had built up its own informer network in this neighboring country. The Disinformation Department of the Foreign Espionage Directorate carried out extensive propaganda operations to discredit Solidarity activists. From the viewpoint of the MfS, Poland had for a time crossed over the threshold between socialist brother country and "operational area."

Among the operational branches of the apparatus, Main Department II (counterespionage) profited the greatest from this expansion: in 1982 it had almost four times as many employees as in 1968. They were supposed to infiltrate the diplomatic representative offices of Western countries and the permanent representative of the Federal Republic and keep them under surveillance. They were also supposed to observe all journalists accredited in the GDR and to track down all GDR citizens who made or sought contact with any of the aforementioned. Thus the seemingly classic system-neutral "counterespionage" developed into a means of reinforcing the MfS function of domestic repression. The reason for this was the basic belief of the party and the State Security Service that dissidence and divergent behavior among the population of the GDR could be traced back to the direct or indirect influence of "imperialist" intelligence services.

However, the expansion of the "long 1970s" (1968–1982) was not at all limited to counterespionage. Based on the principle of the division of labor, all branches of the apparatus profited from the constant influx of staff. The degree and intensity of penetration of all spheres of East German society thereby took on a new quality. The guiding question with respect to "Chekist prevention" that Mielke asked time and again could be reliably answered for an ever-increasing number of GDR citizens: "Who is who?"

In the political security climate of that time, the MfS large-scale bureaucracy was able to become considerably more independent. Branches like cadre and financial administration and the "rear" service units were given considerably more personnel. The Berlin central offices grew continually at a faster pace than the district and area offices. This trend was not unusual for the state and economic apparatus of "bureaucratic socialism." However, it was reinforced by the fact that the secret apparatus was, to a great extent, factually excluded from the planning mechanisms of the national economy and the budget, and not externally supervised. For this reason, cost-use analyses played no role in strategic perspectives during the 1970s.

The most important branches of the MfS apparatus in the 1970s and 1980s will be presented in a brief portrait in order to illustrate the variety of areas of responsibility and the way they worked together.

Main Department I supervised the area of responsibility of the Ministry for National Defense, particularly the National People's Army and the border troops of the GDR. It operated there under the name Administration 2000, and its head was a "permanent participant" in the staff meetings in the Ministry of Defense. In the army and the border units it ran a tight network of *inoffizieller Mitarbeiter* (IMs). Under the pressure of military discipline it was easier to enlist young recruits for informer services; furthermore, particular security regulations were in force. Additionally, Main Department I also had reconnaissance tasks to fulfill: the military espionage service of the Ministry of National Defense was closely connected to the MfS by liaison officers and IMs. The reconnaissance unit of the border troops, who did espionage work in the immediate area of the GDR's national border, consisted exclusively of full-time MfS employees (the departments Reconnaissance Border Detachment North/Central/South of Main Department I).

Among the tasks of Main Department II (counterespionage), in addition to surveillance of diplomatic missions and foreign journalists, were counterespionage in the Foreign Ministry of the GDR as well as at any other "target" of enemy intelligence services. It maintained operational groups in Moscow, Warsaw, Prague, Budapest, and Sofia. As a special assignment area it also secured, using intelligence service methods, the cooperation of the SED and the FDGB (the official association of labor unions in the GDR) with the West German Communist Party (DKP) and the Socialist Unity Party of

West Berlin (SEW). Moreover, the DKP had a secret military organization at its disposal, with approximately two hundred members who had been trained by the MfS. Main Department II grew rapidly in the 1970s; in its Berlin office alone, it had approximately fifteen hundred employees in 1989.

In 1970 the units for passport control and "safeguarding holiday traffic" were combined into Main Department VI. In the area of responsibility of this service unit, close dovetailing developed with the border troops who, among other things, were in command at the border crossings of the GDR, and the customs administration of the GDR. The head of customs from 1963 on was customs chief inspector Gerhard Stauch, who was at the same time MfS colonel on special assignment. Besides the immediate border controls and the accompanying intelligence service activities, all matters regarding holiday traffic control to and from the GDR, including surveillance of the "Interhotels," fell within the competence of Main Department VI.

Similar to the function of Main Department I for the GDR's armed forces was the function of Main Department VII for the People's Police and other institutions under the supervision of the Ministry of the Interior. These included not only the paramilitary "combat groups of the working class," the civil defense staff, but also the State Archive Administration. Supervision and cooperation played similarly important roles here. The police frequently served as an auxiliary support organ in the context of "political-operational interaction" (POZW). Assignment Sector I of the criminal investigation department (political crime) already cooperated permanently with the MfS and ran its own informer network. In addition there existed the People's Police section assignees with their intermediaries. Finally, there were close relations to the Penal System Administration of the MdI, to which the detention centers of the GDR were subordinate. The most important prison used by the MfS—in addition to its own interrogation/detention centers—was the Bautzen II prison. This was formally under the supervision of the Ministry of the Interior but factually controlled to a great extent by the MfS. Prominent political prisoners who had been pursued by the MfS served their sentences here.

Further operational service units to be mentioned are the Main Departments XVIII (national economy) and XIX (traffic, post, telecommunications), which monitored the national economy and the infrastructure of the GDR. In the monitoring area of the Main Department (HA) XVIII (until 1964 HA III) and its district branch offices were not only the enterprises and the collective combines, the planning bureaucracy up to and including the numerous ministries for industry and other economic areas, the apparatus of the Council of Ministers and that of the State Planning Commission but also the various scientific academies. In the area of responsibility of Main Department XVIII, six site offices (*Objektdienststellen*—OD) were established (in the chemical collective combines Buna, Leuna, and Bitterfeld, the gas collective combine Schwarze Pumpe, the collective combine Carl Zeiss Jena, and the nuclear power station in Lubmin/Greifswald); an additional OD could be found at the technical university in Dresden, which belonged to line XX. In addition, two site offices were established in the 1970s in the oil refineries of Schwedt and Böhlen. The competence of Main Department XIX included the transport police in addition to the *Reichsbahn* (East German national railways), the postal system, and airports.

Main Department XVIII was given an important function due to the central organization of the national economy and its significance for SED policy. The spectrum ranged from providing protection to enterprises and industrial counterespionage to security checks in militarily relevant high-technology areas to stopgap functions in the planning process and technical modernization help through espionage. The effects of MfS influence on the East German economy seem contradictory. On the one hand, there are cases in which State Security, through its parallel apparatus, was able to uncover and remedy economic mismanagement. On the other hand, for example, the rigid doctrine of secrecy contributed to the removal of innovative specialists "for security reasons."

Main Department XX is often described as the real core of the Ministry for State Security. In view of its comparatively small size (about 460 employees in 1989 and about twice this number in the district administrations), this is of course exaggerated, but it was nonetheless of central importance in the battle against opposition movements in the GDR. This is where the sections against PID and the exacerbated form thereof, "political underground activity" (PUT), were located. The Christian churches and other religious communities as well as the entire areas of culture and media were monitored from here. Additionally, Main Department XX was responsible for supervision of the bloc parties and social organizations of the GDR, the health and education systems, and sports groups. Leaving aside the SED, which the MfS was prohibited from monitoring systematically, the Main Department XX and its branches in the districts and local areas covered practically all areas of public life in the GDR. Intelligence service "processing" of "PID/PUT centers" ("centers of subversion and underground activity") in West

Germany and West Berlin was also part of the monitoring of opposition activities by Main Department XX. Among these centers were German political institutions and research institutes as well as dissidents who had left the GDR or been expatriated. In some cases they were tormented with psychological intimidation and assassination attempts.

It was particularly important to the State Security Service to penetrate the churches using intelligence service methods because they were the only social institutions that remained ideologically estranged from the system. They were not subject to the principles of democratic centralism and thus also not subject to the direct intervention of the Unity Party. In the 1970s and 1980s, a great deal of opposition potential converged in the freedom made possible by these circumstances. With the help of so-called influence agents, the MfS was supposed to enforce SED policy and interests by conspiratorial means. Particularly great importance was attached to the theological faculties of the state universities and to church lawyers. How far the influence of the MfS on the leading church committees actually reached is disputed, but not how intense the efforts were: in 1988–1989 the MfS had at least eight hundred unofficial informers on the "church line."

A main area of focus of the Main Department XX in the 1970s was the penetration of the literature and theater scene in the GDR, which had the important function of articulating social moods and criticism that could not be formulated in a directly political manner. Because of the public reputation of these intellectuals, who for the most part were critically loyal to the GDR, the State Security Service placed emphasis on preventive surveillance of the literary scene, making use not least of all of numerous artists and cultural functionaries serving as unofficial informers. Parallel to the state and SED cultural bureaucracy and the artists' associations, the MfS Cultural Department functioned in the background as a censorship authority. It endeavored to do everything in its power to hinder the production of critical literature and to criminalize authors who had fallen out of favor—for instance, using the pretext that they had breached exchange control regulations by publishing their works in the West.

In addition to these large main departments, which had essentially existed since the founding of the MfS (partly under other structural names), some important service units should be mentioned that rounded off the range of responsibilities of the MfS in the 1970s and 1980s (or had reached such a magnitude by then that they eventually became areas of responsibility in their own right).

In 1972 the Working Group XVII was created, which ran the so-called visitors' offices in West Berlin, where West Berlin residents had to apply for entry to the GDR. The staff of the visitors' offices consisted of full-time employees and unofficial informers of the MfS. After 1975, as a reaction to the worldwide increase in terrorist attacks, the State Security Service built up its own "Terror Defense" unit (Department XXII). The range of responsibilities of this unit soon reached far beyond the original one of hindering terrorist attacks against the GDR. This unit observed not only the entire spectrum of left- and right-wing extremists in the Federal Republic (as long as they were not closely connected to the DKP, the German Communist Party) but also numerous other West German organizations and institutions from which activities critical of the GDR could be expected. Special attention was given to the attempts of these organizations to extend their sphere of action to the GDR. Thus, in the 1970s, the attempt of the Maoist, later pro-Albanian Communist Party of Germany/Marxist-Leninists to set up an East German section was thwarted with the use of considerable resources.

Above and beyond this "repulsion of danger," Department XXII soon played an active role in the international terror scene. Among other things, it kept surveillance on Arab terrorists who (with the department's knowledge) used the GDR as a "safe area" and for transit purposes. One of the most spectacular operations of Department XXII was the accommodation of ten "dropouts" of the West German terrorist group Red Army Faction (RAF) at the beginning of the 1980s. They were equipped with new identities and integrated professionally into the GDR. Between 1980 and 1982, RAF members made repeated visits to the GDR, where they were trained in the use of weapons by the MfS. Until now, the logic behind these strictly secret operations, which were connected to a high foreign policy risk, has not been conclusively established. Apparently, motives of "anti-imperialist solidarity" mingled with endeavors to keep the terrorist activities under control and to influence them.

In 1976 the Central Coordination Group (ZKG) and the corresponding district coordination groups began their work of battling against escapes to the West and emigration. Originally the ZKG was supposed to coordinate MfS activities against the flight of East Germans and the Western organizations aiding them in their escape efforts. As of 1977, it was also responsible for the applications for legal exit, which had risen dramatically after the signing of the final agreement of the Helsinki accords. Together with the People's Police and other government agencies, the ZKG was supposed to cut down the number of applications by means of reprisals against applicants, to fight against Western institutions and organizations that supported those seeking an exit visa, and to thwart attempts within the GDR to pressure for the support of exit visas through public campaigns and the formation of groups.

Although the number of escapes and attempted escapes declined constantly until 1985, the number of applicants for "permanent exit" rose inexorably. In 1984, when a level of 50,000 applications was reached, the East German leadership opened the sluices for a short time and let almost 30,000 East Germans leave. But the calming effect it had hoped for failed to materialize; the undertow effect was stronger. Already by the end of 1985 there were 53,000 applications for exit; by the summer of 1989 the number had increased to 125,000. Thus the "exit movement" became one of the most important spheres of action for the MfS. Yet the "sword" of the party proved too dull: neither with repression and criminalization nor by approval of emigration for particularly stubborn applicants was it able to keep the problem under control.

Furthermore, in 1983 an independent working group of the sector "Commercial Coordination" (AG BKK) was formed. The AG BKK took over (from Main Department XVIII) the intelligence service control and monitoring of the Commercial Coordination (KoKo) sector, which had been set up in 1966 in the Ministry for Foreign and Inner-German Trade. KoKo was initially headed by MfS officer Horst Roigk. Then, in 1967, Alexander Schalck-Golodkowsi was named head after first being given the rank of colonel and being sworn in as OibE. Other leading positions were also filled by OibEs. This sector had the task of improving the foreign currency situation of the GDR "outside the plan" by weapons sales and other commercial activities and of secretly acquiring products that were subject to Western embargo regulations. In Kavelstorf near Rostock the MfS and the KoKo firm IMES had an extensive weapons depot for transactions with weapons dealers and countries at war. In the 1980s they delivered weapons to both Iran and Iraq—then at war with each another.

The practice of "ransoming prisoners," which had already begun in 1963, and other humanitarian efforts by the Federal Republic became more and more significant in this context. The GDR's negotiator, lawyer Wolfgang Vogel, led the talks under the close supervision of the MfS. Within the framework of the German-German agreements, a total of 33,755 political prisoners were discharged to the Federal Republic, 2,000 children who had been separated from their parents by the construction of the Berlin Wall were handed over to them, and 250,000 other moves to the West were organized. For this the GDR received goods and foreign currency to the tune of about 3.5 billion DM.

In addition to prosecution, the State Security had instructions to keep the SED Party leadership in East Berlin and the local party leadership informed about dissidents' endeavors and the public mood. To do so, it had evaluation and control groups at its disposal in all branches of the apparatus whose reports were gathered in the Central Evaluation and Control Group (ZAIG). The heads of the district offices had to file reports frequently, for the most part weekly, with the first secretary of the SED district office. In 1988, for example, the party leadership around Erich Honecker received about three hundred individual reports from the ZAIG about events, moods, and developments in the country: for example, travel statistics; private visits by West German politicians to the GDR; increased efficiency in industry; meetings of groups of dissidents, rebellious artists, and young "rowdies"; hard currency income from the required minimum exchange by visiting West Germans; actions planned by people wishing to leave the country; and internal matters from the leadership of the Protestant Church. It is possible that the same amount of information was gathered by foreign espionage. Thus the MfS had the chance to contribute quite fundamentally to the information level of decision makers in the GDR. The reports described facts and events relatively broadly and precisely but abstained from analyzing the causes. A "concept of the enemy" was ultimately established, which invariably sought the reason for discord and unrest in the influence of the "imperialistic" West. The MfS was, then, potentially very well informed through its unofficial network, its cooperation with other agencies, and its surveillance techniques. Nonetheless, the compulsion to report only successes and the ideological disciplining of the involved employees hampered its effective function as a "substitute public." And if the MfS did supply the Politburo bureaucracy with negative reports, it frequently met with ignorance. Looking back, SED Secretary General Erich Honecker said for the records: "I paid little attention to the reports, because everything that was in them could be learned from the reports of the Western media"(Andert and Herzberg 1990, 312).

In addition to these most fundamental "subject" and dovetailing lines, the MfS had a number of further operational and operational-technical service units at its disposal—for example, the government news/information connections. A "backup" apparatus had taken shape behind it in the course of the 1970s that considerably contributed to its immense size. The

Main Department for Cadre and Training alone increased its size fivefold from 1968 to 1982.

Preparation for possible scenarios regarding defense or domestic disturbances was also one of the tasks of the MfS in the 1970s and 1980s. Among other things, the Minister's Working Group (AGM) built and maintained the protective bunker installations for the state and party leadership. A special troop with military or paramilitary training also belonged to the AGM, the Central Specific Forces of the AGM/S ("S" for its head, Heinz Stöcker). Until 1987 the AGM/S, together with Department IV, carried out, among other things, activities in preparation for acts of sabotage in the "Operational Area." Traveling agents of these service units scouted, for example, high-tension masts that the MfS planned to blow up in an emergency. Large "dead letter boxes" were set up near the masts as depots for detonators and explosives, which were stocked with the necessary materials by West German citizens. In cooperation with the Foreign Espionage Directorate, the AGM/S trained the appropriate cadre from third world countries as well.

How the planned isolation camps would have been used could be seen in Poland in 1981, when the government there imposed martial law: the security organs interned a large number of activists of the independent trade union Solidarity in such camps. However, the East German planning of a "preventive complex" went substantially further. In 1988, on the lists of the MfS service units, updated regularly, about three thousand "hostile-negative" East German citizens were noted down for arrest, eleven thousand were supposed to be locked up in the planned isolation camps, and more than seventy thousand were to be kept under heightened surveillance.

The MfS guard regiment Feliks E. Dzierzynski grew from barely eight thousand in the early 1970s to about eleven thousand, thereby achieving division strength. In contrast to the rest of the MfS apparatus, the majority of the soldiers serving here did so for only a limited time: in 1989 there were about twenty-five hundred professional soldiers, as opposed to more than eighty-five hundred soldiers serving temporarily. These were subject to a strict recruiting procedure and were bound to serve for three years. The guard regiment was kept separate from the MfS apparatus in organizational terms; military counterespionage (Main Department I) and the cadre administration even recruited unofficial informers for surveillance from among the regular soldiers. These were at the same time an important source of cadre for the MfS service. The military core of the guard regiment consisted of the five command areas, with altogether four motorized rifle regiments, ten rifle regiments, and four rifle companies. In periods of peace they primarily guarded the buildings of the MfS as well as the buildings of the state and party leadership, and they served as standby reserves at large events or for economic purposes, such as helping with the grain harvest. In the event of war or domestic tension, the guard regiment was supposed to militarily protect the government and party sites under its care. In view of its considerable size, it can be assumed that this responsibility would have also included offensive operations if necessary.

The guard regiment had, among other things, armored personnel carriers and mortars at its disposal, but no heavy military equipment. As a rule, the MfS employees of the other service units were equipped with pistols, in addition to which large numbers of submachine guns were available. The immense scope of military preparedness clearly indicates that the Ministry for State Security was to be equipped for a civil war. It was to be ready to defend the central positions in the power structure in the event of a new "June 17," the experience of which was always the point of reference of such planning.

In the end phases of the SED regime, the Stasi became less and less successful in keeping things under control in its main areas of responsibility. The constantly increasing number of individuals applying for exit visas to the West became a fundamental problem. Increasing private and official contacts wore holes in the Iron Curtain. From the end of the 1970s a political opposition had formed among peace, human rights, and environmental groups under the umbrella of the Protestant Church. The latitude of the MfS to fight against activities critical of the system was narrowed by the great public response in the Western media to direct repression of dissidents. Even using the perfidious psychological intimidation of covert "demoralization measures," coercive deprivation of citizenship, and the excessive deployment of unofficial informers, who stirred up as much conflict as possible in the opposition groups, the MfS did not succeed in breaking this movement. It turned out again and again that the mobilization potential was substantially greater than the originally small core of activists, which had at first consisted of only a few individuals.

With respect to the economy, the MfS increasingly assumed the role of a dogsbody forced to bear the results of misguided investment policies and to find the "guilty ones" responsible for losses, which were steadily piling up due to antiquated means of production. Criticism of the economic policy decisions of the Politburo bureaucracy was not permitted, however, not even by the State Security. On the other hand, many economic function-aries in the State Security, as the head of Main Department XVIII already complained in 1983, wanted "sheet anchors" in order to "get the chairman of the State Planning Commission to free up additional funds" (Haendcke-Hoppe-Arndt 1997, 97).

In addition, many other individuals in the economy faced with constant bottlenecks and supply shortages tried to use the ostensibly all-powerful secret apparatus as "grease in the wheels of the economy," expressing their concerns and difficulties directly to State Security. Yet they overestimated the capacities of the MfS, failing to understand its instructions and modus operandi.

The accumulation of system deficits and the additional checking and surveillance tasks resulting from it were a burden above all to the district offices: while only 13 percent of the full-time employees worked in these offices, they monitored more than half of the network of unofficial inform-ers. "Because of the changed political situation," Mielke explained at a service conference in October 1988, the tasks of the district offices were fundamentally expanded. He cited the most important problems: fighting "political underground activities," "repelling applications for emigration," security checks in connection with the "enormously increasing holiday traffic," analysis of the population's reactions to political decisions, and the "carrying out of measures to encourage stability" in important sectors of the national economy. Given these burdens, many employees had come to think that a large portion of their activities had "hardly anything to do with work against the enemy" and "had reached the limits of their operational capacity" (Süß 1996, 117f.).

Note

1. Editors' note: What started as a strike of East Berlin construction workers on June 16 became a major political demonstration on the following day. Upward of twenty thousand people gathered in Berlin near government buildings while a much smaller number actually stormed the seat of government. The uprising was violently suppressed by Soviet troops.

Bibliography

Andert, Reinhold, and Wolfgang Herzberg. 1990. *Der Sturz: Erich Honecker im Kreuzverhör.* Berlin: Aufbau-Verlag.
Bailey, George, Sergei Kondrashew, and David Murphy. 1997. *Battleground Berlin: CIA vs. KGB in the Cold War.* New Haven, CT: Yale University Press.

Beleites, Johannes. 2004. *Anatomie der Staatssicherheit Abteilung XIV: Haftvollzug, MfS-Handbuch*. Berlin: Der Bundesbeauftragte für die Unterlagen des Staatssicherheitsdienstes der Ehemaligen Deutschen Demokratischen Republik, Abteilung Bildung und Forschung.

Bruce, Gary. 2003. *Resistance with the People: Repression and Resistance in Eastern Germany, 1945–1955*. Lanham, MD: Rowman and Littlefield.

Childs, David, and Richard Popplewell. 1996. *The Stasi: The East German Intelligence and Security Service*. Houndmills, UK: Macmillan.

Dennis, Mike. 2003. *The Stasi: Myth and Reality*. Harlow, UK: Pearson Longman.

Engelmann, Roger, and Clemens Vollnhals, eds. 1999. *Justiz im Dienste der Parteiherrschaft: Rechtspraxis und Staatssicherheit in der DDR*. Berlin: Ch. Links Verlag.

Fricke, Karl Wilhelm. 1989. *Die DDR-Staatssicherheit: Entwicklung, Strukturen, Aktionsfelder*. 3rd ed. Cologne: Verlag Wissenschaft und Politik.

———. 1991. *MfS intern: Macht, Strukturen, Auflösung der DDR-Staatssicherheit; Analyse und Dokumentation*. Cologne: Verlag Wissenschaft und Politik.

Fulbrook, Mary. 1995. *Anatomy of a Dictatorship: Inside the GDR, 1949–1989*. Oxford: Oxford University Press.

Gellately, Robert. 1997. "Denunciations in Twentieth-Century Germany: Aspects of Self-Policing in the Third Reich and the German Democratic Republic." In *Accusatory Practices: Denunciation in Modern European History, 1789–1989*, edited by Sheila Fitzpatrick and Robert Gellately, 185–221. Chicago: University of Chicago Press.

Gieseke, Jens. 2000a. *Die hauptamtlichen Mitarbeiter der Staatssicherheit: Personalstruktur und Lebenswelt, 1950–1989/90*. Berlin: Ch. Links Verlag.

———. 2000b. "Von der Deutschen Verwaltung des Innern zum Ministerium für Staatssicherheit 1948 bis 1950: Die politische Polizei in den Weichenstellungen der DDR-Gründung." In *Das letzte Jahr der SBZ: Politische Weichenstellungen und Kontinuitäten im Prozeß der Gründung der DDR*, edited by Dierk Hoffmann and Hermann Wentker, 133–48. Munich: Oldenbourg Wissenschaftsverlag.

———. 2001. *Mielke-Konzern: Die Geschichte der Stasi*. Stuttgart: Deutsche Verlag-Anstalt.

Gieseke, Jens, and Doris Hubert. 2002. *The GDR State Security: Shield and Sword of the Party*. Berlin: Bundeszentrale.

Gill, David, and Ulrich Schröter. 1991. *Das Ministerium für Staatssicherheit: Anatomie des Mielke-Imperiums*. Berlin: Rowohlt.

Haendcke-Hoppe-Arndt, Maria. 1997. *Anatomie der Staatssicherheit: Die Hauptabteilung XVIII: Volkswirtschaft. MfS-Handbuch*. Berlin: Der Bundesbeauftragte für die Unterlagen des Staatssicherheitsdienstes der Ehemaligen Deutschen Demokratischen Republik, Abteilung Bildung und Forschung.

Henke, Klaus-Dietmar et al., eds. 1995– (installments). *Anatomie der Staatssicherheit: Geschichte, Struktur, Methoden. MfS-Handbuch*. Berlin: Der Bundesbeauftragte für die Unterlagen des Staatssicherheitsdienstes der Ehemaligen Deutschen Demokratischen Republik, Abteilung Bildung und Forschung.

Jarausch, Konrad. 1993. *The Rush to German Unity*. New York: Oxford University Press.

Krüger, Dieter, and Armin Wagner, eds. 2003. *Konspiration als Beruf: Deutsche Geheimdienstchefs im Kalten Krieg*. Berlin: Ch. Links Verlag.

Kukutz, Irena, and Katja Havemann. 1990. *Geschützte Quelle: Gespräche mit Monika H. alias Karin Lenz.* Berlin: BasisDruck.

Lindenberger, Thomas. 2003. *Volkspolizei: Herrschaftspraxis und öffentliche Ordnung im SED-Staat, 1952–1968.* Cologne: Böhlau.

Maier, Charles. 1997. *Dissolution: The Crisis of Communism and the End of East Germany.* Princeton, NJ: Princeton University Press.

Major, Patrick, and Jonathan Osmond, eds. 2002. *The Workers' and Peasants' State: Communism and Society in East Germany under Ulbricht, 1945–71.* Manchester: Manchester University Press.

Miller, Barbara. 1999. *Narratives of Guilt and Compliance in Unified Germany: Stasi Informers and Their Impact on Society.* London: Routledge.

Müller-Enbergs, Helmut, ed. 1996. *Inoffizielle Mitarbeiter des Ministeriums für Staatssicherheit: Richtlinien und Durchführungsbestimmungen.* Berlin: Ch. Links Verlag.

Naimark, Norman M. 1997. *The Russians in Germany: A History of the Soviet Zone of Occupation, 1945–1949.* Cambridge, MA: Harvard University Press.

Neubert, Ehrhart. 1997. *Geschichte der Opposition in der DDR, 1949–1989.* Bonn: Ch. Links Verlag.

Raschka, Johannes. 2001. *Zwischen Überwachung und Repression—Politische Verfolgung in der DDR 1971 bis 1989.* Opladen: Leske and Budrich.

Ross, Corey. 2002. *The East German Dictatorship: Problems and Perspectives in the Interpretation of the GDR.* London: Arnold.

Süß, Walter. 1996. "Die Durchdringung der Gesellschaft mittels de MfS—Fallbeispiel: Jen im Jahr 1989." In *Die SED-Herrschaft und ihr Zusammenbruch,* edited by Eberhard Kuhrt. Opladen: Leske und Budrich.

Tantzscher, Monika. 1994. "Maßnahme Donau und Einsatz Genesung." *Die Niederschlagung des Prager Fruhlings 1968/69 im Spiegel der MfS-Akten.* Berlin: Bundesbeauftrage für die Unterlagen des Staatssicherheitsdienstes der ehemaligen DDR.

———. 1998. "Die Vorläufer des Staatssicherheitsdienstes in der Polizei der Sowjetischen Besatzungszone—Ursprung und Entwicklung der K-5. " *Jahrbuch für Historische Kommunismusforschung,* 125–56.

———. 2003. "A New Apparatus Is Established in the Eastern Zone—The Foundation of the East German State Security Service." In *Secret Intelligence in the Twentieth Century,* edited by Heike Bungert, Jan G. Heitmann, and Michael Wala, 113–27. London: Frank Cass.

Veen, Hans-Joachim, ed. 2000. *Lexikon Opposition und Widerstand in der SED-Diktatur.* Berlin: Propyläen.

Werkentin, Falco. 1995. *Politische Strafjustiz in der Ära Ulbricht.* Berlin: Ch. Links Verlag.

Wilfriede, Otto. 2000. *Erich Mielke—Biographie: Aufstieg und Fall eines Tschekisten.* Berlin: Dietz.

Wolf, Markus, and Anne MacElvoy. 1997. *Man without a Face: The Autobiography of Communism's Greatest Spymaster.* New York: Times Books.

ACKNOWLEDGMENTS

The chapters by Cantor, Scott, and Taylor first appeared (in somewhat different form) in *Perspectives on Political Science,* April–June 2011, Vol. 40, No. 2. We thank *Perspectives* for permission to reprint here. The chapter by Wilke first appeared in German as "Fiktion oder erlebt Geschichte? Zur Frage der Glaubwürdigkeit des Films *Das Leben der Anderen,*" in *German Studies Review* 2008, Vol. 31, No. 3. We thank *German Studies Review* and Johns Hopkins University Press for permission to publish an English translation here. The chapter by Biermann first appeared in German in *Die Welt* on March 22, 2006, and then in English at signandsight.com on March 29, 2006. We thank signandsight.com and Pamela Biermann for permission to reprint here. The chapter by Gieseke first appeared in *A Handbook of the Communist Security Apparatus in East Central Europe, 1944–1989,* edited by Krzysztof Persak and Łukasz Kamiński (Warsaw, 2005). We thank Jens Gieseke and the Institute of National Remembrance for permission to reprint here.

The costs associated with permissions, translations, photographs, and the interview with Gauck were all covered by a generous grant from Skidmore College. Many thanks are due to Paul Hockenos for his willingness to undertake the interview and his persistence in securing it. Thanks also to Dirk Johnson for his translation of the Wilke chapter. We are also grateful to Peter Grieder for his expertise on East Germany. We benefited from the wisdom of Marketa Goetz-Stankiewicz on many questions related to the film and this volume.

We also thank the anonymous reviewers for the University Press of Kentucky both at the proposal stage of the project and after the submission of the manuscript. Their suggestions have improved the volume immensely. Steve Wrinn and Allison Webster at the press are models of professionalism. We are very grateful for Steve's patience and guidance throughout the process. We can't imagine a better editor.

CONTRIBUTORS

Wolf Biermann is a prominent German singer-songwriter and poet. At the age of seventeen, Biermann emigrated from West to East Germany to fulfill his attachment to communism. He was later refused membership in the Socialist Unity Party of the GDR, publicly denounced, and then stripped of his East German citizenship while on tour in West Germany. Living in exile, he became a fierce critic of the GDR.

Paul A. Cantor is the Clifton Waller Barrett Professor of English and Comparative Literature at the University of Virginia. He is the author of *Shakespeare: Hamlet* (1989), *Gilligan Unbound: Pop Culture in the Age of Globalization* (2003), and *The Invisible Hand in Popular Culture* (2012). He writes regularly on film and popular culture.

Joachim Gauck is currently the president of Germany and was the first federal commissioner for the Stasi Archives, serving from 1990 to 2000. So integral was Mr. Gauck to administering the archives and investigating the past crimes of East Germany's state security that the office was nicknamed the Gauck Commission. He is a founding signatory of the Prague Declaration on European Conscience and Communism. Since 2003 he has been the chairman of the association Gegen Vergessen—Für Demokratie (Against Forgetting—For Democracy).

Jens Gieseke is a senior researcher at the Zentrum für Zeithistorische Forschung in Potsdam. He is the author of *Mielke-Konzern: Die Geschichte der Stasi, 1945–1990* (2001), *The GDR State Security: Shield and Sword of the Party* (2002), and *Die Stasi, 1945–1990* (2011), among other works.

Marketa Goetz-Stankiewicz is professor emerita in the central, eastern, and northern European studies department at the University of British Columbia. She is the author of *The Silenced Theatre: Czech Playwrights without a Stage* (1979) and editor of *Goodbye Samizdat: 20 Years of Czechoslovak*

Underground Writing (1992). She is currently editing, with Paul Wilson, a collection of Václav Havel's writings on the theater.

Peter Grieder is lecturer in twentieth-century history at the University of Hull, United Kingdom. He is the author of *The East German Leadership, 1946–1973: Conflict and Crisis* (1999) and *The German Democratic Republic* (2012). The latter was selected by *Choice* as an Outstanding Academic Title of 2013.

Paul Hockenos is a journalist based in Berlin. He is currently Germany and Central Europe correspondent for the *Chronicle of Higher Education*. His works include *Joschka Fischer and the Making of the Berlin Republic: An Alternative History of Postwar Germany* (2008) and *Homeland Calling: Exile Patriotism and the Balkan Wars* (2003).

Dirk R. Johnson is professor of German in the department of modern languages at Hampden Sydney College and the author of *Nietzsche's Anti-Darwinism* (2010).

James F. Pontuso is Charles Patterson Professor of government and foreign affairs at Hampden Sydney College. He is the author of *Václav Havel: Civic Responsibility in a Postmodern Age* (2004) and editor of *Political Philosophy Comes to Rick's: Casablanca and American Civic Culture* (2005).

Carl Eric Scott has taught at Hampden-Sydney College, Skidmore College, Washington and Lee University, and Christopher Newport University. He writes on politics, philosophy, film, and music for the blog *Postmodern Conservative* and currently is working on a book about American conceptions of liberty.

F. Flagg Taylor IV is associate professor of government at Skidmore College. He is the editor of *The Great Lie: Classic and Recent Appraisals of Ideology and Totalitarianism* (2011) and coauthor of *The Contested Removal Power, 1789–2010* (2013). He is writing a book on the political thought of the Czech dissidents.

Lauren Weiner, who has contributed articles and reviews to such publications as the *American Interest, Policy Review, First Things*, the *Weekly Stan-*

dard, American Communist History, and the *Wall Street Journal*, is writing a book on communism and American popular culture.

Manfred Wilke, external project leader at the Institut für Zeitgeschichte Munich/Berlin, was professor of sociology at Fachhochschule für Wirtschaft Berlin and codirector of the Forschungs-verbund SED-Staat at the Freie Universität Berlin until his retirement in 2006. He is the author or coauthor of over a dozen books and numerous articles on East and West German labor unions, communism, party rule, opposition, and resistance in East Germany.

INDEX

www.ingramcontent.com/pod-product-compliance
Lightning Source LLC
Chambersburg PA
CBHW021543260326
41914CB00001B/137